T0203236

Visual Inspection Technology in the Hard Disk Drive Industry

Series Editor
Jean-Charles Pomerol

Visual Inspection Technology in the Hard Disk Drive Industry

Edited by

Paisarn Muneesawang
Suchart Yammen

WILEY

First published 2015 in Great Britain and the United States by ISTE Ltd and John Wiley & Sons, Inc.

ISTE Ltd
27-37 St George's Road
London SW19 4EU
UK

www.iste.co.uk

John Wiley & Sons, Inc.
111 River Street
Hoboken, NJ 07030
USA

www.wiley.com

Library of Congress Control Number: 2015930754

British Library Cataloguing-in-Publication Data
A CIP record for this book is available from the British Library
ISBN 978-1-84821-591-7

Contents

CHAPTER 9. INSPECTION OF STYROFOAM
BEADS ON ADAPTER OF HARD DISK DRIVES   225
Suchart YAMMEN

CHAPTER 10. INSPECTION OF
DEFECT ON MAGNETIC DISK SURFACE
AND QUALITY OF THE GLUE DISPENSER ROUTE   237
Anan KRUESUBTHAWORN

Preface

Ever-increasing amounts of hard disk drives (HDDs) have been made largely due to the immense technological advances in the field of machine vision. *Visual Inspection Technology in the Hard Disk Drive Industry* covers the recent progress and developments in computer vision technology in HDD manufacturing. This is the first book to present selected topics in computer vision technology concerning the manufacturing process and product quality in data storage media. It highlights early efforts from corporative research works with world leading companies in HDD manufacturing. By featuring pertinent issues in industrial vision, this book provides engineers and graduate students in computer science and electrical engineering a solid practical perspective and foundation for grasping the different topics.

The book begins with a discussion on pole tips, the key component for reading and writing data in magnetic recording. The first two chapters are devoted to tribology, a highly challenging area in HDD studies which deals with the reliability and corrosion of the head and media. Covering the various defects on the head gimbals assembly (HGA), Chapter 3 focuses on the high impact defects on the small circuits of the HGA, Chapter 4 discusses micro contamination on the air baring surface (ABS), and

Chapter 5 presents the analysis methods of the solder bump of the integrated circuit (IC) die package on the actuator arm. The application of machine learning method for lamination process modeling, actuator arm control chart and machine clustering are discussed in Chapter 6. In Chapter 7, the panoramic image construction method is used for the measurement of the boreholes of pivot arms. Chapter 8 presents the technologies for visualizing visible electrostatic discharge (ESD) events for proactive ESD prevention and control. The inspection of styrofoam beads on adapter cards is presented in Chapter 9.

Next, Chapter 10 discusses various sensor technologies for inspection of defects on media plates, as well as the quality of the glue dispenser route. Chapter 11 provides an overview of the emerging technologies, such as nanoparticles in the field of data storage materials and transmission electron microscope (TEM) image processing and analysis. Magnetic nanoparticles are being researched for ultrahigh density recording applications. This chapter is dedicated to the pattern inspection of prototypes of the heat assisted magnetic recording media where the data are coded in the form of magnetization of magnetic nanoparticles.

Feature Fusion Method for Rapid Corrosion Detection on Pole Tips

Due to its high magnetic moment, FeCo film is a type of ferromagnetic material commonly used for recording pole tips in modern hard disk drives (HDDs). These FeCo pole tips are prone to corrosion because of the corrosive environment and wide pH variations during HDD production. The machine vision is then utilized for automatically auditing of these corroded pole tips. The developed image-processing approach comprises three steps: extraction of top-shield region, fusion of extracted features and decision-making. The key step, fusion of extracted features, employs two types of features which are area-based and contour-based features. The second feature is extracted by image filtering with a specially designed filter kernel. It is capable of extracting the position of corrosion from the top shield of the pole tip. The experiments show that the algorithm reveals corrosion with high accuracy, precision, specificity, as well as sensitivity, and the overall processing time satisfies the industrial environment.

Chapter written by Suchart YAMMEN and Paisarn MUNEESAWANG.

1.1. Introduction

In magnetic recording drive, a recording head consists of both write and read elements embedded at the end of an air-bearing slider. The strength of the magnetic field generated by write heads is determined by the magnetic flux density inside the head poles. The $Fe_{65}Co_{35}$ alloy used in today's write heads has the highest saturation magnetic flux density, of 2.45 Tesla (T), compared to any existing magnetic materials. Thus, the head pole material has changed over the years from permalloy (Ni_8, Fe_{19}), with a magnetic flux density of 1.0 T, to $Ni_{45}Fe_{55}$, with a magnetic flux density of 1.50 T, to the $Fe_{65}Co_{35}$ alloy. In addition to the write element, both Fe and Co are also applied in the construction of giant magnetoresistive (GMR) read sensors in HDDs.

The alloy Fe and Co magnets have outstanding magnetic properties, but these properties are greatly deteriorated by corrosion [CHE 12]. This is caused by a corrosive environment, where pH varies over a wide range [MAB 12]. In order to provide protection against such deterioration, a protective film (PF), typically sputter-deposited carbon on adhesion film, is formed on the air-bearing surface to protect the pole tips [WAN 11, TAN 09]. The PF is a single layer, or a bilayer, of an outer film of carbon formed on an adhesion film of silicon. In order to provide enhanced corrosion resistance, Flint *et al.* [FLI 06] study the modification of the magnet alloy itself by modifying the magnet composition. It simultaneously provides both good corrosion resistance and high coercivity.

The aforementioned methods display corrosion resistance on the thin film material. Nevertheless, FeCo pole tips are susceptible to corroding on the surface. Figure 1.1 shows the different corrosion configurations on the top shield of the pole tips. The components of FeCo pole tip, as shown in

Figure 1.2, have the thin films at the top shield and the bottom shield. The top shield consists of S3 and S4 layers and the bottom shield consists of S1, S2 and P1 layers. The detection of corrosion performed by the expert is based on the following criteria. The corrosion, or pitting, typically occurs outsides the free-zone, within the top shield, at a size of less than 0.2 mm, and a quantity of less than 3 points (at 200× microscope). However, if the corrosion or pitting is inside the free-zone or bottom shield, the pole tip is rejected.

During the HDD production process, these corroded specimens are rejected prior to assembly by relying on human visual inspection. Specifically, inspectors perform 100% inspection using microscopes with a magnification ratio of 1200× for many hours without adequate resting time. Such inspections force the operators to be highly concentrated, inspecting the small product for nonconformities. Due to the nature of the industrial production, a large quantity of FeCo pole tips must be inspected in a short time. Taking into account the fatigue of the operators, it is nearly impossible to maintain the desired inspection accuracy over long working hours. Hence, a more reliable solution is needed to detect the imperfections in pole tips.

In this chapter, a novel approach to detect corrosion on FeCo pole tip is presented. The developed approach aims to improve the accuracy, specificity, robustness, as well as rapidness of detection in order to handle the problem under the time constraint imposed by the industrial environment. The approach starts by extracting the top-shield region of the FeCo pole tip from the input images. A specially designed filter is then applied to the top-shield region to highlight possible corrosion on the bottom contour of the top shield. Only the feature values that follow the criteria are used for decision fusion with the second feature (the area-based feature) to detect a defect. The experiment with several images showing different corrosion configurations demonstrates the high accuracy and specificity with low computational cost. The algorithm is readily implementable in industrial productions lines.

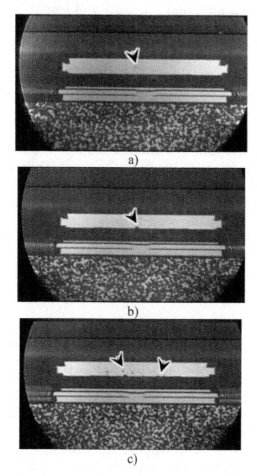

Figure 1.1. *FeCo pole tip images, some of which bearing the corrosions indicated by the arrowheads. a) The corrosion occurs inside the top shied area. b) The corrosion occurs on the bottom contour of the top shield. c) The corrosion occurs at the positions as in (a) and (b)*

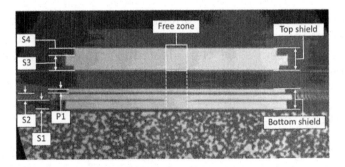

Figure 1.2. *FeCo pole tip and its components revealing the thin films within the top shield and the bottom shield*

Processes in diagnostics and fault detections are commonly composed of several steps including signature detection, decision-making, and final feedback to user interface system. Signature detection characterizes features from various sensor signals including mechanic-based sensors, image [ACC 11, TAN 12, TSA 11, LI 12b], speech [KIM 11], optical-based sensor [SIL 11] and current [CHO 11, PON 11]. A review of the literature revealed only limited previous research focused on visual inspection of pole tips in the HDD manufacturing. Earlier, image processing algorithms have been implemented for automated defect detection in different materials. These include fabric [CHO 05, CUI 08, KUM 08, MAK 09], liquid crystal display (LCD) [LI 13, LI 11], metal stencil [CHO 07, BEN 13], steel [JAG 08, ZHU 07, LI 06, LIN 09], cork parquet [FER 09], and food [GIN 04]. These approaches have met with success to some extent; however, the previous success depends on the peculiar objectives of a production system, and on products to be inspected. There is no generally accepted industrial standards for automated inspections. In this chapter, the extracted features are specific for corrosion detection on FeCo pole tip image, which is very tiny and considered as a different type of surface to those previously studied. The chapter is organized as follows: section 1.2 discusses an effective approach for corrosion detection and section 1.3 shows the results of the algorithm tested with several images.

1.2. Algorithm for corrosion detection

The image processing approach introduced in this chapter comprises three major steps: extraction of top-shield region, extraction of features characterizing corrosion and decision-making for classification. Since the top shield of FeCo pole tips is the corrosion area advised by the expert, it is necessary to determine the top shield area in the image prior to corrosion detection. The extracted top shield is then examined to characterize area-based and contour-based features. While the two features are sensitive enough to pick up each type of corrosions, a single feature could not capture the information which is available on other modality. Hence, in order to increase the specificity of the algorithm, at the final stage, decision fusion rules are applied to further distinguish the possible corrosion regions.

1.2.1. *Extraction of top-shield region*

In Figure 1.1, it is clear that the corrosion is at the top shield of the pole tip image. This top shield area can then be used to define the region of interest. The extraction of the top shield area comprises three steps: template matching, locating top-shield region on the test image and binary conversion of the selected top-shield image. Prior to the automated top-shield region detection, a single template image, of approximately 150×1250 pixels containing only the top-shield region, is manually extracted from a perfect pole tip image chosen by a professional inspector. As this template contains only the region of interest, the selected image covers the top shield of the pole tip, as shown in

Figure 1.3(a). This image is kept as a reference template for test images.

In the following step, the matching of a reference template and a test image is obtained. The grayscale value at each pixel of this image is correlated to that in the reference template, from which the corresponding pixel locations are mapped to the test image. The template matching method is based on the calculation of cross-correlation function (CCF). It can be defined as follows. Let $\{f[m,n]\}$ be the grayscale test image of size 2048×2048 pixels, and $\{w[m,n]\}$ be the grayscale template image of size 150×1250 pixels. Then, we can have:

$$r_{fw}[m,n] = \sum_{s=0}^{149} \sum_{t=0}^{1249} f[m+s, n+t]w[s,t] \qquad [1.1]$$

where m and n are the coordinates $m,n \in \{0,1,\dots,2047\}$, and s,t are integers [GON 87, LIA 10]. The mapped image can be considered as the probability of finding a pixel with a particular gray value in the template. Hence, from this process, the mapped image shows a high probability in the area of the top shield and a low probability elsewhere. This concept is demonstrated by the application of CCF for an effective process of fault detection of one-dimensional (1D) signal [CHO 11].

By finding the maximum value of the CCF, the best matching image can be obtained. This follows the problem of finding a suitable constant value:

$$r_{fw}[m_0, n_0] = \max_{m,n} r_{fw}[m,n] \qquad [1.2]$$

where the coordinate $[m_0, n_0]$ gives the maximum value of the function. This coordinate is used to generate the output top-shield image; that is, $\{f[m_0+m, n_0+n]\}$ for the index $m \in \{0,1,\dots,199\}$ and the index $n \in \{0,1,\dots,1199\}$.

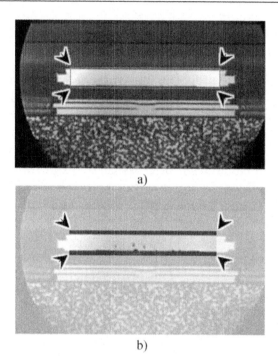

a)

b)

Figure 1.3. *Extraction of top-shield region from the pole tip image in Figure 1.1(c). a) The test image composes with the template at the maximum CCF value. The template is highlight with the orange color. b) The mapped image is obtained at the template position in (a) where the top-shield region is located*

The mapped image is then the threshold, resulting in the binary image where a majority of the corrosion region is highlighted. The graylevel image $\{f[m_0 + m, n_0 + n]\}$, of size 150×1250 pixels, is segmented into a two-level image using the Otsu threshold selection method [GON 87, OTS 79]

$$b[m,n] = \begin{cases} 1, & \text{if}\{f[m_0 + m, n_0 + n]\} \geq t^* \\ 0, & \text{if}\{f[m_0 + m, n_0 + n]\} < t^* \end{cases} \qquad [1.3]$$

where $b[m,n]$ is the two-level image with horizontal index $m \in \{0,1,2,...,199\}$ and vertical index $n \in \{0,1,2,...,1199\}$, t^* is a suitable threshold value. We can obtain the value of parameter t^* by the selection criterion:

$$\min_{t \in 0,1,\dots,255} \sigma_T^2[t] = \sigma_T^2[t^*] \tag{1.4}$$

where $\sigma_T^2[t]$ is the total variance, which is defined as:

$$\sigma_T^2[t] = w[t]\sigma_0^2[t] + (1 - w[t])\sigma_1^2[t] \tag{1.5}$$

where $w[t]$ is the summation of the probability that the gray value of image $\{f[m_0 + m, n_0 + n]\}$ is less than t. Here $\sigma_0^2[t]$ and $\sigma_1^2[t]$ are the class variances of the gray value, less than t and greater than or equal to t, respectively. When an image $\{f[m_0 + m, n_0 + n]\}$ is composed of dark objects (i.e. the potential corrosions) on a light background of the top shield, then the foreground is clearly distinguished from the background. In this case, the graylevel histogram of the image will be bimodal so that the threshold value will lie in the valley of the histogram ensuring that the objects can be extracted by comparing pixel value with the threshold t^* as in equation [1.3].

1.2.2. Area-based feature

In Figure 1.1, it is clear that the top shield area has a pale white color with no texture, in contrast to surrounding materials. The top shield areas which are corroded have different features from the areas which are not corroded. The differences are observed at the bottom contour of the un-corroded top shield revealing as a straight line. However, chips on the bottom contour and black holes, as demonstrated in Figures 1.1(a)–(c), can exist in corroded top shields. Hence, we can characterize the corrosion by two features: (1) corrosion area within the top-shield region as the first feature, and (2) number of corrosion points at the bottom contour as the second feature. These two features and their fusion are then used for the classification of pole-tip images.

The extraction of area-based feature starts with invert transformation of the two-level image $b[m,n]$ in equation [1.3]. The image pixel value of 1 is changed to 0, and the image pixel value of 0 is changed to 1:

$$b_{inv}[m,n] = 1 - b[m,n] \qquad [1.6]$$

It is observed that the two-level image $b_{inv}[m,n]$ has the areas above and below the top shield with white pixel value. If the top shield is corroded, the white holes can be observed within its inside area.

The binary image $\{b_{inv}[m,n]\}$ obtained as a result of image inversion is used for finding the corrosion area within the top shield. The corrosion areas are characterized by the small linked components in the image, which form a closed contour. The process of connected component labeling [BAR 89] assigns a distinct label to each object present in the binary image. The image is scanned in a raster-scanned manner by moving along a row until reaching a white pixel p (where p denotes the pixel to be labeled at any stage in the scanning process). When this is true, the process examines the four neighbors of p, i.e. the neighbors (1) to the North-East of p, (2) to the North of p and ((3) and (4)) to the North-West and West of the current value. The labeling of p occurs as follows:

– if all four neighbors are dark pixels, a new label is labeled to p;

– if one of the neighbors is white pixel, its temporary label is assigned to p.

After completing the scan, the equivalent label pairs are sorted into equivalent classes; each of which is assigned with a unique class index. As a final step, a second scan is made through the image, where each label is replaced by the corresponding class index.

As a result of the labeling process, the objects are formed by the connected components with the corresponding class labels. The corrosion area can be characterized by a small connected component, and its area is calculated by counting the number of the pixels having the same class label. Particularly, we associate each object class $O_c, c = 1, ..., C$ from the connected component labeling with a subset $\mathcal{R}_c \subset \mathcal{X}$, where $\mathcal{X}$ denotes the set of points in an $M \times N$ image lattice.

$$\mathcal{X} = \{(i_1, i_2) : 1 \leq i_1 \leq M, 1 \leq i_2 \leq N\}, \qquad [1.7]$$

and where the regions $\mathcal{R}_c$ form a partition of $\mathcal{X}$.

$$\mathcal{R}_{c_1} \cap \mathcal{R}_{c_2} = \emptyset \quad c_1 \neq c_2 \qquad [1.8]$$

$$\bigcup_{c=1}^{C} \mathcal{R}_c = \mathcal{X} \qquad [1.9]$$

In this way, we can define a binary object, $b_{obj}(i_1, i_2)$ of class c as:

$$b_{obj,c}(i_1, i_2) = \begin{cases} 1, & (i_1, i_2) \in \mathcal{R}_c \\ 0, & (i_1, i_2) \notin \mathcal{R}_c \end{cases} \qquad [1.10]$$

The set of binary objects, $b_{obj,c}, c = 1, ..., C$ contains objects associated with noise, corrosion and the two dark regions at the border of the top shield. In order to select only the objects of the possible corrosion, the following thresholding is applied:

$$T_S \leq |b_{obj,c}(i_1, i_2)| \leq T_L, \qquad [1.11]$$

$$\left|b_{obj,c}(i_1, i_2)\right| = \sum_{i_1}^{M_p} \sum_{i_2}^{N_p} b_{obj,c}(i_1, i_2),$$ [1.12]

$$i_1 \in \{1, ..., M_p\}, i_2 \in \{1, ..., N_p\}, (i_1, i_2) \in \mathcal{R}_c.$$ [1.13]

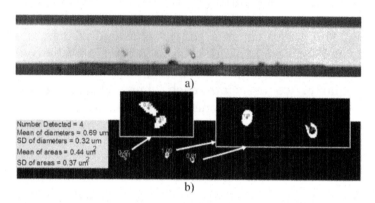

a)

b)

Figure 1.4. *Corrosion area feature extraction: a) input images
and b) the possible corrosion regions extracted*

In equation [1.11], the threshold T_S removes the small object, regarding noise, and T_L removes the two large dark regions at the border of the top shield. As a result, we obtain the set of selected binary objects associating with the corrosion by $b_{obj,c'}, c' = 1, ..., C', C' \leq C$, where $b_{obj,c'}$ denotes the binary object that follows the two threshold values in equation [1.11]. From this set, we obtain the feature of corrosion area, f_A by:

$$f_A = \frac{\sum_{c'=1}^{C'} \left|b_{obj,c'}(i_1, i_2)\right|}{M \times N}$$ [1.14]

In this way, f_A gives a measure of the normalized area between the corrosion and the top shield. On the basis of its definition, the feature f_A assumes value being in the range $[0, 1]$. It is observed that if no corrosion occurs, $f_A = 0$, and the test image has not been corroded within the top shield.

On the contrary, $f_A > 0$ reveals the potential corrosion within the top shield of the test image.

Figure 1.4 shows the results of area-based feature extraction. This figure is the result of pole tip image in Figure 1.3(b). It is observed that all possible regions regarding corrosion are effectively highlighted by the application of connected component labeling and the thresholding in equation [1.11]. The output also shows the distribution of corrosion in terms of area and diameter.

1.2.3. *Contour-based feature*

As individual characteristics of corrosion are displayed onto the top shield surface along with the bottom contour, the detecting of corrosion positions along this direction can enhance useful information for image classification. Projecting the bottom contour along horizontal direction results in a 1D signal, $\{x[n]\}$, for $n \in \{0,1,2,\dots,N-1\}$, describing the image profile—the index of the contour along the horizontal direction. The resulting image profile provides a compact, faithful representation of top-shield contour, which contributes to efficiency of comparison (see Figure 1.6(b)). The key issue in the feature extraction process is the determination of the corrosion position on the contour, which can be accomplished by a filter in the subsequent step. By application of high-pass filtering, a feature profile only composed of individual characteristic of corrosion can be acquired (see Figure 1.6(c)). The two-step feature extraction is discussed in the following sections.

1.2.3.1. *Contour extraction*

In order to obtain an image profile in terms of sequence $\{x[n]\}$, the binary image subtraction is first applied to remove a non-relevant portion from the processing image area. The image subtraction operator is processed on the two-level image $\{b_{inv}[m, n]\}$ from equation [1.6] and the image $\{b_{obj,c'}[m, n]\}$. The binary objects in the image $\{b_{obj,c'}[m, n]\}$ have already been to address the corrosion area feature. Therefore, they are considered as a non-relevant portion for the current feature extraction process:

$$b_{dif}[m, n] = b_{inv}[m, n] - b_{obj,c'}[m, n] \qquad [1.15]$$

Figure 1.6(a) shows the result after the application of equation [1.15] to the pole tip image in Figure 1.3(b). Next, the resulting image $\{b_{dif}[m, n]\}$ is passed through a Canny edge detector [BIN 09] to obtain the edge image. The bottom half of the edge image is then selected as the processing area. The Canny edge detector can work efficiently to detect the contour since the top shield pole tip has a high contrast. In the case of the heterogeneous background, detection could be less effective and the system would require a different operator, such as the entropy method [TSA 11].

Let **b** be the binary image containing only the lower part contour of the top shield:

$$\mathbf{b} = \{\mathbf{b}[m, 0] \cdots \mathbf{b}[m, N - 1]\} \qquad [1.16]$$

$$= \{b[m, n]\}, \qquad [1.17]$$

$$m = 0, 1, \dots, \frac{M}{2} - 1, \qquad [1.18]$$

$$n = 0, 1, \dots, N - 1 \qquad [1.19]$$

Also, let the point (m^*, n^*) be the point at the edge contour where the value of $b[m^*, n^*] = 1$. For contour abstraction, the binary image $\mathbf{b} = \{b[m, n]\}, \in \mathbf{B}^{\frac{M}{2} \times N}$, where $\mathbf{B} = \{0, 1\}$, representing the binary values of the current image is mapped to an integer-valued vector $\mathbf{x} \in \mathbf{I}^{1 \times N}$, where

$I = \{0, ..., \frac{M}{2} - 1\}$. To achieve this purpose, we define the mapping $Q: B^{\frac{M}{2} \times N} \rightarrow I^{1 \times N}$ as follows:

$$\mathbf{x} = Q(\mathbf{b}) = [q(b[m^*, 0]) \cdots q(b[m^*, N-1])] \in I^{1 \times N} \quad [1.20]$$

where the component mappings $q: B \rightarrow I$ are specified as:

$$q(b[m^*, n]) = \begin{cases} 0, & if\, m^* = \min\{M^*\} \\ m^* - \min\{M^*\}, & if\, m^* > \min\{M^*\} \end{cases} \quad [1.21]$$

$$M^* = \{m^* \in I | b(m^*, n^*) = 1\} \quad [1.22]$$

For valid contour configuration, the integer vector $\mathbf{x}$ is in a form $\mathbf{x} = \{x[n]\}, n = 0,1, ..., N-1$.

Figure 1.6(b) reveals the image profile in terms of sequence $\{x[n]\}$. In this figure, the peaks on the data plotted belong to the corrosion occurring on the input image in Figure 1.6(a). In the image profile, the corrosion exhibits itself as a burst noise on the contour of the bottom part of the top shield. It consists of sudden step-like transitions between two or more pixels at random and unpredictable times.

1.2.3.2. *Filtering feature profile*

Up to this stage, we have prepared the image profile of the top shield image. This 1D representation of an image contour consists of noises and individual characteristics of corrosion. Accurate separation of these two parts is the key issue for detection. This line feature of the corrosion is elaborated in a spatial domain, and a threshold can be applied for detecting the corrosion positions. However, the problem of choosing a good and accurate threshold value is a difficult task in this case, where the individual characteristics of the corrosion are exhibited unclearly by the current form of the 1D signal. Hence, it is necessary to engage a problem-specific algorithm before thresholding. This has to be generalized for all possible form of corrosion. Convolving the 1D signal with a direction filter kernel is proven to be an effective solution, particularly under the time constraint in the current application. Principally, the convolution process can be expressed as follows:

$$d[n] = \sum_{k=0}^{N-1} x[n-k]h[k] \qquad [1.23]$$

where $\{d[n]\}$ is the filtered signal, $\{x[n]\}$ is the original signal (the 1D image profile) and $\{h[n]\}$ is the filter kernel.

The specially designed filter for enhancing the peak value of possible corrosion is given in Figure 1.5. A new filter is based on this practical application, and its type is a finite impulse response (FIR) filter [PRO 96] with a design to cope with all possible forms of corrosion for effective detection. The 1D signal $\{x[n]\}$ is first passed through a twofold downsampling operator, followed by a sequence transpose, resulting in signal $\{x[-2n]\}$ with the side reduced to half of the original signal. The signal is transformed with the filter $H(z)$, which is the z-transform of the filter kernel $\{h[n]\}$:

$$H(z) = \sum_{-\infty}^{\infty} h[n]z^{-n}. \qquad [1.24]$$

The filter signal can be obtained by the convolution in the spatial domain (see equation [1.24]):

$$y[n] = \sum_{k=0}^{N-1} x[-2n+2k]h[k]. \qquad [1.25]$$

Finally, the output signal is transposed, resulting in $d[n] = Tr(y[n])$,

$$d[n] = \sum_{k=0}^{N-1} x[2n+2k]h[k]. \qquad [1.26]$$

The filter kernel $\{h[n]\}$ is designed to have its coefficients as $\{h[n]\} = \{+1, -1\}$ so that the filter displays as a moving difference filter.

This kernel is based on the assumption that the corrosion has a form of a spike-like noise lying in the vertical direction. The downsampling operation allows the filter to differentiate the current signal component with the previous two components in order to detect the sudden change at the corrosion. The filter in equation [1.27] reveals that it functions as a high-pass filter in the vertical direction. The high-pass filter picks up a rapid variation in the signal across corrosion and at the same time ignores a flat region.

Figure 1.6(c) represents the filtered feature profile of an image with corrosion. Compared to the input image profile in Figure 1.6(b), the filtered feature profile shows an enhancement in the corrosion lying on the horizontal direction. It is observed that the filtered feature profiles capture all possible corrosion locations.

Therefore, it is convenient to apply thresholding to locate possible corrosions on the filtered feature profile $\{d[n]\}$. The index n reveals the corrosion locations upon the thresholding the magnitude of $d[n]$. Let $\mathcal{P}$ be the set of index n that $d[n] > 1$ as follows:

$$\mathcal{P} = \{n \in \{0,1,2, ..., (N/2 - 1)\} | n \quad if \quad d[n] > 1\} \qquad [1.27]$$

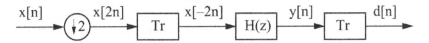

Figure 1.5. *Filtering process of a feature profile. Tr denotes a transpose operator of the data sequence, and $H(z)$ is the z-transform of the filter kernel $\{h[n]\}$*

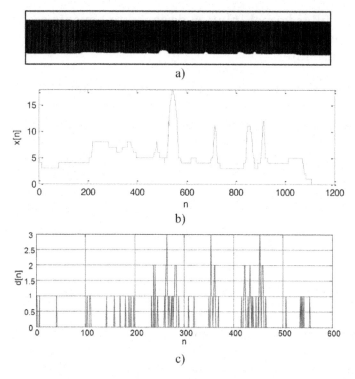

Figure 1.6. *a) Image subtraction result* $\{b_{dif}[m, n]\}$*, b) the corresponding image profile* $\{x[n]\}$ *and c) individual feature profile*

Thus, if $\mathcal{P}$ is an empty set, the test images have no corrosion on the bottom contour of the pole tip; otherwise, they would have been corroded.

1.2.3.3. *Fusion*

In order to allow the classifier to take into account the corrosion occurring on the bottom contour and inside the area of the top shield, it is necessary to employ both area-based and contour-based features. This is accomplished by the logical operation:

$$AP = \Gamma\{D_A, D_C\} \qquad [1.28]$$

$$D_A = (f_A > 0) \hspace{4cm} [1.29]$$

$$D_C = (N(P) > 0) \hspace{3.5cm} [1.30]$$

where Γ is the fusion rule which represents the output of the logical OR operator, and $N(P)$ is the total number of the members of set P. Therefore, if the logical value of AP is false, the test pole tip image will have no corrosion on the top shield, and the logical true value of AP indicates that there is a corrosion on the top shield image. This type of fusion process is considered as a decision fusion [GUN 12, CHO 11, LI 12b]. The fusion method captures two outputs of the decision making modules, instead of concatenating the features into a single vector. It is assumed that the individual features are independent to each other.

1.3. Experimental result

In section 1.2, the corrosion detection approach, consisting of three major stages, was discussed in detail. Section 1.3 completes the chapter with a number of pole tip images inspected by the proposed algorithm. A total of 647 pole tip images of size 2048 × 2048 pixels were prepared, using the 1200× DUV optical microscope. This test set consists of 289 non-corrosion images (class I) and 358 corrosion images (class II). The best top-shield region, of size 150 × 1250 pixels, an area which is usually susceptible to corrosion, was selected as a template by an expert. This is used as the reference template for obtaining CCF values in order to select a region of interest by cross correlation method. A program has been developed, which automated the methods discussed in section 1.3. The testing platform is Intel CPU Core 2 Duo running at 3.16 GHz. The computational time for each 4.2-megapixel image is approximately 0.44 s.

1.3.1. *Distribution of corrosion*

The classification of pole tip images employed three feature extraction methods: (1) area-based feature, (2) contour-based feature and (3) the fusion of the two features. Table 1.1 shows corrosion detection results of all samples from the two classes. Based on 647 detections, the corrosion in images from Class II (average diameter 0.333 µm, area 0.149 µm^2) are much larger than those in images from Class I (average diameter 0.093 µm, area 0.011 µm^2). For Class II, the system correctly detected 171 samples that have been corroded inside the area of the top shield and 320 samples corroded on the lower contour of the top shield. However, the system also shows a small false negative; 10 images from Class I were detected as corroded samples. Figure 1.7 also illustrates the application of feature extraction methods on some samples. As observed from the figures, corrosions appear as dark dots on a lighter background. The conversion from grayscale to binary images gives rise to high contrast between black corrosion and the white background but several tiny 'noise' dots are introduced in the background. These noise dots are subsequently eliminated in the connected component labeling and thresholding (see equation [1.11]). All corrosion regions passed through this application are accounted for in the average diameter and area in Table 1.1. It can also be observed from Figure 1.7 that the contour-based feature shows the high peak amplitude at all corrosion points. This effectively detected the corrosion at the lower contour of the top shield.

1.3.2. *Performance metric*

Four measures of the detection efficiency [HAN 06], sensitivity, specificity, precision and accuracy, were studied in the experiment. Table 1.2 shows the definition of all four measures, and Table 1.3 shows the corresponding data dictionary. The sensitivity of a test refers to the ability of the detector to correctly identify pole tips without corrosion. It is the true positive rate that gives the ratio between the number of non-corrosion pole tip images, which have been validated, and the total number of non-corrosion images. The specificity, or the true negative rate, is given by the ratio between the number of corrosion pole tip images, which have been validated, and the total number of corrosion images. The third measure is the precision describing the positive predictive value. The last measure, the accuracy, is the ratio of the total number of correctly detected images and the total number of images.

	Class I			
	Image detected	Corrosion area per image	Area (μm^2)	Diameter (μm)
Corrosion inside the top shield	6	1.5±0.7	0.011±0.026	0.093±0.740
		Point per image	Min	Max
Corrosion on the contour	4	2.5±3	1	7(4)
	Class II			
	Image detected	Corrosion area per image	Area (μm^2)	Diameter (μm)
Corrosion inside the top shield	171	10.6±14.3	0.149±0.290	0.333±0.280
		Point per image	Min	Max
Corrosion on the contour	320	9.4±11.9	1	152(76)

Table 1.1. *Corrosion detection result*

Methods	Definition
Sensitivity	The true positive rate, $\frac{tp}{tp+fn}$.
Specificity	The true negative rate, $\frac{tn}{tn+fp}$.
Precision	The positive predictive value, $\frac{tp}{tp+fp}$
Accuracy	The proportion of true results in the population, $\frac{tp+tn}{tp+tn+fp+fn}$.

Table 1.2. *The measurement methods and their definition*

	Predicted Class (examined by program)	
Actual Class (examined by expert)	Positive	Negative
Class I: non-corrosion	tp (true positive)	fn (false negative)
Class II: corrosion	fp (false positive)	tn(true negative)

Table 1.3. *The data dictionary of classification*

Automatic corrosion audits were used to confirm or refute the presence of a corrosion or further the inspection process. Ideally, such audits correctly identify all pole tips with corrosion, and similarly correctly identify all pole tips which are corrosion free. In other words, a perfect test is never negative in a pole tip which is corrosion free, and is never positive in a pole tip which is in fact corroded. In Table 1.2, the sensitivity and specificity are terms used to evaluate an audit test. As described by their definition, the two measures are independent of the population of interest subjected to the audit. In comparison, the precision, or positive predictive value, is dependent on the prevalence of the corrosion in the population of interest. Since a negative test is used to confirm the presence of corrosion and the test sample is subjected to further investigation, an auditing system which can achieve high specificity (true negative rate) is of importance when considering the quality assurance. A test with 100% specificity correctly identifies all pole tips with the corrosion. A test with 80% specificity detects 80% of pole tips with corrosion (true negatives) but 20% with corrosion go undetected (false positive).

Table 1.4 summarizes the corrosion detection results obtained by all feature extraction methods. According to the experimental results, it can be observed that the fusion method (area-based and contour-based features) outperformed all other methods discussed, which effectively applied to detect the corrosion on pole tip images with regards to accuracy, precision and specificity. This system can attain the highest accuracy at 96.60%. As discussed above, the specificity is of importance to the corrosion audit, and the system employing the fusion method can achieve the specificity at 96.65% (i.e. only 3.35% of corroded tips go undetected). It can also be observed from the result that the sensitivity of the fusion method is at 96.54%. This indicates that 3.46% of non-corrosions are undetected. However, these pole tips which are initially negative to the audit are subjected to the second audit with an expert. In this way, nearly all of the false negatives may be correctly identified.

Methods	Sensitivity	Specificity	Precision	Accuracy
Area-based feature	0.9792	0.4777	0.6021	0.7017
Contour-based feature	0.9861	0.8938	0.8823	0.9350
Fusion	0.9654	0.9665	0.9588	0.9660

Table 1.4. *Performance evaluation of the classifiers*

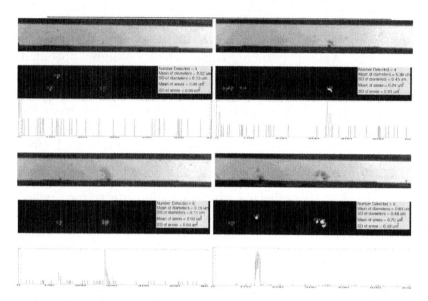

Figure 1.7. *Corrosion detection result. For each case, the top row is the input image, the middle row is the detected corrosion area; the last row is the corrosion position detected at the lower contour of top shield*

1.3.3. Robustness

In order to study the robustness of the algorithms for corrosion detection, all 647 pole tip images were added an additive white noise before auditing. Figure 1.8 shows the performance of the corrosion detection at 10 different settings of noise level, corresponding to the signal-to-noise ratio (SNR) from 28.8 dB to 70.4 dB. This result can be used in comparison with the case of an SNR = ∞ dB, reported in Table 1.4. It can be observed that the system employing the contour-based feature is the most robust in which it performed steadily, regardless of the SNR ranges discussed. In comparison, the system employing the area-based feature and the fusion has performance dropped rapidly at SNR equal or lower than 32.3 dB (i.e. noise standard deviation

(STD) is 4). The fusion method facilitates the system to perform with high accuracy if the signal has an SNR equal or greater than 34.8 dB (i.e. noise STD is 3). In other words, this study shows that the system can effectively identify either non-corrosion or corrosion images with various SNR values, from 34.8 dB to ∞ dB.

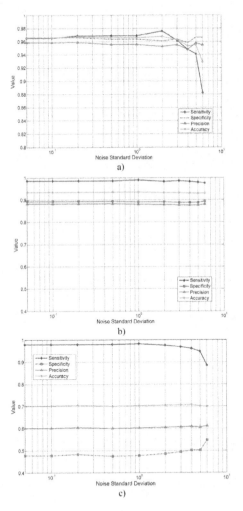

Figure 1.8. *Performance plotted for various levels of noise, obtained by a) fusion, b) contour-based feature and c) area-based feature. The measured SNR is at 28.8–70.4 dB*

From the result in Figure 1.8(c), the system employing the area-based feature is sensitive to noise. Sensitivity drops by 9.6% if the level of noise STD increases from 1 to 6. The noise at high STD exhibits itself as corrosion on the top shield background. Thus, the system that employs a fix threshold value can't cope with the increasing of noise level adaptively. The increasing of levels of noise also increases the dark dots on the images. As a result, the system detected more negative samples. This observation is shown by the result in Figure 1.8(c); the specificity (true negative rate) increased at the high noise STD.

It is worth noting that the threshold value Ts is applied for distinguishing corrosion regions forming the noise (see equation [1.11]). The selection value for Ts when SNR = ∞ dB was obtained and the plot of system performance against the threshold value is shown in Figure 1.9. At $Ts = 2$, the system performs effectively to characterize regions associated with corrosion. However, the high value of Ts introduced the degradation in system specificity.

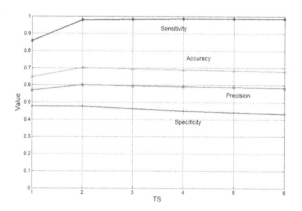

Figure 1.9. *Performance of corrosion detection obtained by area-based feature at six setting of threshold Ts*

The success in detecting corrosion is ascribed to the fusion of area-based and contour-based features, which help increase the discriminant power of the system. Despite this, some pole tip images with corrosions are still missed by the algorithm. The missing detections mainly result from variations in intensity of the camera system and dust on the specimens. The variation in intensity results in the detection error by the system employing area-based feature. Note that, during the tests, all of the relevant parameters, such as the top shield template and thresholding values, are kept unchanged. Hence, the algorithm can be considered to be fully automated.

1.4. Conclusion

In this chapter, we introduced the area-based and contour-based features to characterize corrosion on the top shield of pole tip of the HDD. These features and their fusion offer an effective approach for decision-making in a corrosion audit. This automated detection system plays a very important role for HDD production lines, where a large number of pole tips must be inspected before being assembled into HDDs. The proposed algorithm performs successfully on test samples, with very high accuracy and robustness. The small detection error, 3.35% of false positives, is in the expectable margin allowed by experts, where 3.46% of false negatives are subjected to a second audit validated by the expert for correct identification. This detection algorithm for the corrosion on the pole tips is developed in answer to the needs of users at the company. The moderate computational complexity of the algorithm satisfies the time constraint imposed by the industrial environment. Further improvements are possible at the expense of computational time.

1.5. Bibliography

[ACC 11] ACCIANI G., FORNRELLI G., GIAQUINTO A., "A fuzzy method for global quality index evaluation of solder joints in surface mount technology", *IEEE Transactions on Industrial Informatics*, vol. 7, no. 1, pp. 115–124, 2011.

[BAR 89] BARAGHIMIAN G.A., "Connected component labeling using self-organizing feature maps", *Proceedings of the Annual International Conference on Computer Software and Applications*, CA, pp. 680–684, 1989.

[BEN 13] BENEDEK C., KRAMMER O., JANOCZKI M., *et al.*, "Solder paste scooping detection by multi-level visual inspection of printed circuit boards", *IEEE Transactions on Industrial Electronics*, vol. 60, no. 6, pp. 2318–2331, 2013.

[BIN 09] BING W., SHAOSHENG F., "An improved Canny edge detection algorithm", *Proceedings of the International Conference on Computer Science and Engineering*, Washington, DC, vol. 1, pp. 497–500, 2009.

[CHE 12] CHENG C.-P., YANG C.-I., CHUDASAMA J., *et al.*, Method of reducing main pole corrosion during aluminum oxide etch, U.S. Patent 0 181 181 A1, July 19, 2012.

[CHO 05] CHO C.-S., CHUNG B.-M., PARK M.-J., "Development of real-time vision based fabric inspection system", *IEEE Transactions on Industrial Electronics*, vol. 52, no. 4, pp. 1073–1079, 2005.

[CHO 07] CHOI K.-J., LEE Y.-H., MOON J.-W., *et al.*, "Development of an automatic stencil inspection system using modified Hough transform and fuzzy logic", *IEEE Transactions on Industrial Electronics*, vol. 54, no. 1, pp. 604–611, 2007.

[CHO 11] CHOI S., AKIN B., RAHIMIAN M.M., *et al.*, "Implementation of a fault-diagnosis algorithm for induction machines based on advance digital-signal-processing Techniques", *IEEE Transactions on Industrial Electronics*, vol. 58, no. 3, pp. 937–948, 2011.

[CUI 08] CUI B., LIU H., XUE T., "Application of a new image recognition technology in fabric defect detection," *Proceedings of the International Seminar on Future BioMedical Information Engineering*, Washington, DC, pp. 67–70, 2008.

[FER 09] FERREIRA M.J., SANTOS C., MONTEIRO J., "Cork parquet quality control vision system based on texture segmentation and fuzzy grammar," *IEEE Transactions on Industrial Electronics*, vol. 56, no. 3, pp. 756–765, 2009.

[FLI 06] FLINT E., HSIAO W.-C., HSIAO Y., "Disk drive thin-film inductive write head with pole tip structure having reduced susceptibility of corrosion", U.S. Patent 0 198 048 A1, September 7, 2006.

[GIN 04] GINESU G., GIUSTO D.D., MARGNER V., *et al.*, "Detection of foreign bodies in food by thermal image processing," *IEEE Transactions on Industrial Electronics*, vol. 51, no. 2, pp. 480–490, 2004.

[GON 87] GONZALEZ R.C., WINTZ P.A., *Digital Image Processing*, Reading, MA, Addison-Wesley, 1987.

[GUN 12] GUNAY O., TOREYIN B.U., KOSE K., *et al.*, "Entropy-functional-based online adaptive decision fusion framework with application to wildfire detection in video," *IEEE Transactions on Image Processing*, vol. 5, no. 5, pp. 2853–2865, 2012.

[HAN 06] HAN J., KAMBER M., *Data Mining: Concepts and Techniques*, 2nd ed., San Francisco, CA, Elsevier, Morgan Kaufmann, 2006.

[JAG 08] JAGER M., HUMBERT S., HAMPRECHT F.A., "Sputter tracking for the automatic monitoring of industrial laser-welding process", *IEEE Transactions on Industrial Electronics*, vol. 55, no. 5, pp. 2177–2184, 2008.

[KIM 11] KIM J., YOU B.-J., "Fault detection in a microphone array by intercorrelation of features in voice activity detection", *IEEE Transactions on Industrial Electronics*, vol. 58, no. 6, pp. 2568–2571, 2011.

[KUM 08] KUMAR A., "Computer-vision-based fabric defect detection: a survey", *IEEE Transactions on Industrial Electronics*, vol. 55, no. 1, pp. 348–363, 2008.

[LIA 10] LIANG P., ZHIWEI X., JIGUANG D., "Fast normalized cross-correlation image matching based on multiscale edge information", *in International Conference on Computer Application and System Modeling (ICCASM)*, Fuxin, China, vol. 10, pp. 507–511, 2010.

[LI 06] LI X., TSO S.K., GUAN X.-P., *et al.*, "Improving automatic detection of defects in castings by applying wavelet technique", *IEEE Transactions on Industrial Electronics*, vol. 53, no. 6, pp. 1927–1934, 2006.

[LIN 09] LIN J., LUO S., LI Q., *et al.*, "Real-time rail head surface defect detection: A geometrical approach", *IEEE International Symposium on Industrial Electronics*, China, pp. 769–774, 2009.

[LI 11] LI W.C., TSAI D.-M., "Defect inspection in low-contrast LCD images using Hough transform-based nonstationary line detection", *IEEE Transactions on Industrial Informatics*, vol. 7, no. 1, pp. 136–147, 2011.

[LI 12] LI W., WANG D., CHAI T., "Flame image-baed burning state recognition for sintering process for rotary kiln using heterogeneous features and fuzzy integral", *IEEE Transactions on Industrial Electronics*, vol. 8, no. 4, pp. 780–790, 2012.

[LI 13] LI T.-Y., TSAI J.-Z., CHANG R.-S., *et al.*, "Pretest gap mura on TFT LCDs using the optical interference pattern sensing method and neural network classification", *IEEE Transactions on Industrial Electronics*, vol. 60, no. 9, pp. 3976–3982, 2013.

[MAB 12] MABUCHI K., AKAHOSHI H., Corrosion control method of metal, U.S. Patent 0 202 010 A1, August 16, 2012.

[MAK 09] MAK K.L., PENG P., YIU K.F.C., "Fabric defect detection using morphological filters", *Image and Vision Computing*, vol. 27, pp. 1585–1592, 2009.

[OTS 79] OTSU N., "A threshold selection method from gray-level histograms", *IEEE Transactions on Systems, Man, and Cybernetics*, vol. 9, no. 1, pp. 62–66, 1979.

[PON 11] PONS-LLINARES J., ANTONINO-DAVIU J.A., RIERA-GUASP M., *et al.*, "Induction motor diagnosis based on a transient current analytic wavelet transform via frequency B-splines", *IEEE Transactions on Industrial Electronics*, vol. 58, no. 5, pp. 1530–1544, 2011.

[PRO 96] PROAKIS J.G., MANOLOAKIS D.G., *Digital Signal Processing*, 3rd ed., Upper Saddle, New Jersey, Prentice Hall, 1996.

[SIL 11] SILVA A.F., GONCALVES A.F., FERREIRA L.A.A., *et al.*, "A smart skin PVC foil based on FBG sensors for monitoring strain and temperature", *IEEE Transactions on Industrial Electronics*, vol. 58, no. 7, pp. 2728–2735, 2011.

[TAN 09] TAN M., YAN Y., ZHANG H., *et al.*, "Corrosion protection of ultra-thin ta-C films for recording slider applications at varied substrate bias", *Surface & Coatings Technology*, vol. 203, pp. 936–966, 2009.

[TAN 12] TAN W.R., CHAN C.S., YOGARAJAH P., *et al.*, "A fusion approach for efficient human skin detection", *IEEE Transactions on Industrial Informatics*, vol. 8, no. 1, pp. 138–147, 2012.

[TSA 11] TSAI D.-M., LUO J.-Y., "Mean shift-based defect detection in multicrystalline solar wafer surfaces", *IEEE Transactions on Industrial Electronics*, vol. 7, no. 1, pp. 125–135, 2011.

[WAN 11] WANG G.-G., KUANG X.-P., ZHANG H.-Y., *et al.*, "Silicon nitride gradient film as the underlayer of ultra-thin tetrahedral amorphous carbon overcoat for magnetic recording slider", *Materials Chemistry and Physics*, vol. 131, pp. 127–131, 2011.

[ZHU 07] ZHU J., MAE Y., MINAMI M., "Finding and quantitative evaluation of minute flaws on metal surface using hairline", *IEEE Transactions on Industrial Electronics*, vol. 54, no. 3, pp. 1420–1429, 2007.

2

Nonlinear Filtering Method for Corrosion Detection on Pole Tips

New magnetic recording technology has been developed to achieve high-area densities. This requires reduced thickness of thin films to develop pole tips, an element continually challenged by corrosion. A detection method with high sensitivity and accuracy is therefore necessary to ensure the reliability of hard disk drives (HDDs). This chapter presents two corrosion detection methods based on the contour information of the pole tip. The first method estimates contour length of the pole tip in order to analyze the occurrence of corrosion. The second method implements nonlinear analysis to detect pitting corrosion. The nonlinear filter shows higher accuracy for detecting minute corrosion and is more favorable than the previous studies.

2.1. Introduction

Chapter 1 covered the automatic detection of corrosion on pole tip based on longitudinal recording technology.

Chapter written by Paisarn MUNEESAWANG and Suchart YAMMEN.

Although the recording technology has changed to perpendicular architecture, corrosion is still the main challenge, especially when meeting the requirement of high area density of the new technology. The new designs of thin films, including lubricant layers and overcoat layers, need to focus more on corrosion resistance, as the film layers are thinner than before, in order to meet recording magnetic spacing. Moreover, corrosion is thermodynamically favored under hot and humid conditions, and is also a problem during the manufacturing of recording heads/sliders. The feature extraction methods discussed in Chapter 1 are independent of the types of pole tip. They can be applied to longitudinal recording technology as well as perpendicular types. Once a region of interest is detected, the area-based feature focuses on corrosion spots, whereas the contour-based feature characterizes imperfections on the contour of the pole tip.

When pole tip protrusion renders slider–disk clearances down to a few nanometers, the size of the corrosion particles is a significant determinant in the reliability of HDDs. Therefore, a more accurate characterization of pitting corrosion is necessary. In this chapter, new contour-based features are discussed. This follows on from the experimental study in Chapter 1, which demonstrated that contour-based features play an important role for accurate detection of defects, offering robustness. For the high area density recording, sizing of thin-film components is critical, and thus, the minute corrosion particles need to be sensed effectively. This chapter presents two methods: length-estimator and nonlinear filtering methods. Both can be applied to the contour of pole tips.

Section 2.2 covers the recent developments in perpendicular magnetic recording (PMR) and its challenges with corrosion. These include the selection of lubricants and overcoat layers, thermal effects and pole tip manufacturing. Then, section 2.4 presents the length estimator method for measuring the length of pole tips, and section 2.5 provides nonlinear filtering method for corrosion detection. Section 2.6 discusses the applications and section 2.7 summarizes the chapter.

2.2. Perpendicular magnetic recording

The first magnetic heads, discovered more than 100 years ago by Valdemar Poulsen, were perpendicular recording heads. However, this type was not efficient enough to generate a suitable write field for wire media, and hence, for the past 50 years, the disk drive industry has extensively focused on longitudinal magnetic recordings. In the current HDD technology, however, write heads have switched back to the perpendicular type, since longitudinal recording technology reached its limit a few years back. In 2006, perpendicular recording technology was re-introduced, where the magnetization of each data bit is aligned vertically – or perpendicularly – in relation to the disk drive's platter (Figure 2.1(a)). This recording technology represents an important opportunity for companies in the HDD industry to continue to grow and expand at a reasonable pace.

Figure 2.1(b) shows one configuration of perpendicular recording heads based on a single-pole-type (SPT) head, which is discussed in [ISE 06]. This SPT head is composed of a shield yoke surrounding a quadrangular-shaped pole piece. The specific shape of the main pole generates a large additional field, and the shield narrows the field distribution, resulting in a sharp, confined field with a high maximum field strength [HON 10]. This design structure has been studied in order to reduce track widths, and thus, increase areal density [YAM 08].

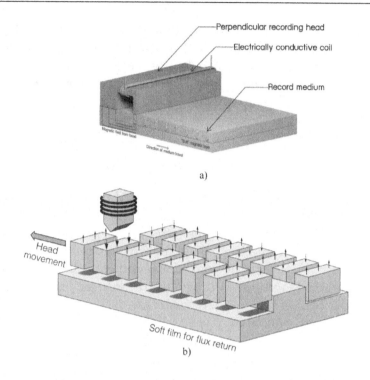

Figure 2.1. *Illustration of a) magnetic fields of perpendicular magnetic recording and b) top view of single-pole head*

Figure 2.2 shows the practical structure configuration of a perpendicular pole tip taken by scanning-electron microscope-based critical dimension (SEM-CD) measurement system. The shield is generally composed of a large soft magnetic layer placed at the trailing edge of the main pole. For narrow track width recordings, it is necessary to design the dimension of the tip widths to produce field sharpness. The critical parameters are concerned with the width, thickness and angles of the writer. In the inspection-based screening operations, the dimension of the writer is monitored at various points in the slider process. Row bars of wafer are passed through air-baring surface (ABS) metrology for measurement and also for corrosion audit. In this process, the SEM-CD helps for automatic measurement at operator level and 100% screening of ABS and pole defects.

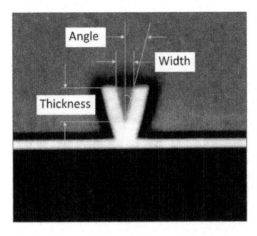

Figure 2.2. *Air-bearing surface view of shielded heads*

2.3. Perpendicular magnetic recorder and corrosion

Figure 2.3 illustrates the components of a thin-film magnetic recording head. Between the pole tip and the magnetic layer, there are the needs for overcoat and lubricant layers. According to Wallace equation [WAL 51], magnetic signal increases exponentially with a decrease in magnetic spacing, which is the space between the head and the magnetic layer [POH 10]. Thus, in order to increase the magnetic areal density, we need to reduce magnetic spacing [POH 10, SAM 11b]. The high-density HDD of more than 1 Tbit/inch^2 needs to reduce the magnetic spacing below 10 nm [KIM 11]. To that end, the overcoat thickness of less than sub-2 nm is required [POH 10]. However, reducing the

thickness of the protective film is not the only requirement –
another important requirement is maintaining its durability
during contact between the head and the disk [MIY 05]. The
aforementioned requirements control the surface topography
of both the disk media and the read/write head [ABE 11,
MOS 06].

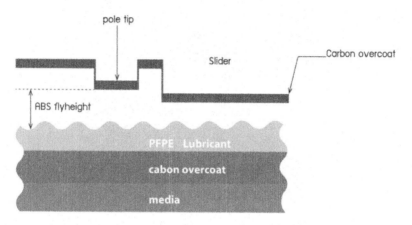

Figure 2.3. *Components of a thin film*

2.3.1. *Lubricant layer*

The lubricant layer contributes to reducing the friction
and wear of the slider and disk, which are tribologically soft
and poor in wear and corrosion resistance. It works together
with the carbon overcoat on the hard disk surface to protect
the magnetic layer from corrosion. As discussed previously,
reducing thickness of lubricant layers contributes to
reducing magnetic spacing. The lubricant layer of current
HDDs is typically 10–20 Å thick. If the head–disk interface
could be stable without a lubricant layer, removing part or
the entire lubricant layer can contribute to a significant
reduction of the magnetic spacing in this spacing range

[KIM 11]. However, the reduction of the lubricant thickness is a challenging problem regarding wear and corrosion resistance. Tribological researchers have studied the material structure to explore this problem, in particular to understand the behavior of lubricant particles on the atomic scale [MIY 05]. For new lubricant design and development, the molecular property of lubricant structure is considered an important issue. Specifically, the material composition and mobility of a lubricant are key factors in determining the composition, distribution and morphology of corrosion products [JI 09].

2.3.1.1. *Perfluoropolyether (PFPE)*

PFPEs are currently used as lubricants at head–disk interfaces to reduce friction and wear [XU 04] and lower surface energy [KIM 09]. Various types of PFPEs, including Z-Dol, A20H and Lubel, can inhibit corrosion due to their hydrophobicity [JI 09]. A good corrosion-resistant lubricant can be achieved by having water-repellent properties and low mobility. In this regard, Z-Dol is not a good choice. In contrast, Lubel offers high thermal stability and good fictional property by synthesization. Kim *et al.* [KIM 11] attempted to reduce the thickness by first classifying the lubricant layers into three types, and then studying their properties by baking. The normal lubricants have a thickness of more than 7 Å, whereas the partial lubricants have a thickness of 3.5 Å, and bared lubricants have a thickness of 0.5 Å. Baking the partial lubricanted disks provides increased wear resistance, as good as the normally lubricanted disks, and thus, the thickness can be reduced to half of the normal lubricant. However, baking decreases corrosion resistance.

Reduced thickness encounters issues with corrosion, but also the following problems. At the decrease in head–disk clearance, there is an increasing probability of interaction between the slider and lubricant film [MAR 03, MA 07]. This causes the problem of lubricant transfer from disk surface to slider, flying stiction [KIM 09, RAM 99] and lubricant depletion [AMB 09], which reduces the stability of head–disk interface [LI 11]. Lubricant thickness and molecular structures are all relevant to the transfer of lubricants [WAN 05]. The less lubricant used in manufacturing, the better it is for solving this problem. The dynamic behavior of molecularly thin lubricant film, such as its spring constants and damping coefficients, can determine the durability and reliability of the head–disk interface [MIT 07].

2.3.1.2. *Overcoat*

In Figure 2.3, the magnetic medium and the read–write head elements are coated with a thin overcoat of diamond-like carbon (DLC). The primary role of an overcoat is to protect the devices from oxidation and wear [SAM 11a, SAM 11b]. In a HDD of 1 Tb/inch^2 areal density, the overcoat is approximately 1 and 2 nm on head and magnetic media, respectively. If the requirement is up to 10 Tb/inch^2, the overcoat on media should be reduced to the range of less than a nanometer without compromising their tribological and corrosion properties. DLC surfaces are chemically inert, continuous, densely packed and free of pinholes [SAM 11b]. They must have the ability to bond well with the lubricant. Denser DLC is produced by chemical vapor deposition (CVD) and cathodic arc deposition of silicon nitride [WAL 10].

In order to reduce the overcoat thickness, there are two solutions. The first solution involves techniques to improve the decomposition for fabricating thinner and denser carbon films with enhanced properties [PIR 03]. The second solution involves finding alternative overcoat materials such as Zirconia, SiO_2 and SiN_x that can provide better corrosion than carbon [YEN 03]. However, the techniques belonging to the second solution may not be easily implemented in the production process as they involve many changes from the existing process in recording media. Recently, a hybrid magnetic overcoat (Hy-MOC) has been studied [POH 08, POH 10]. It contains two layers with different purposes: an amorphous carbon overcoat at the top and a magnetic overcoat at the bottom. The Hy-MOC may provide a solution of further reduction in the magnetic spacing at the same time, providing the sufficient protection against corrosion.

2.3.2. *Thermal effect results in corrosion*

Tribological reliability remains challenged by the heat, especially when the thickness of DLC and lubricant films has been continuously decreasing [XU 04]. Since corrosion is thermodynamically favored [WAL 10], magnetic media and the pole tip must demonstrate corrosion resistance under hot, humid conditions. The cobalt dissolution in the magnetic alloy is galvanically coupled to the O_2/OH^- system [NOV 88]. This is confirmed by the studies of Pourbaix diagram for $Co-H_2O$ system [CHI 08, HEM 94, POU 66]. Co will be oxidized by aerated water with the formation of Co^{2+} for all pH values at the redox potential values above the equilibrium. This indicates that at higher pH and/or potential values, various oxides of cobalt are produced.

Wal *et al.* [WAL 10] studied the critical overcoat film thickness for corrosion inhibition at 20°C temperature and 50% relative humidity for cobalt clothing by ion beam-deposited nitrogenated carbon (IBDN), SiC and SiN_x. In their study, corrosion decreases with increasing overcoat film thickness in all cases. The critical film thicknesses are approximately 25, 25 and 20 Å for IBDN, SiC and SiN_x, respectively. In addition to the DLC, PFPE is sensitive to temperature, especially its mobile fraction. Thus, movement of the PFPE molecules will allow the magnetic media to be exposed to the environment through the micropores existing in DLC overcoat. In a study by Xu *et al.* [XU 04], during heating, the lubricant decomposition and the diffusion of elements out of magnetic media layer thorough amorphous carbon overcoat cause the corrosion of the disk media. The heat increases the number of corrosion spots and their depth.

2.3.3. *Recording head/slider manufacturing and corrosion*

The slider is a multicomponent material, wherein the read and write elements mainly consist of the alloy of soft magnetic materials such as CoNiFe and NiFe [AZU 04, FEK 04, THO 64], while the slider substrate is made up of a hard ceramic material (Al_2O_3-TiC) [ABE 11, PHO 12]. The variety of materials offer a plethora of opportunities for electrostatic discharge [JIA 03] and electrochemical corrosion during ABS formation process [CHA 11]. The read and write elements of recording heads are fabricated on ceramic substrates using thin-film processing technology, as shown in Figure 2.4. In the first step, the wafer processing involves several sequential lithography and etching steps with many photo mask plates. The wafers are built with multilayers and then sliced. The surface of the head is finished by lapping. The ABS is formed and coated by thin DLC film before the bars are diced to individual heads.

The by-products of photoresist from the etching process in slider fabrication are very prone to corrosion. The thinner protection DLC coating (<17 Å for recording density of 500 Gb/inch^2 or more [LEE 05]) on the slider bar surface cannot provide sufficient protection for the corrosion during etching process. A more optimized solution is the selection of photoresist materials to minimize slider corrosion during the etching process. The type of wet photoresist AZ4999 is more suitable in the photography process than the dry photoresist [CHA 11].

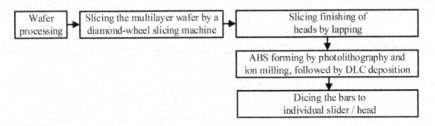

Figure 2.4. *Thin-film magnetic recording head / slider manufacture*

The lapping process serves for surface finishing of a slider. The materials are removed to control important step heights of the individual material components of a slider (i.e. across multilayer of thin metal film and AlTiC hard substrate). This process contributes to the final head–disk gap [ABE 11], thereby to minimize space loss and reduce flying height variation. The finishing process also critically affects the magnetic, electrical and mechanical performance of the recording heads and their stability [JIA 03]. Nanogrinding is a slider abrasive finishing process [GAT 96, GAT 97] used to remove metal for the surface of the slider to give it a good planar finish and improve the topographical variation of the slider. This process is completed by embedding abrasive particles in a lapping plate and passing the lubricant between the workpiece and the lapping plate. A suitable type of lubricant can be chosen to achieve this process. The oil-soluble lubricant can prevent metal corrosion of the magnetic read elements, whereas the water-soluble lubricant can be chemically selective, through pH adjustment, leading to a preference for the removal of one type of materials over another [ABE 11].

2.4. Length estimator for pole tip

When pole tip protrusion reduces slider–disk clearances to a mere 2–4 nm, the size of the corrosion particles is a significant determinant in the reliability of HDDs [HUA 97]. A corrosion particle on the overcoat surface that exceeds these clearances will have an increased possibility of contact with the low-flying slider, causing unwanted failures of the HDD [WAL 10]. In order to detect corrosion particles in this range, contour information of the pole tips can be used. In this chapter, it is shown that the contour of the top shield has been corrupted by corrosion, and thus, analyzing the contour characteristics provides a clue for detection of corrosion. The methods for contour analysis presented in this chapter are the length estimator method (discussed in this section) and the nonlinear filtering method (discussed in section 2.5).

In order to estimate the length of contours in digital image, there have been many studies in the past. An image contour can be viewed as a digital arc which is equivalent to chain codes, i.e. sequence of vectors whose slopes are multiples of $45°$ and whose lengths are 1 (if horizontal or vertical) or $\sqrt{2}$ (if diagonal) [JI 09]. Using this definition, the contour of pole tips in Figure 2.5 can be viewed as a sequence of chain codes $i(0), i(1),...$ with $i(n) \in A = \{0,...,7\}, n \geq 0$. Thus, the method for length estimation can be applied to this sequence.

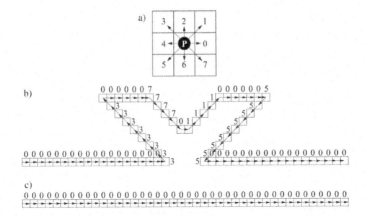

Figure 2.5. *Change codes of pole tips: a) 8-neighbor change codes,*
b) schematic view of change codes of perpendicular pole tip and
c) schematic view of change codes of longitudinal pole tip

In the simplest terms, n-characterization is defined for
the length estimator [DOR 87]:

$$L(n) = an \qquad\qquad [2.1]$$

where a is a constant value. If $a = 1$, $L_o(n) = n$, which is the
number of strings (codes) in the chain codes. Although
simple, this estimator gives very high error of RDEV = 10%,
where RDEV is the root mean square difference between
original length and estimated length of overall strings of n
elements, and divided by n this can achieve an RDEV of
0.8%. The second length estimator is the (n_e, n_o)
characterization:

$$L(n_e, n_o) = an_e + bn_o \qquad\qquad [2.2]$$

where n_e is the number of even chain code elements aligned
along the grid, and n_o is the number of old chain code
elements aligned diagonally. The parameters a and b are the
coefficients characteristics of the length estimator, which are
chosen to minimize the error of the measurements

[RIV 09]. The Freeman formula [FRE 70, MOB 11] used to determine the parameters is:

$$L_F(n_e, n_o) = n_e + \sqrt{2}n_o = 1.000n_e + 1.414n_o \qquad [2.3]$$

This formula gives no error when slopes are 0 and 1, i.e. only line segments lying on the octant lines [RIV 09]. For all other segment slopes, the values of L_F exceed the true length with an error which depends on the slope. This length estimator gives the RDEV = 6.6% [TAJ 03]. The statistical analysis has been used to find those parameters that minimize the error [DOR 87]. Kulpa [KUL 77] proposed a length estimator in which the parameters a and b were adjusted to minimize the expected error. This defines the following length estimator:

$$L_F(n_e, n_o) = 0.948n_e + 1.343n_o \qquad [2.4]$$

It gives RDEV = 2.6%. The last length estimator is the (n_e, n_o, n_c)-characterization which is the *cornercount* length estimator [COE 04]:

$$L_F(n_e, n_o, n_c) = an_e + bn_o + cn_c \qquad [2.5]$$

where n_c is the number of odd–even chain code transitions. In [VOS 82], the coefficients are estimated by minimizing the mean square error, which results in the formula:

$$L_F(n_e, n_o, n_c) = 0.980n_e + 1.406n_o - 0.091n_c \qquad [2.6]$$

With regard to the error, the estimator for contour length measurements depend on image resolution, i.e. pixel size [RIV 09]. The larger the pixel size (low resolution), the larger the amount of undetected contour, and thus, the higher the length estimation error. For all methods discussed earlier, the error is reduced at the higher grid resolution [COE 04]. However, as it is evident from the study in [TAJ 03], although the pixel size is very small (resolution tends to infinity, i.e. continuous curve), the estimator cannot be used because of the lack of convergence of the estimators [TAJ 03].

We may refer to the formulas in equations [2.1]–[2.6] as approaches based on local metrics (i.e. weighted metrics) which are linear in characterizing the parameters [COE 04]. These estimators are popular because of their computational simplicity [DOR 87]. Given the sequence of chain codes, there are also two approaches based on polygonalizations of digital curves which are directed to subsequent calculations of two parameters. These are maximum-length digital straight segments (DSSs) and minimum length polygons (MLPs). In the DSS method, the boundary is considered as a collection of DSSs [KLE 99]. Thus, the method detects each maximum-length DSS and calculates the length of each DSS using Euclidean distance. The sum of the lengths is finally used as the length of the given digital arc. The MLP method is characterized by the calculation of the MLP circumscribing a given inner boundary and being in the interior of an outer boundary [COE 04].

If the Euclidean convex region is digitized with increasing grid resolution, the two polygonalization-based techniques converge toward the true values of perimeters [KLE 99]. DSS runs considerably faster than MLP and with faster convergence, as well as offering a lower error than MLP. However, in practice, polygonalization-based estimators are much slower than local metric methods, especially for higher grid resolutions [COE 04].

In this chapter, the automatic visual inspection for corrosion detection is implemented using the length estimation method. To keep the computation of the contour length simple, the commonly used (n_e, n_o)-characterization is applied in the experiment section. The length of the contour is characterized by image feature. The corroded pole tip has this image feature varied from the non-corroded pole tip. Thus, a threshold value can be applied for image classification.

2.5. Nonlinear filtering as a corrosion detector

In a filtering process, the goal is to identify the signal samples that are corrupted by noise and restored them to the original signal values. It is equally important for the filtering process to preserve the details of the signal, thereby maintaining uncorrupted signal samples. Similarly, in the corrosion detection process, the first goal is to detect the location of corrosion, and the second goal is to, without obtaining false detection by mistake, detect the uncorroded signal samples. Therefore, it is necessary to explore the filter type that can effectively detect the noise, together with preserving signal details as much as possible. The noise removal methods can be categorized as linear and nonlinear methods [SHA 12]. Moving average filters are examples of linear process, whereas media, stack, min and max filters are the nonlinear processes [JIN 07, COY 88]. In this chapter, convolution techniques have been used to implement the weighting kernels as a neighborhood function, which represent a linear process. Alternatively, a median filter can be performed for this purpose, as nonlinear neighborhood operations.

2.5.1. *Median filter techniques*

The ranked-order filters [ARC 89] are nonlinear processes and can be classified into two categories: adaptive and non-adaptive ranked-order filters. The second category has less complexity because there is no requirement for prior information of the signal samples. The median filter is a non-adaptive ranked-order filter, which was first introduced by Tukey [TUK 71, TUK 74] in 1971. In order to calculate a filtered signal value at a particular time, the median filter sorts an odd number of sample values and takes the middle value as the filter output [YIN 96], i.e.:

$$y[n] = \mathrm{MED}\left[x[n-k],...,x[n],...,x[n+k]\right] \qquad [2.7]$$

for the filter length $N = 2k + 1$, and the sample values $X[n-k],...,X[n+k]$.

The two intrinsic properties of median filter are edge preservation and efficient noise attenuation particularly for impulsive-type noise. These are elementary to the success of median filters [YIN 96]. However, there are some problems associated with its application. First, the filtering performance is dependent on the window size (i.e. N). A smaller N must be used to preserve smaller detail in signals [YAN 95]. Unfortunately, the smaller N is, the poorer its noise reduction capability becomes [JUS 81]. In addition, when the number of the samples in the filter's window is large, the ordering procedures in equation [2.7] become cumbersome [HEI 87]. Second, the median filter may cause edge jitter or get rid of important signal detail [SHA 12, NIE 87, ARC 89]. The main reason for this is that the filter uses only rank-order information of the input data, and discards its original temporal-order information [YIN 96]. For example, some input vectors have distinct and varied patterns. However, their corresponding sorted vectors are identical [BAR 94]. Temporal order is relevant for non-constant signals corrupted by noise [PAL 89].

In order to exploit both rank- and temporal-order information, the weight median filters and other rank-order-based filters have been developed [KOT 94, COY 88, HEI 87, BAR 94, BRO 84]. Among these, the weight median filters are the simplest rank-order-based filters. It offers much greater flexibility in design specifications than the median filter [YIN 96]. The weights control the filter behavior to trade off detail preservation against noise reduction [JIN 07, YAN 95]. The weight median filter spans N associated input samples with the integer weights:

$$W = [w_1, w_2, ..., w_N] \qquad\qquad [2.8]$$

and obtains the output by:

$$y[n] = \mathrm{MED}\left[w_1 \Diamond x[n-k], ..., w_n \Diamond x[n], ..., w_N \Diamond x[n+k]\right] \qquad [2.9]$$

where $\Diamond$ denotes the duplication, i.e.:

$$w \Diamond x = \overbrace{x, x, ..., x}^{w \text{ times}} \qquad\qquad\qquad [2.10]$$

There are a number of works that have been done to determine the weight vector to achieve the optimum balance between noise smoothing and detail preservation, e.g. the varying-weight trim [ZHA 05] and the distance-weighted vector [CHA 03]. In principle, the central signal sample in the filter window is emphasized with a maximal weight [KO 91]. All weight parameters can also be determined adaptively by learning algorithms according to statistic characteristics of signal and noise [YAN 03]. The psychophysical phenomena of human visual contrast sensitivity are studied to characterize the weights in [BEL 00, JIN 07]. Thus, signal values are classified as contour points based on the contrast sensitivity, and are not disturbed by the filtering operation.

2.5.2. *Median ε-Filter*

Weight media filters require a high degree of calculation for obtaining weight through learning process. Recently, the median ε-filter has been introduced by Matsumoto *et al.* [MAT 09a] with low calculation cost. It has the advantage of the ε-filter, which requires only switching operation, while at the same time, it can reduce impulsive noise by persevering edge information [SHA 12]. The conventional ε-filter was introduced by Harushima *et al.* [HAR 82] for reducing stationary noise as well as non-stationary noise. It is easy to design and computation costs are small. In [ABE 07], this type of filter is improved to handle large non-stationary noise by the application of time–frequency analysis method.

In this study, the median ε-filter [MAT 09a] is adopted for detection of corrosion on the contour of pole tips. The filter applies median operation to the output of the ε-filter demonstrated in [MAT 09b], instead of direct application to the signal sequence. The ε value is used to select the noise positions so that the signal samples are unselected and undisturbed. The selection of ε parameter is essential to reduce the noise appropriately. Using small value of ε, the filter behavior is similar to the median filter, while using the large value of ε, the signal values being processing are replaced with the same value and the filter dose nothing to reduce the noise [MAT 09a].

2.5.3. Corrosion detection procedure

Figure 2.6 shows the nonlinear filter process for corrosion detection. An adoption of median ε-filter [MAT 09a] is proposed to detect pitting corrosion on the contour of pole tip. An input data $\{x[n]\}$, which is an image contour, is passed through the median ε-filter to obtain the output response $\{s[n]\}$. The filter can perform the job of rejecting corrosion points, in which some individual signal components have extreme values. This enables the data sequence $\{e[n]\}$, which is the difference between $\{x[n]\}$ and $\{s[n]\}$, to be able to indicate the position of corrosion. Compared to the convolution technique that uses a moving difference filter to discover the change in the amplitude of data $\{x[n]\}$, with limited capability to detect data with low gradient, the output sequence $\{e[n]\}$ in the filtering process of Figure 2.6 is more sensitive than the small corrosion points.

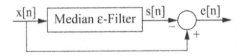

Figure 2.6. *Illustration of nonlinear filter*

The process of implementing the median ε-filter with q order is detailed as follows. Letting the input data point be $\{x[n]\}$ and the output data point be $\{s[n]\}$:

STEP 1. Select an odd number q to obtain a new data sequence containing data points around $\{x[n]\}$:

$$\left\{x\left[n-\left((q-1)/2\right)\right],...,x[n-1],x[n+1],...,x\left[n+\left((q-1)/2\right)\right]\right\} \quad [2.11]$$

STEP 2. Sort the data sequence in equation [2.11] resulting in a new data sequence:

$$\left\{\hat{x}_1[n],\hat{x}_2[n],...,\hat{x}_{q-2}[n],\hat{x}_{q-1}[n]\right\} \quad [2.12]$$

Then, obtain the median value $\mu[n]$ of the data sequence:

$$\mu[n]=0.5\left\{\hat{x}_{((q-1)/2)}[n]+\hat{x}_{((q+1)/2)}[n]\right\} \quad [2.13]$$

STEP 3. Obtain the data sequence $\{d_i[n]\}$ whose member is the difference between the data points in sequence (equation [2.12]) and $x[n]$, where $d_i[n]$ is defined as:

$$d_i[n]=\begin{cases} \hat{x}_i[n]-x[n], & x[n]\le\mu[n] \\ x[n]-\hat{x}_{q-1-i}[n], & x[n]>\mu[n] \end{cases} \quad [2.14]$$

where $i=1,2,...,(q-1)/2$.

STEP 4. Find the location of possible corrosion at $n=n_0$, where $n=n_0$ if both values $d_{(q-1)/2}[n]$ and $d_{(q-3)/2}[n]$ are greater than a threshold value ε.

STEP 5. Assign $s[n]=\mu[n]$ if there exists n_0 in step 4, otherwise, assign $s[n]=x[n]$.

It is noted that the input data elements $x[n]$ being processed contain a relatively small number of small corrosion points. The median ε-filter provides an effective way of ignoring these corrosion points, while leaving relatively undistorted long-term trends and yet preserving non-corrosion points in the input data sequence. It is apparent that the response value of $\{s[n]\}$ is obtained from running through the input data entry by entry, replacing each entry with either the median of neighboring entries, if the conditions in step 4 hold, or the input data entry, if not. Without any doubt, using the above procedure, the improved median filter can be used to detect the positions of small corrosion points. Remember we now determine the responses of the difference filter to the nonlinear filtering output data sequence $\{s[n]\}$ and the data sequence $\{x[n]\}$ as the error data sequence $\{e[n]\}$ governed by:

$$e[n] = x[n] - s[n] \tag{2.15}$$

At a small corrosion point, the bottom shield of the pole tip has a small indented contour with low slope. The convolution technique tends to miss detecting this since it uses a linear weighting function on the neighborhood data points. In the median ε-filter, the neighboring components are ranked according to ordered values and the median position becomes the corrosion location. Thus, a small change can be detected at the corrosion location which requires finding all the values of n_0; that is:

$$e[n]\big|_{n=n_0} > 0 \tag{2.16}$$

Furthermore, the non-corrosion location requires finding all values of n_0; that is:

$$e[n]\big|_{n=n_0} = 0 \tag{2.17}$$

In order to detect the corrosion, the standard signal-to-noise ratio is obtained:

$$SNR = 10\log_{10}\left(\frac{\sum_{n=1}^{N}(s[n])^2}{\sum_{n=1}^{N}(e[n])^2}\right)[dB] \qquad [2.18]$$

The level of *SNR* can be used in the detection of the corrosion on the pole tip, in comparison with a predefined threshold value.

2.6. Application

The nonlinear filter discussed in section 2.5 is applied in corrosion detection. Its performance is compared to the length-estimator method as discussed in section 2.4 and the convolution-based filtering method as discussed in this chapter. A total of 647 pole tip images of 2,048 × 2,048 pixels were prepared by an expert, using a 1,200× Deep Ultraviolet (DUV) optical microscope. This is the same set of data used in the experiments reported in this chapter. This test set consisted of 289 non-corrosion images (class I) and 358 corrosion images (class II). The best top shield region of size 200 × 1,200 pixels was used as the reference template for obtaining cross-correlation function (CCF) values, in order to select the region of interest. A program was developed to automate the methods as discussed in section 2.5. The testing platform was an Intel CPU Core 2 Duo computer running at 3.16 GHz. The computational time for each 4.2-megapixel image was approximately 0.41 sec.

Figure 2.7 shows edge images of four configurations of top shield pole tips. The image profile of the lower contour on each image was obtained and normalized to the value in the interval [0,1], as shown in Figure 2.8. These image profiles were used as the input signals, and were passed through the nonlinear filter. Figures 2.9 and 2.10 show the output signals at each stage of the nonlinear filter. It can be observed from Figure 2.10 that the corrosion points on the contour of the top shield have effectively been detected. The fault detection does not occur for the pole tips that have not been corroded at the contour area. The procedural parameter for the filter (filter order, q, and threshold value, ε) are determined experimentally. At the calibration process, the value of q was set from [5,99] with a step size of 2, and the value of ε was set from [0.005, 0.35] with the step size of 0.005. It was found that best detection rate was obtained at $q = [71,75]$ and $\varepsilon = [0.205, 0.210]$.

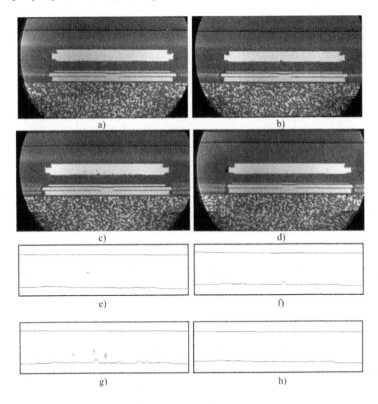

Figure 2.7. *Top shield pole tips and the extracted edge images: a) and e) corrosion inside the top shield area; b) and f) corrosion on the bottom contour of the top shield; c) and g) corrosion at both the positions in a) and b); d) and h) the reference non-corrosion image*

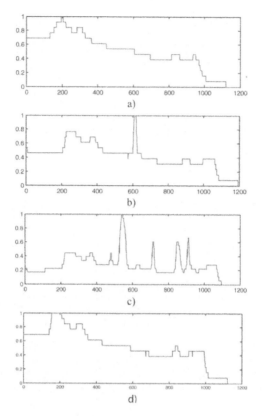

Figure 2.8. *Image profiles of the top shield pole tips in Figure 2.7(e)–(h), each of which shows the input signal* {$x[n]$} *to the nonlinear filter*

The implementation of the length-estimator method used (n_c,n_o)-characterization (see equation [2.3]). The estimated length, L_F, was obtained from the edge image. The pole tips which have $L_F \geq 1212.12$ were classified as corroded pole tips. It was observed that this estimated length was slightly longer than the actual length of the extracted top shield region whose size is 200 × 1,200 pixels. The implementation of the convolution-based filtering was based on the same setting of procedural parameters as the experiment discussed in Chapter 1.

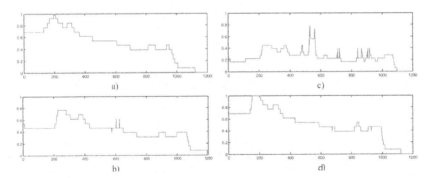

Figure 2.9. *Output signal* $\{s[n]\}$ *for the corresponding input signal in Figure 2.8*

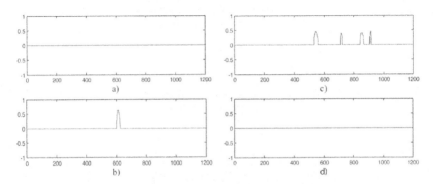

Figure 2.10. *Output of the improved median filter* $\{e[n]\}$ *for the corresponding input signal in Figure 2.9. The peak values indicate possible corrosions*

Table 2.1 shows the results for corrosion detection, in the case where all images were corroded, together with the corresponding signal-to-noise ratio (*SNR*). These images were in class I (corrosion class) and all were detected as corroded samples by the nonlinear filter. It is observed that the *SNRs* measured fall within a certain range. This allows effective image classification. In comparison, Table 2.2 shows 14 samples of non-corrosion analyzed by the system. In this case, the level of *SNR* is ∞ as the noise level becomes zero.

Index	Top shield image	SNR [dB]
1		22.9207
2		38.2491
3		21.0567
4		22.6791
5		26.4667
6		25.2545
7		33.6214
8		74.5545
9		44.4470
10		46.3268
11		39.0430
12		72.7457
13		37.4460
14		38.9023

Table 2.1. *Corrosion detection results obtained by the nonlinear filter: 14 images from class I (corrosion class), each of which was detected as corrosion using the corresponding SNR*

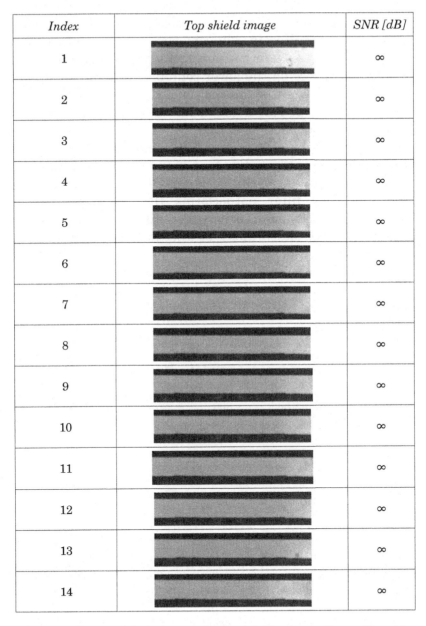

Index	Top shield image	SNR [dB]
1		∞
2		∞
3		∞
4		∞
5		∞
6		∞
7		∞
8		∞
9		∞
10		∞
11		∞
12		∞
13		∞
14		∞

Table 2.2. *Corrosion detection results obtained by the nonlinear filter: 14 images from class II (non-corrosion class), each of which was detected as non-corrosion using the corresponding SNR*

The visual inspection of 647 pole tip images obtained by an operator resulted in 329 corrosion images and 318 non-corrosion images. Here, the operator examined corrosion only for its occurrence on the lower contour of the top shield, and not inside the area of the top shield, in order to study the discriminating power of the three methods. The results of automatic inspection obtained by the three methods are shown in Table 2.3, and the evaluation of the system performance based on the four standard measurements is given in Table 2.4. It can be observed from the tables that the nonlinear filter outperforms the other methods as discussed. It can achieve very low false positive and false negative rates. Regardless of the measurement methods used for the evaluation, detection rates of more than 99% can be obtained. In comparison, the convolution-based filtering method comes in second at 97.5% accuracy and the length-estimator method has the lowest accuracy at 95.8%.

Method	Corosion		Non-corrosion	
	Correct	Miss	Correct	Miss
Nonlinear filter	326	3	315	3
Length-estimator method	309	20	311	7
Convolution-based filtering	318	11	313	5

Table 2.3. *Automatic visual inspection results, obtained by detection of corrosion on the contour of the top shield pole tips of 647 samples*

Method	Performance			
	Sensitivity	Specificity	Precision	Accuracy
Nonlinear filter	0.9906	0.9909	0.9906	0.9907
Length-estimator method	0.9780	0.9392	0.9396	0.9583
Convolution-based filtering	0.9843	0.9666	0.9660	0.9753

Table 2.4. *Performance evaluation of automatic visual inspection results in Table 2.3, using four standard measurements*

Next, the system considered all positions of corrosion for image classification, in which the pole tips have been corroded on any part on the top shield. The methods based on a single feature (contour-based/area-based feature) were applied to the pole tip images and the results are shown in Table 2.5. As anticipated, the methods using a single feature cannot cope with all configurations of corrosion. The nonlinear filter can obtain an accuracy rate of 95.2% which is the highest compared to the methods which used single features. Table 2.6 shows the results obtained by the three fusion methods, and Table 2.7 summarizes the detection results based on the four measurements. The fusion of the decisions from the nonlinear filter and the area-based feature can obtain a corrosion detection performance at 98.2% accuracy. The specificity is of importance in the corrosion audit, and the system using the fusion method can achieve a specificity of 98.6% (e.g. only 1.4% of corrosion goes undetected). It can also be seen from the result that the sensitivity of the fusion method is 97.6%. This indicates that 2.4% of non-corrosions go undetected.

| | *Method* | *Image class* | *Detection result* | |
			Correct	*Miss*
Contour-based feature	Nonlinear filter	Non-corrosion	288	1
		Corrosion	328	30
		Total	*616 (95.2%)*	*31*
	Length-estimator method	Non-corrosion	279	10
		Corrosion	317	41
		Total	*596 (92.1%)*	*51*
	Convolution-based filtering method	Non-corrosion	285	4
		Corrosion	320	38
		Total	*605 (93.5%)*	*42*
Area-based feature		Non-corrosion	283	6
		Corrosion	169	189
		Total	*452 (69.9%)*	*195*

Table 2.5. *Corrosion detection result, obtained by a single feature (contour-based / area-based feature)*

Method	Image class	Detection result	
		Correct	*Miss*
Fusion I: Nonlinear filter and area-based feature	Non-corrosion	282	7
	Corrosion	353	5
	Total	635	12
Fusion II: Length-estimator method and area-based feature	Non-corrosion	281	8
	Corrosion	338	20
	Total	619	28
Fusion III: Convolution-based filter and area-based feature	Non-corrosion	281	8
	Corrosion	345	13
	Total	626	21

Table 2.6. *Corrosion detection result, obtained by decision fusion of two features*

Method	Performance			
	Sensitivity	*Specificity*	*Precision*	*Accuracy*
Fusion I	0.9758	0.9860	0.9826	0.9815
Fusion II	0.9723	0.9441	0.9335	0.9567
Fusion III	0.9723	0.9636	0.9557	0.9675

Table 2.7. *Performance evaluation of corrosion detection results in Table 2.6*

2.7. Conclusion

In this chapter, two methods are discussed for corrosion detection on contour of pole tips. The first method encodes the edge image of the pole tips with 8-connected grid, and estimates the contour length. It is concluded that the corroded pole tip has different length from the uncorroded pole tip. Thus, corrosion images can be classified by application of thresholding. The second method is the adoption of median ε-filter, which implements a non-linear approach to characterize minute corrosions. It outperforms previous methods and performs well on test samples with very high accuracy and sensibility. The small detection error rate, 1.4%, of false positives is in the expected margin allowed by an expert inspector, whereas 2.4% of false negatives are subjected to a second audit by the expert to be correctly identified.

2.8. Bibliography

[ABE 07] ABE T., MATSUMOTO M., HASHIMOTO S., "Noise reduction combining time-domain e-filter and time-frequency e-filter", *Journal of the Acoustical Society of America*, vol. 122, pp. 2697–2705, 2007.

[ABE 11] ABENOJAR E.C., HERBER J.P., ENRIQUEZ E.P., "Surface energies of magnetic recording head components", *Tribology Letters*, vol. 41, pp. 587–595, 2011.

[AMB 09] AMBEKAR R.P., BOGY D.B., BHATIA C.S., "Lubricant depletion and disk-to-head lubricant transfer at the head-disk interface in hard disk drives", *Journal of Tribology*, vol. 131, pp. 031901–031908, 2009.

[ARC 89] ARCE G.R., FOSTER R.E., "Detail-preserving ranked-order based filters for image processing", *IEEE Transactions on Acoustics Speech and Signal Processing*, vol. 37, pp. 83–98, 1989.

[AZU 04] AZUMA S., KUDO T., MIYUKI H., *et al.*, "Effect of nickel alloying on crevice corrosion resistance of stainless steels", *Corrosion Science*, vol. 46, pp. 2265–2280, 2004.

[BAR 94] BARNER K.E., ARCE G.R., "Permutation filters: a class of nonlinear filters based on set permutations", *IEEE Transactions on Signal Processing*, vol. 42, pp. 782–798, 1994.

[BEL 00] BELKACEM-BOUSSAID K., BEGHDADI A., "A new image smoothing method based on a simple model of spatial processing in the early stages of human vision", *IEEE Transactions on Image Processing*, vol. 9, pp. 220–226, 2000.

[BRO 84] BROWNRIGG D.R.K., "The weighted median filter", *Communications of the ACM*, vol. 27, pp. 807–818, 1984.

[CHA 03] CHARLES D., DAVIES E.R., "Distance-weighted median filters and their application to colour images", *Proceedings of the International Conference on Visual Information Engineering*, pp. 117–120, 2003.

[CHA 11] CHATRUPRACHEWIN S., SUPADEE L., TITIROONGRUANG W., "Polymer film selection for corrosion protection of data storage magnetic materials", *Journal of Nanoscience and Nanotechnology*, vol. 11, pp. 10579–10583, 2011.

[CHI 08] CHIVOT J., MENDOZA L., MANSOUR C., *et al.*, "New insight in the behaviour of Co–H2O system at 25–150 °C, based on revised Pourbaix diagrams", *Corrosion Science*, vol. 50, pp. 62–69, 2008.

[COE 04] COEURJOLLY D., KLETTE R., "A comparative evaluation of length estimators of digital curves", *IEEE Transactions on Pattern Analysis and Machine Intelligence*, vol. 26, pp. 252–258, 2004.

[COY 88] COYLE E.J., LIN J.-H., "Stack filters and the mean absolute error criterion", *IEEE Transactions on Acoustics, Speech, and Signal Processing*", vol. 36, pp. 1244–1254, 1988.

[DOR 87] DORST L., SMEULDERS A.W.M., "Length estimators for digitized contours", *Computer Vision, Graphics, and Image Processing*, vol. 40, pp. 311–333, 1987.

[FEK 04] FEKRY A.M., HEAKAL F.E., "Electrochemical behavior of passive films on molybdenum-containing austenitic stainless steels in aqueous solutions", *Electrochimica Acta*, vol. 50, pp. 43–49, 2004.

[FRE 70] FREEMAN H., "Boundary encoding and processing", in LIPKIN B.S., ROSENFELD A., (eds.), *Picture Processing and Psychopitorics*, 1st Edition, Academic Press, INC, New York, 1970.

[GAT 96] GATZEN H.H., MAETZING J.C., SCHWABE M.K., "Precision machining of rigid disk head sliders", *IEEE Transactions on Magnetics*, vol. 32, pp. 1843–1849, 1996.

[GAT 97] TATZEN H.H., MAETZING J.C., "Nanogrinding", *Precision Engineering*, vol. 21, pp. 134–139, 1997.

[HAR 82] HARASHIMA H., ODAJIMA K., SHISHIKUI Y., *et al.*, "e-Separating nonlinear digital filter and its applications", *IEICE Transactions on Fundamentals*, vol. J65-A, pp. 297–303, 1982.

[HAR 05] HARON H., SHAMSUDDIN S.M., MOHAMED D., "A new corner detection algorithm for chain code representation", *International Journal of Computer Mathematics*, vol. 82, pp. 941–950, 2005.

[HEI 87] HEINONEN P., NEUVO Y., "FIR-median hybrid filters", *IEEE Transactions on Acoustics, Speech, and Signal Processing*, vol. ASSP-35, pp. 832–839, 1987.

[HEM 94] HEMMI Y., ICHIKAWA N., SAITO N., *et al.* "Protective oxide film on alloy X750 formed in air at 973 K", *Journal of Nuclear Science and Technology*, vol. 31, pp. 552–561, 1994.

[HON 10] HONDA N., YAMAKAWA K., OUCHI K., "Simulation study of bit patterned media with weakly inclined anisotropy", *IEEE Transactions on Magnetics*, vol. 46, no. 6, pp. 1806–1808, 2010.

[HUA 97] HUANG L.J., HUNG Y., CHANG S., "Surface and lubricant/overcoat interface properties of the rigid disks after corrosion", *IEEE Trans. Magn.*, vol. 33, pp. 3154–3156, 1997.

[ISE 06] ISE K., TAKAHASHI S., YAMAKAWA K., *et al.*, "New shielded single-pole head with planar structure", *IEEE Transactions on Magnetics*, vol. 42, no. 10, pp. 2422–2424, 2006.

[JI 09] JI R., ZHANG J., XU B., *et al.*, "A study of the corrosion-resistant property of media lubricant", *IEEE Transactions on Magnetics*, vol. 45, pp. 5065–5068, 2009.

[JIA 03] JIANG M., HAO S., KOMANDURI R., "On the advanced lapping process in the precision finishing of thin-film magnetic recording heads for rigid disc drives", *Applied Physics A – Materials Science & Processing*, vol. 77, pp. 923–932, 2003.

[JIN 07] JIN L., LI D., LU Z., "Improved adaptive spatial distance-weighted median filter", *Optical Engineering*, vol. 46, pp. 1–7, 2007.

[JUS 81] JUSTUSSON B.J., "Median filtering: statistical properties", in HUANG T.S., (ed.), *Two Dimensional Digital Signal Processing II*, Springer-Verlag, Berlin, 1981.

[KIM 09] KIM H.J., JANG C.E., KIM D.E., *et al.*, "Effects of self-assembled monolayer and PFPD lubricant on wear characteristics of flat silicon tips", *Tribology Letters*, vol. 34, pp. 61–73, 2009.

[KIM 11] KIM S.H., GUO X.-C., WALTMAN R.I., *et al.*, "Durability against contact wear of nonlubricated disks in the head-disk interface of disk drives", *IEEE Transactions on Magnetics*, vol. 47, pp. 239–243, 2011.

[KLE 99] KLETTE R., KOVALEVSKY V., YIP B., "On the length estimation of digital curves", Technical Report, CITR-TR-45, University of Auckland, 1999.

[KO 91] KO S.J., LEE Y.H., "Center weighed median filters and their applications to image enhancement", *IEEE Transactions on Circuits and Systems*, vol. 38, pp. 984–993, 1991.

[KOT 94] KOTROPOULOS C., PITAS I., "Multichannel L filters based on marginal data ordering", *IEEE Trans. Signal Process.*, vol. 42, pp. 2581–2595, 1994.

[KUL 77] KULPA Z., "Area and perimeter measurement of blobs in discrete binary pictures", *Computer Graphics and Image Processing*, vol. 6, pp. 434–454, 1977.

[LEE 05] LEE C.H., PARK H.B., LEE Y.M., "Importance of proton conductivity measurement in polymer electrolyte membrane for fuel cell application", *Industrial and Engineering Chemistry Research*, vol. 44, pp. 7617–7626, 2005.

[LI 11] LI N., MENG Y., BOGY D.B., "Effects of PFPE lubricant properties on the critical clearance and rate of the lubricant transfer from disk surface to slider", *Tribology Letters*, vol. 43, pp. 275–286, 2011.

[MA 07] MA Y.S., LIU B., "Lubricant transfer from disk to slider in hard disk drives", *Applied Physics Letters*, vol. 92, pp. 143516–143518, 2007.

[MAR 03] MARCHON B., KARIS T., DAI Q., *et al.*, "A model for lubricant flow from disk to slider", *IEEE Transactions on Magnetism*, vol. 39, pp. 2447–2449, 2003.

[MAT 09a] MATSUMOTO M., "Parameter optimization of median e-filter based on correlation maximization", *Proceedings of the IEEE International Congress Digital Image and Signal Processing*, pp. 1–5, 2009.

[MAT 09b] MATSUMOTO M., "Adaptive e-filter based on signal-noise decorrelation", *Proceedings of the IEEE International Symposium on Intelligent Signal Processing and Communication Systems*, pp. 611–614, 2009.

[MIT 07] MITSUYA Y., OHSHIMA Y., ZHANG H., *et al.*, "Stiffness and damping of thin PFPD lubricant bridging between magnetic disk and diamond probe tip", *Journal of Tribology*, vol. 129, pp. 720–728, 2007.

[MIY 05] MIYAKE S., WAKATSUKI Y., WANG M., *et al.*, "Amplitude dependence of the lateral-vibration wear test for perpendicular recording magnetic treated by heat curing", *Japanese Journal of Applied Physics*, vol. 44, no. 5A, pp. 3209–3217, 2005.

[MIY 06] MIYAKE S., WANG M., NINOMIYA S., "Nanotribological properties of perfluoropolyether-coated magnetic disk evaluated by vertical and lateral vibration wear tests", *Surface & Coatings Technology*, vol. 2, pp. 6137–6154, 2006.

[MOB 11] MOBAHI H., RAO S.R., YANG A.Y., "Segmentation of natural images by texture and boundary compression", *International Journal of Computer Vision*, vol. 95, pp. 86–98, 2011.

[MOS 06] MOSER A., BONHOTE C., DAI Q., *et al.*, "Perpendicular magnetic recording technology at 230 Gbit/in^2", *Journal of Magnetism and Magnetic Materials*, vol. 303, pp. 271–275, 2006.

[NIE 87] NIEMINEN A., HEINONEN P., NEUVO Y., "A new class of detail-preserving filters for image processing", *IEEE Transactions on Pattern Analysis and Machine Intelligence*, vol. PAMI-9, pp. 74–90, 1987.

[NOV 88] NOVOTNY V., STROUD N., "Correlation between environmental and electrochemical corrosion of thin film magnetic recording media", *Journal of the Electrochemical Society*, vol. 135, pp. 2931–2938, 1988.

[PAL 89] PALMIERI F.R., BONCELET C.G., JR., "Ll-filter – a new class of order statistic filters", *IEEE Transactions on Acoustics, Speech and Signal Processing*, vol. 37, pp. 691–701, 1989.

[PHO 12] PHOLPRASIT P., ATTHI N., THAMMABUT T., *et al.*, "Pattern transfer characterization after double-level lithography for a fabrication of the three-dimensional aluminum titanium carbide air bearing surface of the hard disk slider", *Japanese Journal of Applied Physics*, vol. 51, no. 06FF08, pp. 1–5, 2012.

[PIR 03] PIRZADA S.A., LIU J.J., PARK D.W., *et al.*, "Ultrathin carbon overcoats: processing, characterization and tribological performance", *IEEE Transactions on Magnetics*, vol. 39, pp. 759–764, 2003.

[POH 08] POH W.C., PIRAMANAYAGAM S.N., LIEW T., "Nobel hybrid magnetic overcoats: a prospective solution for low magnetic spacing", *Journal of Applied Physics*, vol. 103, no. 07F523, pp. 1–3, 2008.

[POH 10] POH W.C., PIRAMANAYAGAM S.N., LIEW T., "Magnetic properties and corrosion resistance studies on hybrid magnetic overcoats for perpendicular recording media", *IEEE Transactions on Magnetics*, vol. 46, pp. 1069–1076, 2010.

[POU 66] POURVAIX M., *Atlas of Electrochemical Equilibrium in Aqueous Solutions*, Pergamon, New York, 1966.

[RAM 99] RAMMAN V., JEN D., GILLIS D., *et al.*, "Component level investigations of liquid accumulation on sliders–fly stiction", *IEEE Transactions on Magnetism*, vol. 35, pp. 2412–2414, 1999.

[RIV 09] RIVETTI C., "A simple and optimized length estimator for digitized DNA contours", *Cytometry Part A*, vol. 75A, pp. 854–861, 2009.

[ROS 74] ROSENFELD A., "Digital straight line segments", *IEEE Transactions on Computers*, vol. c-23, pp. 1264–1269, 1974.

[SAM 11a] SAMAD MA., RISMANI E., YANG H., *et al.*, "Overcoat Free magnetic media for lower magnetic spacing and improved tribological properties for higher areal densities", *Tribology Letters*, vol. 43, pp. 247–256, 2011.

[SAM 11b] SAMAD M.A., YANG H., SINHA S.K., *et al.*, "Effect of carbon embedding on the tribological properties of magnetic media surface with and without a perfluoropolyether (PFPE) layer", *Journal of Physics D: Applied Physics*, vol. 44, pp. 1–7, 2011.

[SHA 12] SHANEH M., MAHYARI A.G., "Impulse noise reduction based on improved median e-filter", *International Journal of Electronics*, vol. 99, pp. 1489–1496, 2012.

[TAJ 03] TAJINE M., DAURAT A., "On local definitions of length of digital curves", *Proceedings of the International Conference on Discrete Geometry for Computer Imagery*, pp. 114–123, 2003.

[THO 64] THOMASOV N.D., CHERNOVA G.P., MARCOVA O.N., "Effect of supplementary alloying elements on pitting corrosion susceptibility of 18Cr-14Ni stainless steel", *Corrosion*, vol. 20, pp. 166t–173t, 1964.

[TUK 74] TUKEY J.W., "Nonlinear (nonsuperposable) methods for smoothing data", *Proceedings of the Congress Record (EASCON 74)*, pp. 673, 1974.

[TUK 77] TUKEY J.W., *Exploratory Data Analysis*, Addison-Wesley, Menlo Park, CA, 1977.

[VOS 82] VOSSEPOEL A.M., SMEULDERS A.W.M., "Vector code probability and metrication error in the representation of straight lines of finite length", *Computer Graphics and Image Processing*, vol. 20, pp. 347–364, 1982.

[WAL 10] WALTMAN R.J., JOSEPH J., GUO X.-C., "An AFM study of corrosion on rigid magnetic disks", *Corrosion Science*, vol. 52, pp. 1258–1262, 2010.

[WAL 51] WALLACE R.L., "The reproduction of magnetically recorded signals", *Bell System Technical Journal*, vol. 30, pp. 1145–1173, 1951.

[WAN 05] WANG M., MIYAKE S., MATSUNUMA S., "Nanowear studies of PFPE lubricant on magnetic perpendicular recording DLC-film-coated disk by lateral oscillation test", *Wear*, vol. 259, pp. 1332–1342, 2005.

[XU 04] XU D., LIU E., LIU B., *et al.*, "Corrosion study of hard disks by OSA and XPS", *International journal of nanoscience*, vol. 3, pp. 853–857, 2004.

[YAM 08] YAMAKAWA K., ISE S., TAKAHASHI N., *et al.*, "Shielded planar write head," *Journal of Magnetism and Magnetic Materials*, vol. 320, pp. 2854–2859, 2008.

[YAN 03] YANG P., BASIR O.A., "Adaptive weighted median filter using local entropy for ultrasonic image denoising", *Proceedings of the International Symposium on Image and Signal Processing and Analysis*, vol. 2, pp. 799–803, 2003.

[YAN 95] YANG R., YIN L., GABBOUJ M., *et al.*, "Optimal weighted median filtering under structural constraints", *IEEE Transactions on Signal Processing*, vol. 43, pp. 591–604, 1995.

[YEN 03] YEN B.K., WHITE R.L., WALTMAN R.J., *et al.*, "Coverage and properties of a-SiNx hard disk overcoat", *Journal of Applied Physics*, vol. 93, pp. 8704–8706, 2003.

[YIN 96] YIN L., YANG R., GABBOUJ M., *et al.*, "Weighted median filters: a tutorial", *IEEE Transactions on Circuits and Systems – II: Analog and Digital Signal Processing*, vol. 43, pp. 157–190, 1996.

[ZHA 05] ZHANG D.S., KOURI D.J., "Varying weight trimmed mean filter for the restoration of impulse noise corrupted images", *Proceedings of the IEEE International Conference Acoustics, Speech and Signal Processing*, vol. 4, pp. 137–140, 2005.

3

Micro Defect Detection
on Air-bearing Surface

This chapter presents texture analysis methods for detection of contaminations (i.e. microparticle, stain and metal) on the air-bearing surface (ABS). A complete system is developed composed of a image acquisition module, a feature extraction module and a decision-making module. The input ABS image is first analyzed by the texture unit and the co-occurrence matrix to obtain texture features which are then transformed by the principle component analysis (PCA) for effective classification of the defective samples.

3.1. Introduction

Currently, inspection processes on the small parts of the read/write head of hard disk drives (HDD) is carried out by human operators using microscopes. The problem with this process is the decrease in performance over operating time which makes the operators fatigued. The automatic inspection machine is used to solve this problem.

In the past, many techniques have been used in the inspection machine. This aims to detect the contamination

Chapter written by Pichate KUNAKORNVONG and Pitikhate SOORAKSA.

particle based on the theory of light scattering technologies: laser, detector and optic. Most light scattering techniques are used for counting particles. Blesener [BLE 92] studied the non-imaging laser particle counter (LPC) for detection of a single particle. Bhushan [BHU 99] utilized LPC instruments and sampling techniques for detecting and determining the size of particle contamination in rigid disk drives. Kochevar [KOC 12] proposed the next generation of contamination monitoring using nanotechnology. However, light scattering techniques cannot determine the type of particle appearing on objects.

Equipment which is helpful for inspecting and determining the type of particle is based on image processing, e.g. automatic force microscopy (AFM) [BIN 86], scanning electron microscope (SEM) and machine vision (MV). Both AFM and SEM create an image from the surface of scanning object. AFM creates the three-dimensional (3D) image by scanning the surface with the probe tip. The advantage of AFM is that it offers a very high resolution (i.e. smaller than 0.1 nm) imaging technology. The type of contamination on the surface can be determined from the characteristics of the surface that is analyzed by the moving probe tips. Similarly, the advantages of SEM include high magnification, high resolution and large depth of fields (DOFs). However, the major disadvantages of AFM and SEM are that they eliminate the surfaces of the scanned object and are too slow for analyzing said surface. AFM and SEM are only truly compatible in lab tests.

MV is capable of detecting and determining the type of defect. Various defect detection algorithms have been proposed and can be categorized into four main groups: statistical, structural, spectral and filtering, and model-based approaches. Table 3.1 shows some example applications of these algorithms.

Approach	Method/algorithm	Application
Statistical	Graylevel statistics (Histogram)	Textiles [SUN 12], texture [POP 07]
	Co-occurrence matrix	Textile [ZUO 12], ABS [KUN 12]
	Texture unit texture spectrum	Blood cell [BAR 07]
	Principle component analysis	Wood [TOM 06, TOM 07]
	Mean shift	Solar wafer [TSA 11]
	Weibull	SAR [AYE 06]
Structural algorithms	Edge detection	PZT [WIT 13], ceramic [ATI 09], flash thermography (FT) [SHA 08]
	Morphological operation	Textiles [MAK 09, MAL 00, SON 96], ceramic [ELB 07]
Spectral and filtering methods	Fourier transforms	IC wafer [LIU 10], textiles [MIR 13, CHA 00], metal [ZHA 11], texture [TSA 03]
	Gabor wavelet	Texture [ASH 11, HOU 05]
	Gabor filter	Textiles [BOD 02, KUM 02], industrial texture [TSA 00]
	Wavelet transform	Textiles [YAN 05, FAT 12, GHA 09], color texture [LIN 07]
	Discrete cosine transform	Textiles [AZI 13]
Model-based	Neural network	Textiles [RIM 05]
	Generic algorithm	Metallic surface [FRA 06], [ZHE 02]
	Support vector machines	Texture [HOU 05], metallic surface [ZHA 11]
	Independent component analysis	Textile [GÖK 04], LCD [TSA 06]
	Texem model	Marble [XIE 05, XIA 07]

Table 3.1. *Methods for defect detection*

In this chapter, the statistical approach is adopted for the texture analysis of the ABS image, and the texture features are used in the classification of defective samples. Section 3.2 presents the components of the ABS which can be affected by the defect. Section 3.3 presents the design of the imaging system. Section 3.4 starts with feature extraction, defect classification methods, and then provides the experimental results. Section 3.5 concludes this chapter.

3.2. Air-bearing surface

Figure 3.1 shows the ABS attached on a head gimbal assembly (HGA). The ABS is the crucial part on the slider which carries the read/write head and holds the head microinches above the disk media. For very high density HDDs, the read/write head flies extremely close to the disk platter, within a couple of nanometers above the media [WOO 06], under high gravity force conditions. Figure 3.2 shows the schematic of the flying height. Air passing under the ABS provides the required lift, for which the design has to take into account the weight, velocity and skew in order to achieve a uniformed flying height. The low flying height requires a tight control of the operating environment. Changes in the flying height can lead to disk failure or a decrease in the performance of the HDD.

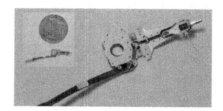

Figure 3.1. *ABS on HGA and size comparison with a Thai One-Baht coin*

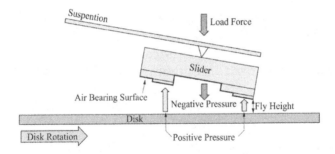

Figure 3.2. *Schematic of flying height*

Contamination (dust particle, finger print and chemical vapor) can cause the head to crash on the disk surface. The damage from contact between the head and media leads to loss of data in the HDD. Figure 3.3 illustrates the relative dimensions of some possible contaminants compared to the flying height. The contamination on the ABS could affect the performance of read/write data transfer. In order to maintain the high efficiency performance of HDD, the ABS must have the least possible amount of contamination.

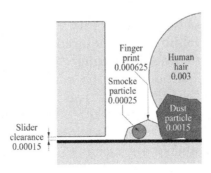

Figure 3.3. *Dimensions of contaminants versus flying height*

3.3. Imaging system

This section discusses the imaging system used for the inspection process. The system comprises of a camera, lens and illumination components.

There are two requirements for the camera: resolution and frame rate. The camera resolution design is based on the minimum resolution, which is calculated by the size of the smallest contaminant. Minimum resolution is calculated by equation [3.1]:

$$\# pixel = \left(2 \times d_{FOV}\right) / \mathrm{Re}\, s \qquad [3.1]$$

where $\# pixel$ is the minimum resolution, d_{FOV} is the width/height of the field of view (FOV) and Res is the smallest size of contamination that needs to be resolved. In the current application, the dimension of the ABS is approximately 1×0.8 mm^2 which denotes the FOV. In addition, Res is around 1 µm.

The frame rate is based on the number of sample units needed to be detected per hour. It is calculated by equation [3.2]:

$$Frame\ Rate \geq Inspection\ frequency \qquad [3.2]$$

In order to get a high-quality image, devices of high quality and reliability are required. Thus, the industrial charge-coupled device (CCD) camera was used in the current application. In equation [3.1], the minimum pixel dimension of the camera should be at least 1600×2000 pixels. This requirement matches the commercially available 5 megapixel (MP) CCD cameras which have pixel dimensions of 2048×2594 and $(2.5)^{-1}$ inches (5.70×4.28 mm^2), and a frame rate of 30 fps.

Selection of the lens is based on focal length. The design of focal length is obtained by three variables: camera sensor size; working distance, which is the distance between the lens and, ABS; and FOV, which is determined by the actual size of the ABS. The focal length of a lens is calculated by equation [3.3].

$$f = \frac{d_{sensor} \times WD}{d_{FOV} + d_{sensor}}$$
[3.3]

where f is the focal length of the lens, d_{sensor} is the width/height of CCD size and WD is the distance from the lens to the target ABS. For the current system, WD is initially 50 mm, hence the focal length of the lens is equal to 42.537 mm. This specification is matched to the commercial lens with a focal length of 50 mm. However, there is a distortion in the image captured by the system. In such a case, the macrolens is used to reduce image distortion. The magnification of the macrolens is calculated by equation [3.4].

$$Mag = \frac{d_{sensor}}{d_{FOV}}$$
[3.4]

where Mag is the maximum magnification. According to the given information, the magnification of lens is not more than 5.7x. So, the selected lens is a 4x magnification macrolens with –0.073489% distortion. Its magnification is extended by the 5 mm extension ring to be 4.3x.

The illumination system can be designed based on the characteristics of the target. Table 3.2 shows the comparison of different illumination techniques. Overall, the bright field is used. The dark field illuminates the defects on target, whereas the coaxial light is used to eliminate the shadow. Figure 3.4 shows an image sample captured by the setting system.

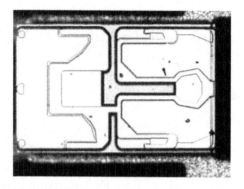

Figure 3.4. *Sample ABS image captured by the system using a camera with a resolution of 5 MP and 4x macrolens included coaxial illumination*

Illumination techniques	Characteristics	Sample defect detected
Direct illumination with bright field	– easy to implement, high-contrast illumination; – cause of unwanted shadows; – illuminates from front direction of target.	– normal particle.
Diffuse illumination with bright field	– relatively easy to implement, uniform illumination, reduces glare on specular surface; – illumination contrast decrease; – illuminates from front direction of target.	– normal particle with glare effect.
Dark field	– illuminates defects, outer edges are bright; – cannot illuminate the flat and smooth surface; – illuminates from side direction of target.	– defect with edge feature e.g. surface contamination, scratch and crack; – any small raised feature.

Back light	– produces the target shape; – needs some space available behind object for illuminator; – illuminates behind the target;	– drill holes; – silhouette opaque; – internal defect of translucent object: glasses and plastic lens;
Coaxial light	– eliminates shadows, uniform across FOV. – complicated implement, intense reflection from specular surfaces; – illuminates from front direction of target.	– microcontamination.

Table 3.2. *Comparison of illumination techniques*

3.4. Contamination detection

The current work studies three types of defects on the ABS: (1) microparticle, (2) stain contamination, and (3) metal contamination. Figure 3.5 shows a range of defects, captured from SEM. The microparticle has two types of defects, including white particle and black particle. This defect is a loose particle, or dry dust, with no bond to the slider. Stain contamination is any discoloration of a surface with no appearance height. Metal contamination is a shiny material which appears as bright as the pole tip surface.

This section introduces two algorithms to detect contamination on ABS images. The detection of contamination has three main steps: feature extraction, feature analysis and contamination identification. The commonly used methods for texture feature extraction are employed in the current application. The first method is the co-occurrence matrix demonstrated by Haralick [HAR 73] in 1973, and the second method is the texture unit texture spectrum demonstrated by He and Wang [HE 90] in 1990. PCA is applied to analyze the features from the previous step. The Euclidean distance is used together with the selecting threshold for the identification of the defected and non-defected ABS.

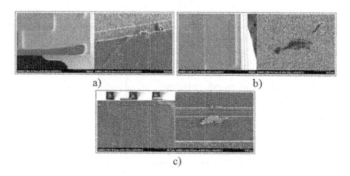

Figure 3.5. *Images representing three types of defect: a) microparticle, b) stain contamination and c) metal contamination*

3.4.1. *Texture unit texture spectrum*

The characteristics of texture can be extracted and clarified by texture unit (TU). The smoothness of intensity in the local TU is represented by the texture unit number (N_{TU}). TU is a small matrix which is calculated from the local texture. The local texture information for the pixel can be extracted from its neighborhood of size 3×3 pixels, $V = \{v_0, v_1, ..., v_8\}$, where v_0 represents the intensity of the central pixel and v_1, $i = 1, 2, ..., 8$, represents the intensity of the surrounding pixels.

v_1	v_2	v_3
v_8	v_0	v_4
v_7	v_6	v_5

Figure 3.6. *The intensity value of its neighboring pixel*

The intensity value of its neighboring pixels is shown in Figure 3.6. For the given values of V, the texture unit, $TU=\{E_1, E_2, ..., E_8\}$, can be determined by the occurrence matrix of v_0 and its neighborhood. The element E_i is expressed as:

$$E_i = \begin{cases} 0 & \text{if} \quad v_i - v_0 < -T \\ 1 & \text{if} \quad -T \leq v_i - v_0 \leq T \\ 2 & \text{if} \quad T < v_i - v_0 \end{cases} \qquad [3.5]$$

where $i = (1,2,...,8)$, and T is the threshold which characterizes a small change of intensity in the local texture ($T = 0$). Each element E_i occupies the same position as pixel v_i. Since E_i is 0, 1, 2, the value of E is $3^8 = 6561$. According to this characteristic, we can create the label of the local texture by N_{TU} as:

$$N_{TU} = \sum_{i=1}^{8} E_i \cdot 3^{i-1} \qquad [3.6]$$

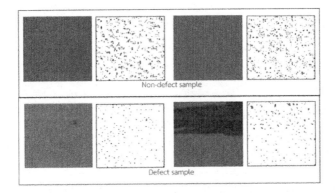

Figure 3.7. *Texture image encoding by texture unit with the threshold T = 2*

The sample texture and graphical characteristic of encoded texture (i.e. TU image) from texture unit are shown in Figure 3.7. The characteristic of the TU image is significant. The uniform distributions can be observed in the TU images of the smooth texture images (i.e. non-defected samples). On the other hand, the TU images of uneven texture images are random distributions which belong to the defect samples.

3.4.2. Graylevel co-occurrence matrix

Graylevel co-occurrence matrix (GLCM) is a well-known technique for texture classification. The co-occurrence matrix is calculated from the repeated intensity of pixel in image. Co-occurrence matrix is expressed by equation [3.7] and the distance matrix is expressed by equation [3.8] [HAR 79].

$$P(i,j;d,0°) = \# \left\{ \begin{array}{l} ((r,c),(r',c')) \in (L_r \times L_c) \times (L_r \times L_c) \\ r'-r=0, |c'-c|=d, I(r,c)=i, I(r',c')=j \end{array} \right\},$$

$$P(i,j;d,45°) = \# \left\{ \begin{array}{l} ((r,c),(r',c')) \in (L_r \times L_c) \times (L_r \times L_c) \\ (r'-r=d, c'-c=d) \text{ or } (r'-r=-d, c'-c=-d) \\ I(r,c)=i, I(r',c')=j \end{array} \right\}$$

$$P(i,j;d,90°) = \# \left\{ \begin{array}{l} ((r,c),(r',c')) \in (L_r \times L_c) \times (L_r \times L_c) \\ |r'-r|=d, c'-c=0, I(r,c)=i, I(r',c')=j \end{array} \right\} \quad [3.7]$$

$$P(i,j;d,135°) = \# \left\{ \begin{array}{l} ((r,c),(r',c')) \in (L_r \times L_c) \times (L_r \times L_c) \\ (r'-r=d, c'-c=-d) \text{ or } (r'-r=d, c'-c=-d) \\ I(r,c)=i, I(r',c')=j \end{array} \right\}$$

where the distance d can be explicitly defined by:

$$d((r,c),(r',c')) = \max \left\{ |r-r|, |c-c'| \right\} \quad [3.8]$$

Figure 3.8 shows the sample of region of interest (ROI) from ABS images and the graphical characteristic of ROI obtained from co-occurrence matrix.

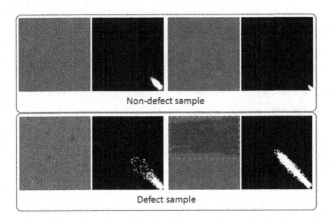

Figure 3.8. *Co-occurrence matrices of non-defected and defected samples*

The selected individual features from the co-occurrence matrix of sample image are used as the identification features, $(f_1, f_2, ..., f_n)$. These are calculated by:

Correlation:

$$f_1 = \sum_{i=1}^{Ng}\sum_{j=1}^{Ng}\frac{(i-\mu_i)(j-\mu_j)\cdot C(i.j)}{\sigma_i\sigma_j}, \qquad [3.9]$$

Sum average:

$$f_2 = \sum_{i=2}^{2Ng} i \cdot C_{x+y}(i) \qquad [3.10]$$

Cluster shade:

$$f_3 = \sum_{i=1}^{Ng}\sum_{j=1}^{Ng}\left((i-\mu_i)+(j-\mu_j)\right)^3 C(i,j), \qquad [3.11]$$

Cluster prominence:

$$f_4 = \sum_{i=1}^{Ng}\sum_{j=1}^{Ng}\left((i-\mu_i)+(j-\mu_j)\right)^4 C(i,j) \qquad\qquad [3.12]$$

where the notations are defined as follows:

– $C(i,j)$ is a value at (i,j) in co-occurrence matrix C;

– $\mu_i = \sum_{i=1}^{M} i \sum_{j=1}^{N} C(i,j)$;

– $\mu_j = \sum_{j=1}^{N} j \sum_{i=1}^{M} C(i,j)$;

– $\sigma_i = \sum_{i=1}^{M} (i-\mu_i)^2 \sum_{j=1}^{N} C(i,j)$;

– $\sigma_j = \sum_{j=1}^{N} (j-\mu_j)^2 \sum_{i=1}^{M} C(i,j)$;

– $C_{x+y}(k) = \sum_{\substack{i=1 \\ i+j=k}}^{Ng}\sum_{j=1}^{Ng} C(i,j).$

for $k = 2,3,\ldots,2Ng$.

Four features from equations [3.9]–[3.12] (correlation, sum-average, cluster shade and cluster prominence) are selected to identify the defected and non-defected cases. *Correlation* is used to measure the linear dependence of element in the matrix, between the specified elements relative to each other. *Sum-average* is used to measure the average of the graylevel within an image. *Cluster shade* and *cluster prominence* are used to measure the skewness of the matrix. The image is symmetric when the value of cluster shade and cluster prominence is low, which means that the image has a little variation. Figure 3.9 shows the plot of four identification features. It shows the trends used to identify the defected and non-defected samples.

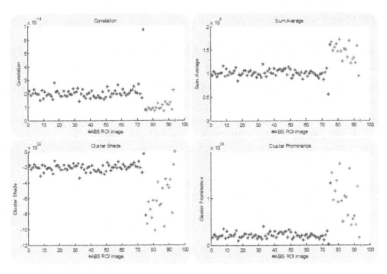

Figure 3.9. *Plot of the four identification features of the defected and non-defected ABS samples*

3.4.3. *Principle component analysis*

PCA is a method to identify the patterns in data, and express the data in a way to highlight their similarities and dissimilarities. It is a numerical procedure for analyzing the basis of variation present in a multidimensional data set. PCA is used in all forms of analysis because it is a simple, non-parametric method of extracting significant information from confusing data sets.

The goals of PCA are as follows:

– to extract the most important information from the data table;

– to compress the size of the data set by keeping only this important information;

– to simplify the description of the data set;

– to analyze the structure of the observations and the variables.

The PCA coefficients of the feature parameter vector obtained in the preceding section are used for defect detection on ABS. The detection algorithm is given by the following steps:

1) Feature parameter vector is defined as:

$$\mathbf{f} = [f_1, f_2, \ldots, f_7]$$

[3.13]

2) Covariance matrix R is calculated by:

$$R = \frac{1}{L}\sum_{i=1}^{L}(\tilde{\mathbf{f}}_i\tilde{\mathbf{f}}_i'), \quad \tilde{\mathbf{f}} = \mathbf{f}_i - \overline{\mathbf{f}}$$

[3.14]

$$\overline{\mathbf{f}} = \frac{1}{L}\sum_{i=1}^{L}\mathbf{f}_i$$

[3.15]

where L is the total number of reference ABS images and $\mathbf{f}_i$ is the feature vector obtained from reference data for a particular ABS image.

3) Eigenvalue λ_k and eigenvector $\mathbf{u}_k$ of covariance matrix R are calculated by

$$R\mathbf{u}_k = \lambda_k\mathbf{u}_k, \quad (k = 1, 2, \ldots, N)$$

[3.16]

4) Transformation matrix U is calculated by

$$U = [\mathbf{u}_1, \cdots, \mathbf{u}_{N^*}]$$

[3.17]

where $N^* < N$

5) PCA coefficient $\mathbf{z}$ is calculated by

$$\mathbf{z} = U'\tilde{\mathbf{p}} \equiv [z_1, z_2, \ldots, z_{N^*}]'$$

[3.18]

where $\tilde{\mathbf{p}} = \mathbf{f}^* - \overline{\mathbf{f}}$ and $\mathbf{f}^*$ are the feature parameter vectors obtained from the ABS image.

Figures 3.10(a) and (b) show the plot of first and second PCA coefficients of ABS images with and without encoded TU on ABS images, respectively.

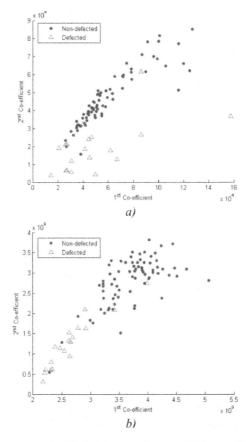

Figure 3.10. *The plot of first and second PCA coefficients: a) non-TU encoded and b) TU encoded*

3.4.4. Identification defect

Let e_1 and e_2 be the false acceptance and false rejection errors, obtained by the set of threshold values. First, an optimum threshold is selected by the minimum value of the summation of the two errors:

$$\eta = \min(e_1 + e_2) \qquad [3.19]$$

Then, the Euclidean distance and the selected threshold are used to identify the defect on ABS sample.

The defect is detected by the mean value from the set of training data. The non-defected and defected are expressed as:

$$\text{Non-defect}: \begin{cases} \bar{x}_1 < \bar{x}_2, & \|f\| > \eta \\ \bar{x}_1 > \bar{x}_2, & \|f\| < \eta \end{cases}$$

$$\text{Defect}: \begin{cases} \bar{x}_1 < \bar{x}_2, & \|f\| \le \eta \\ \bar{x}_1 > \bar{x}_2, & \|f\| \ge \eta \end{cases} \qquad [3.20]$$

where $\| \|$ is the Euclidean distance. In the case of using TU for feature extraction, f is the PCA coefficient. In the case of using co-occurrence matrix for feature extraction, f is the feature parameter obtained from the co-occurrence matrix. In addition, $\bar{x}_1$ and $\bar{x}_2$ are the means of defected and non-defected training samples, respectively.

Figure 3.11(a) and 3.12(a), respectively, show the selection of threshold when using PCA coefficients with and without encoded TU. Figure 3.11(b) and 3.12(b) show the plot of Euclidean distance and the selected threshold to identify the defect and non-defect with and without encoded TU, respectively. It can be observed that TU offers a better margin of separation between the two classes.

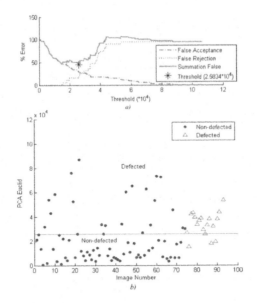

Figure 3.11. *Defect detection on ABS using PCA without encoded TU: a) selection of threshold and b) identifying defect by Euclidean distance and the threshold selected in (a)*

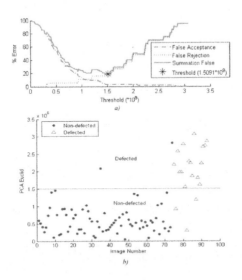

Figure 3.12. *Defect detection on ABS using PCA with encoded TU: a) selection of threshold and b) identifying defect by Euclidean distance and the threshold selected in (a)*

Figures 3.12(a)–3.16(a) show the threshold selection when using the co-occurrence matrix as the features: correlation, sum-average, cluster shade and cluster prominence, respectively. Figures 3.12(b)–3.16(b) show the corresponding plot of the Euclidean distance for the classification.

From the results, it can be observed that the two methods for texture characterization are effective for the classification of defects on ABS. The PCA can highlight the important features, and the classification can be made conveniently by the application of the thresholding.

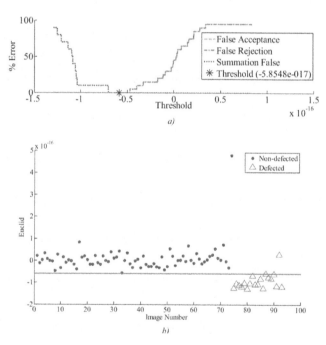

Figure 3.13. *Detect classification result obtained by the correlation identification: a) threshold selection and b) identification of defect by Euclidean distance and the threshold from (a)*

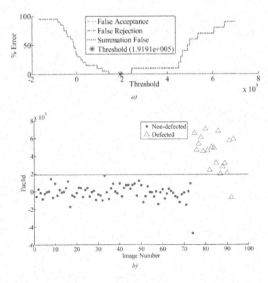

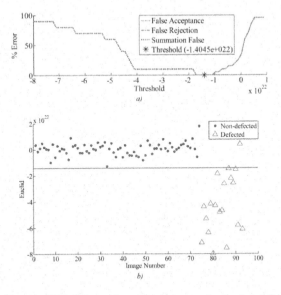

Figure 3.14. *Detect classification result obtained by the sum-average: a) threshold selection and b) identification of defect by Euclidean distance and the threshold from (a)*

Figure 3.15. *Detect classification result obtained by the cluster shade: a) threshold selection and b) identification of defect by Euclidean distance and the threshold from (a)*

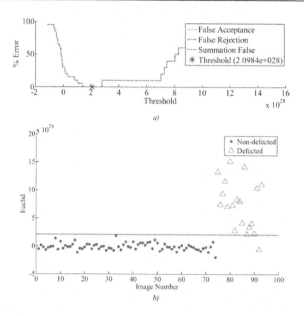

Figure 3.16. *Detect classification result obtained by the cluster prominence: a) threshold selection and b) identification of defect by Euclidean distance and the threshold from (a)*

3.5. Conclusion

This chapter explains the MV system for defect detection and the importance of defect detection on the ABS. The defect detection system has three parts: image capturing, feature extraction and defect identification. The most important factor in the defect detection process is how to capture the defect. In this regard, this chapter is explained in the part of imaging system. Two methods are employed for extracting the features from the input image. Each method has its own advantages and disadvantages. The texture unit encoded is fast, whereas GLCM offers more features to be used. The features from the texture unit or GLCM are analyzed by PCA. The Euclidean distance is very useful and convenient for the identification process.

3.6. Acknowledgment

This work is supported by DSTAR KMITL, HDDI-NECTEC of NSTDA under grant HDD-01-53-03D. Special thanks to Seagate Technology (Thailand).

3.7. Bibliography

[ASH 11] ASHA V., BHAJANTRI N.U., NAGABHUSHAN P., "Automatic detection of texture defects using texture-periodicity and Gabor wavelets", *Computer Networks and Intelligent Computing,* pp. 548–553, vol. 157, 2011.

[ATI 09] ATIQUR R.G.M., MOBARAK H.M., "Automatic defect detection and classification technique from image: a special case using ceramic tiles", *International Journal of Computer Science and Information Security (IJCSIS),* vol. 1, no. 1, pp. 22–30, 2009.

[AYE 06] AYED I.B., HENNANE N., MITICHE A., "Unsupervised variational image segmentation/classification using a Weibull observation model", *IEEE Transactions on Image Processing,* vol. 15, no. 11, pp. 3431–3439, 2006.

[AZI 13] AZIZ M.A., HAGGAG A.S., SAYED M.S., "Fabric defect detection algorithm using morphological processing and DCT", *Communications, Signal Processing, and their Applications (ICCSPA), IEEE,* pp. 1–4, 2013.

[BAR 07] BARCELO A., MONTSENY E., SOBREVILLA P., "Fuzzy texture unit and fuzzy texture spectrum for texture characterization", *Fuzzy Sets and Systems,* vol. 158, pp. 239–252, 2007.

[BHU 99] BHUSHAN B., CHANDRA S., "Detection and sizing of particulate contamination in rigid disk drives: instruments and sampling techniques", *IEEE Transactions on Magnetics,* vol. 35, no. 2, pp. 956–962, 1999.

[BIN 86] BINING G., QUATE C.F., GERBER C.H., "Atomic force microscope", *Physical Review Letters,* vol. 59, no. 9, pp. 930–934, 1986.

[BLE 92] BLESENER J.L., Non-imaging laser particle counter, U.S. Patent no. 5,085,500, 1992.

[BOD 02] BODNAROVA A., BENNAMOUN M., LATHAM S., "Optimal Gabor filters for textile flaw detection", *Pattern Recognition*, vol. 35, no. 12, pp. 2973–2991, 2002.

[CHA 00] CHAN C.H., PANG G.K., "Fabric defect detection by Fourier analysis", *IEEE Transactions on Industry Applications*, vol. 36, no. 5, pp. 1267–1276, 2000.

[ELB 07] ELBEHIERY H., HEFNAWY A., ELEWA M., "Surface defects detection for ceramic tiles using image processing and morphological techniques", *WEC, World Academy of Science, Engineering and Technology*, vol. 5, pp. 158–162, April 2007.

[FAT 12] FATHI A., MONADJEMI A.H., MAHMOUDI F., "Defect detection of tiles with combined undecimated wavelet transform and GLCM features", *International Journal of Soft Computing and Engineering (IJSCE)*, vol. 2, no. 2, pp. 30–34, 2012.

[FRA 06] FRAYMAN Y., ZHENG H., NAHAVANDI S., "Machine vision system for automatic inspection of surface defects in aluminum die casting", *Journal of Advanced Computational Intelligence and Intelligent Informatics*, vol. 10, no. 3, pp. 281–286, 2006.

[GHA 09] GHAZVINI M., MONADJEMI S.A., MOVAHHEDINIA N., *et al.*, "Defect detection of tiles using 2D-wavelet transform and statistical features", *World Academy of Science, Engineering and Technology*, vol. 3, no. 1, pp. 773–776, 2009.

[GÖK 04] GÖKHAN S.O., ERTÜZÜN A., ERÇIL A., "Independent component analysis for texture defect detection", *Pattern Recognition and Image Analysis*, vol. 14, no. 2, pp. 303–307, 2004.

[HAR 73] HARALICK R.M., SHANMUGAM K., DINSTEIN H., "Textural features for image classification", *IEEE Transactions on Systems, Man and Cybernetics*, vol. SMC-3, no. 6, pp. 610–621, 1973.

[HAR 79] HARALICK R.M., "Statistical and structural approaches to texture", *Proceedings of the IEEE*, vol. 67, no. 5, pp. 786–804, May 1979.

[HE 90] HE D.C., WANG L., "Texture unit, texture spectrum, and texture analysis", *IEEE Transactions on Geoscience and Remote Sensing*, vol. 28, no. 4, pp. 509–512, July 1990.

[HOU 05] HOU Z., PARKER J.M., "Texture defect detection using support vector machines with adaptive Gabor wavelet features", *7th IEEE Workshops on Application of Computer Vision, WACV/MOTIONS'05*, vol. 1, pp. 275–280, January 2005.

[KOC 12] KOCHEVAR S., PIETRYKOWSKI T., RODIER D., "Next generation nano-contamination monitoring", *SPIE Optical Engineering+ Applications, International Society for Optics and Photonics*, pp. 84920H–84920H, vol. 8492, October 2012.

[KUM 02] KUMAR A., PANG G.K., "Defect detection in textured materials using Gabor filters", *IEEE Transactions on Industry Applications*, vol. 38, no. 2, pp. 425–440, 2002.

[KUN 12] KUNAKORNVONG P., TANGKONGKIET C., SOORAKSA P., "Defect detection on air bearing surface with luminance intensity invariance", *9th International Conference on Fuzzy Systems and Knowledge Discovery (FSKD)*, pp. 693–696, 2012.

[LIN 07] LIN H.D., "Automated visual inspection of ripple defects using wavelet characteristic based multivariate statistical approach", *Image and Vision Computing*, vol. 25, no. 11, pp. 1785–1801, 2007.

[LIU 10] LIU H., ZHOU W., KUANG Q., *et al.*, "Defect detection of IC wafer based on spectral subtraction", *IEEE Transactions on Semiconductor Manufacturing*, vol. 23, no. 1, pp. 141–147, 2010.

[MAK 09] MAK K.L., PENG P., YIU K.F.C., "Fabric defect detection using morphological filters", *Image and Vision Computing*, vol. 27, no. 10, pp. 1585–1592, 2009.

[MAL 00] MALLIK-GOSWAMI B., DATTA A.K., "Detecting defects in fabric with laser-based morphological image processing", *Textile Research Journal*, vol. 70, no. 9, pp. 758–762, 2000.

[MIR 13] MIRMAHDAVI S.A., AHMADYFARD A., SHAHRAKI A.A., et al., "A novel modeling of random textures using Fourier transform for defect detection", The UKSim 15th International Conference on Computer Modeling and Simulation (UKSim), pp. 470–475, 2013.

[POP 07] POPESCU D., DOBRESCU R., MAXIMILIAN N., "Texture classification and defect detection by statistical features", NAUN International Journal of Circuits, Systems and Signal Processing, vol. 1, pp. 79–84, 2007.

[RIM 05] RIMAC-DRLJE S., KELLER A., HOCENSKI Z., "Neural network based detection of defects in texture surfaces", Proceedings of the IEEE International Symposium on Industrial Electronics, ISIE 2005, vol. 3, pp. 1255–1260, 2005.

[SHA 08] SHAM F.C., NELSON C., LONG L., "Surface crack detection by flash thermography in concrete surface", Journal of Insight-Winston the Northampton, vol. 50, no. 5, pp. 240–243, 2008.

[SON 96] SONG K.Y., KITTLER J., PETROU M., "Defect detection in random colour textures", Image and Vision Computing, vol. 14, no. 9, pp. 667–683, 1996.

[SUN 12] SUNPREET S., MANINDER K., "Machine vision system for automated visual inspection of tile's surface quality", International Organization of Scientific Research (IOSR), vol. 2, no. 3, pp. 429–432, 2012.

[TOM 06] TOMCZAK L., MOSOROV V., SANKOWSKI D., "Texture defect detection with non-supervised clustering", International Conference on Modern Problems of Radio Engineering, Telecommunications, and Computer Science, TCSET, pp. 266–268, February 2006.

[TOM 07] TOMCZAK L., MOSOROV V.D., SANKOWSKI J.N., "Image defect detection methods for visual inspection systems", 9th International Conference of the Experience of Designing and Applications, IEEE, CADSM'07, pp. 454–456, 2007.

[TSA 00] TSAI D.M., WU S.K., "Automated surface inspection using Gabor filters", International Journal of Advanced Manufacturing Technology, vol. 16, no. 7, pp. 1–26, 2000.

[TSA 03] TSAI D.M., HUANG T.Y., "Automated surface inspection for statistical textures", *Image and Vision Computing*, vol. 21, pp. 307–323, 2003.

[TSA 06] TSAI D.M., TSENG Y.H., CHAO S.M., *et al.*, "Independent component analysis based filter design for defect detection in low-contrast textured images", *18th International Conference on Pattern Recognition, ICPR*, vol. 2, pp. 231–234, 2006.

[TSA 11] TSAI D.M., LUO J.Y., "Mean shift-based defect detection in multicrystalline solar wafer surfaces", *IEEE Transactions on Industrial Informatics*, vol. 7, no. 1, pp. 125–135, 2011.

[WIT 13] WITHAYACHUMNANKUL W., KUNAKORNVONG P., ASAVATHONGKUL C., *et al.*, "Rapid detection of hairline cracks on the surface of piezoelectric ceramics", *The International Journal of Advanced Manufacturing Technology*, vol. 64, nos. 9–12, pp. 1275–1283, 2013.

[WOO 06] WOOD R., "Future hard disk drive systems", *Journal of Magnetism and Magnetic Materials*, vol. 321, no. 6, pp. 555–561, 2006.

[XIA 07] XIANGHUA X., MIRMEHDI M., "TEXEMS: texture exemplars for defect detection on random textured surfaces", *IEEE Transactions on Pattern Analysis and Machine Intelligence*, vol. 29, no. 8, pp. 1454–1464, 2007.

[XIE 05] XIE X., MIRMEHDI M., "Texture exemplars for defect detection on random textures", *Pattern Recognition and Image Analysis*, vol. 3687, pp. 404–413, 2005.

[YAN 05] YANG X., PANG G., YUNG N., "Robust fabric defect detection and classification using multiple adaptive wavelets", *IEEE Proceedings-Vision, Image and Signal Processing*, vol. 152, no. 6, pp. 715–723, 2005.

[ZHA 11] ZHANG X.W., DING Y.Q., LV Y.Y., *et al.*, "A vision inspection system for the surface defects of strongly reflected metal based on multi-class SVM", *Expert Systems with Applications*, vol. 38, no. 5, pp. 5930–5939, 2011.

[ZHE 02] ZHENG H., KONG L.X., NAHAVANDI S., "Automatic inspection of metallic surface defects using genetic algorithms", *Journal of Materials Processing Technology,* vol. 125–126, no. 9, pp. 427–433, 2002.

[ZUO 12] ZUO H., WANG Y., YANG X., *et al.*, "Fabric defect detection based on texture enhancement", *5th International Congress on Image and Signal Processing (CISP), IEEE,* pp. 876–880, October 2012.

4

Automated Optical Inspection for Solder Jet Ball Joint Defects in the Head Gimbal Assembly Process

The head gimbal assembly (HGA) is an important component of the read/write part in a hard disk drive (HDD). The HGA consists of a slider and suspension which are connected by a solder jet bond (SJB) machine. In HGA production, there are steps in slider assembly with suspension using an SJB machine that might cause a mistake, and therefore cause defects. This chapter presents detection methods with a very high performance to detect solder jet ball joint defects on HGAs including the vertical edge detection method, chain code descriptor-based method, morphology and template matching method, K-mean and Otsu's method.

4.1. Introduction

The HGA is one of the most important components of the read-write part. It is attached to an actuator arm as shown in Figure 4.1. The HGA is used to support the read and write heads attached at the end of the slider to read or write data onto the disk platter. HGA visual investigation is currently

Chapter written by Jirarat IEAMSAARD and Thanapoom FUANGPIAN.

performed by humans which might cause faulty decisions because of weariness after checking a number of products. Faulty inspection causes problems, production delays, resource waste, and reduces customer confidence. The demand on the company is to develop an automatic inspection system in order to reduce mistakes in visual inspection and achieve a product inspection rate of 3,600 inspected HGA/h. This chapter presents various methods for automatic visual inspection of HGAs to accomplish this requirement.

Section 4.3 focuses on defects in solder joints between the slider and suspension where the solder balls or pads are burned. The characteristic of the defect is that one of the pad's edges is not smooth or the pad's border has a black limb caused by the errors in the soldering process using the SJB machine. Some other HGA defects, such as solder ball bridging and incomplete solder joint on both sides of the slider and suspension have previously been studied using morphological template matching [MUN 12, IEA 12, MUN 13]. However, the defect caused by solder ball burning cannot be detected by either the morphology template matching or other methods based on general shape features such as the area, perimeter and center of mass. Therefore, a new method is proposed to identify the HGA defect caused by solder and pad burning.

Section 4.4 focuses on defects in solder joints between the slider and suspension when the tail of one ball bridges another ball or a solder ball touches other balls, caused by errors in the process of soldering using SJB. The automatic visual inspection employs the morphology operation and template matching method for image processing. This system is compared with the defect inspection method obtained by chain code and discrete Fourier transformation proposed in [IEA 12].

Section 4.5 presents the method for the detection of missing solder balls on the HGA. The image processing is conducted by the segmentation of solder balls using an unsupervised data clustering method. Then, the complete-loop contour feature is extracted for image classification.

4.2. Head gimbal assembly

The HGA is made up of two components: the slider and the suspension. The recording head is at the slider and attached to the gimbal so that it can move for reading or writing signal to the magnetic plate during the operation.

The slider is made up of an electrical circuit for reading/writing signals to the magnetic plate. The front surface of the slider is designed as an air-bearing surface (ABS) which helps in controlling the fly height between the head and the media. The suspension is the part connected to the slider. It is made up of flexure and load beams, which control the bending angle, bending force and distance of the head.

In the assembly process, the slider is attached to the gimbal by the following steps: (1) auto dispensing, (2) slider attachment, (3) solder jet bonding, and (4) infrared curing. The two parts are connected by glue, the size of which can be as small as 320 μm. After the slider is attached to the gimbal, a UV gun is focused on the glue for the correct alignment. The electric path between the two objects is connected by solder jet bonding. Finally, the connection is made rigid by infrared curing.

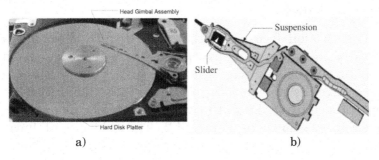

a)   b)

Figure 4.1. *Slider and suspension of HGA*

Several defects can occur on the HGA during the assembly process. These are grouped according to the positions where the defect occurred, which include ABS, slider, suspension, interface between slide and suspension, flexure, and load beam. Table 4.1 summarizes the defect areas.

Assembly Area	Defect at Assembly Area
ABS	– ABS contamination embedded metal on ABS surface and etch surface. – Cracks on ABS surface.
Slider	– Fail location. – Slider reverses. – Slider misaligned.
Suspension	– Dimple separation at suspension. – No slider on suspension.
Slider and suspension	– Bonding between slider and suspension; missing solder ball, solder ball bridging, solder ball not complete on both sides of slider and suspension, solder ball burning, solder ball splash out of pad area.
Flexure	– Flexure bend.
Load beam	– Load beam dent. – Load beam bend.
Flexure and load beam	– Epoxy spread out from flexure to load beam. – Flexure tongue touch load beam.

Table 4.1. *HGA defect at assembly area*

4.3. Vertical edge method for inspection of pad burning defect

This section focuses on the detection of the solder joint between the slider and suspension where the solder balls or pads burn. The characteristic of the defect is that one of the pad's edges is not smooth or the pad's border has a black limb caused by errors in the soldering process using the SJB machine as shown in Figure 4.2. The solder joint burning defect is the most significant problem to be solved. The new vertical edge detection is proposed to identify a burnt pad defect.

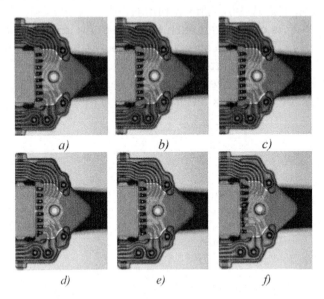

Figure 4.2. *Sample of HGA top view images; a), b) and c) are non-defected images; d), e) and f) are defected images*

4.3.1. *Inspection procedure*

The image processing techniques and the vertical edge detector are implemented in order to identify the defect on the input images. The overall algorithm procedure is shown in Figure 4.3. The proposed algorithm begins with the preprocessing step to find the region of interest, segmenting the region of interest into sub-images and transforming the sub-images into binary images. This is followed by the application of an edge detector to identify the defect. These are described by the following steps.

4.3.1.1. *Preprocessing*

The goal of the preprocessing step is to segment the region of interest or solder ball region, then to transform it into binary images. In order to segment the soldering burn region, we first find the reference point using standard cross correlation [LEW 95]. The input HGA image of size 2,400 × 2,000 pixels is correlated with the template image of size 405 × 36 pixels. The most corresponding point between the input image and the template image is the reference point. From the reference point, we extract the region of interest as the sub-image of size 405 × 36 pixels.

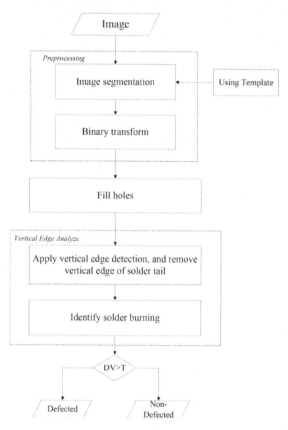

Figure 4.3. *Flow chart of the inspection of a pad burning defect*

The input HGA image is the RGB color image. The blue channel is used to create the binary image because the blue channel presents the difference between the solder balls and the gap region clearer than the other color channels. Then, an optimum threshold is defined by Otsu's criteria and the blue channel image is transformed into a binary image.

Figure 4.4 shows some results after the preprocessing. It can be observed that the binary sub-image may contain solder balls with holes inside their boundary. The next step fills holes in the solder balls using morphological reconstruction [SOI 99]. The holes will be filled except for the small object in a gap area between one solder ball and another solder ball. This small object is characterized as the burning defect.

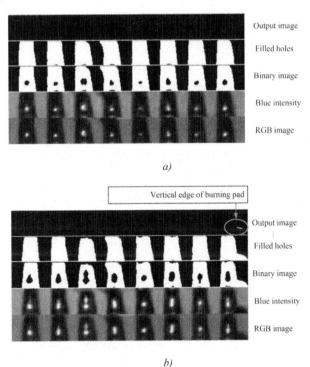

Figure 4.4. *Detection results: a) non-defected image; b) defected image. For a color version of this figure, see www.iste.co.uk / muneesawang / visualinspect.zip*

4.3.1.2. *Vertical edge detector*

We apply the Sobel edge detector demonstrated in [SAE 12, MA 10, DEN 11] to detect the solder ball burning. The Sobel operator is based on convolving an input image with the filter that consists of small, separable and integer values in horizontal and vertical directions. The operator uses two 3 × 3 kernels which are convolved with the input image. The horizontal and vertical edges are computed as:

$$G_x = \begin{bmatrix} 1 & 2 & 1 \\ 0 & 0 & 0 \\ -1 & -2 & -1 \end{bmatrix} * A \qquad [4.1]$$

$$G_y = \begin{bmatrix} 1 & 0 & -1 \\ 2 & 0 & -2 \\ 1 & 0 & -1 \end{bmatrix} * A \qquad [4.2]$$

where A is the input image, and G_x and G_y are the horizontal and vertical derivative approximation images, respectively. Then, images G_x and G_y are combined together to find the absolute magnitude of the gradient at each point and the orientation of that gradient. The gradient magnitude is computed by:

$$|G| = \sqrt{G_x^2 + G_y^2} \qquad [4.3]$$

The angle of orientation of the edge is given by:

$$\theta = \arctan\left(G_x / G_y\right) \qquad [4.4]$$

In this step, only the vertical edge explained in equation [4.2] is used to analyze the vertical edge of the solder balls for identifying the defect.

Some of the solder tails may appear in the binary sub-image after segmentation in the preprocessing step. Thus, we check and remove the vertical edge of solder balls using a threshold value. If the size of the detected vertical edge is larger than the pre-defined threshold value, the detected vertical edge will be removed.

After removing vertical edge of solder balls, the binary sub-image contains only the vertical edge of the burning solder balls, as well as the small burning objects in the gap area between solder balls. Figure 4.4 shows the result of detecting defects on the input HGA image using the proposed method. Figure 4.4(a) shows the result of the good image, and Figure 4.4(b) shows the result of the defective image which contains the solder ball or pad burning defect.

4.3.1.3. *Decision making*

Finally, the algorithm makes a decision whether the test image is defective. After analyzing the vertical edge and removing the edge of the solder tails, the white pixels in the binary sub-image correspond to the vertical edge of the solder balls that are burned and some small burning objects. To make a decision, a decision value (DV) is generated by summation of all pixels of the binary sub-image resulting from the previous step. If the DV is greater than a threshold value, the test image is a defective image; otherwise the test image is a non-defective image.

4.3.2. Experimental result

In an experiment, a total of 622 HGA images (572 good images and 50 defective images) were acquired by a mechanical positioning tool which positions the camera to take a picture. It produces the same size and resolution but may have differences in illumination. The images used in this experiment were RGB with 2,400 × 2,000 pixels, resolution 96 dpi. The samples of the tested images are shown in Figure 4.2.

The result of the experiment obtained by the proposed algorithm is shown in Table 4.2. In order to evaluate the performance of the proposed inspection system, we studied four performance evaluation measurements [HAN 06]: sensitivity, specification, precision and accuracy. The proposed algorithm for solder ball or pad burning defect detection provided a very high performance with 98.60% sensitivity, 100% specification, 100% precision and 98.71% accuracy. The processing time took 0.8400 s per image, measured from an Intel CPU Core™ i5 3210M computer running at 2.50 GHz. In the decision step, we defined a threshold value to classify the test images. The threshold value was experimentally obtained by the minimum size of burning regions in all test images in the experiment. The false detection as show in Table 4.2 was caused by noise and some of the solder ball tails that the system could not remove.

Test set	Result from machine detection		False detection
	Non-defective	Defective	
572 Non-defective images	564	8	8
50 defective images	0	50	0

Table 4.2. *Pad burned defect detection results obtained by the vertical edge method*

4.4. Detection of solder ball bridging on HGA

4.4.1. *Solder ball bridging defect*

The characteristic of a solder joint defect on a 6-pad HGA (shown in Figure 4.5) is described by the tail of one ball bridging another ball, or the solder ball touching another ball. This section presents two methods for detecting this defect. The first method uses chain code and the discrete Fourier transform, and the second method uses morphology and the template matching algorithm.

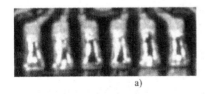 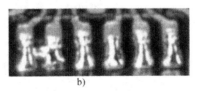

a)   b)

Figure 4.5. *HGA solder ball sub-images: a) non-defective sample; b) defective sample. For a color version of this figure, see www.iste.co.uk / muneesawang / visualinspect.zip*

4.4.2. *Chain code descriptor-based method*

The chain code descriptor is demonstrated in [SAE 11] to detect pads in integrated circuits (IC) of HDDs. Firstly, the region of interest is obtained and the pad area is segmented. Secondly, the chain codes of the edge of the pad are obtained and transformed into the frequency domain using Fourier transformation. The cross correlation is used to evaluate the similarity index of the input image for making a decision.

The method demonstrated in [SAE 11] is employed here for the inspection of a solder joint image of a HGA. This is compared to the newly proposed method.

4.4.2.1. *Preprocessing*

The region of interest is characterized by the normalized cross correlation to find the point that most corresponds with the template image. At the most corresponding point, we assign the sub-image size 242 × 62 pixels. The sub-image is then transformed into binary using Otsu's method, and following with the Sobel filter, to extract the edge of the solder joint. Figure 4.6 shows the edge outputs of the input images shown in Figure 4.5.

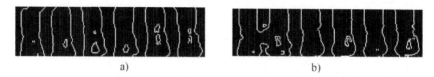

a)   b)

Figure 4.6. *Edge of solder joint image:*
a) non-defective image; b) defective image

4.4.2.2. Chain-code descriptor

In this step, the chain-code with eight neighbors is applied to the contour of the binary sub-image obtained previously. Figures 4.7(a)–(b) show the chain-code of the corresponding non-defective image and defective image, respectively.

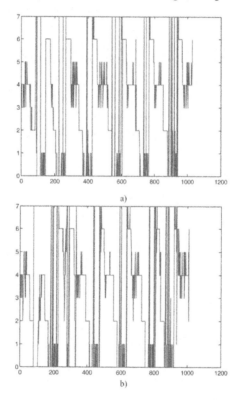

a)

b)

Figure 4.7. *Chain-code of solder joint image:*
a) non-defective image; b) defective image

4.4.2.3. *Similarity measurement*

This step transforms the chain-code signal from the previous step into the frequency domain using Fourier transformation. The transform coefficients are cross correlated with the coefficients of the template image in order to evaluate the similarity index of the input image. Then, the most appropriate threshold is set for making a decision. In this similarity measurement process, the signature of the template image must be evaluated in advance and kept in the database. We use the mean of non-defective images as the template image.

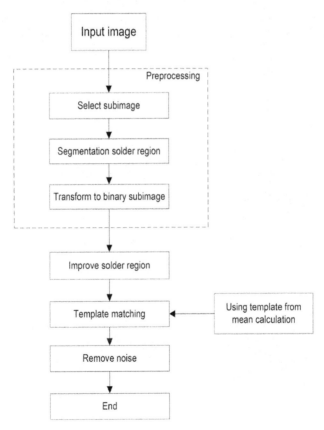

Figure 4.8. *Image processing procedure for detection of solder ball bridging defect, using morphology and template matching method*

4.4.3. *Morphological template-based method*

The proposed method uses morphology operation and the template matching method for identification of defects produced by the SJB machine. Figure 4.8 shows the flow chart of the proposed method. The preprocessing steps are the same as the change code method discussed in the previous section.

4.4.3.1. *Morphology and template matching*

Referring to previous works, Ibrahim *et al.*, [IBR 12] developed an algorithm for defect detection on PCBs by using the flood-fill morphology operator, which changes the color of a region, given an initial pixel in that region on binary and grayscale images. For binary images, this operator is used to fill the holes in a binary image. Putera and Ibrahim [PUT 10] segment images using morphological techniques in preparing the images for defect detection.

From this research, binary dilation is used to improve solder regions, and binary erosion is used to reduce noise from the output image. The method is described by the following steps:

– *Step 1*: improve solder regions. We use morphology [SHI 09, SON 08, GON 02] to improve the solder regions in the binary sub-image which is derived from preprocessing. Binary dilation is an operator of morphology for probing and expanding the shapes contained in the input image by combining two sets using vector addition of set elements. Let A and B be the active image and structuring element; denote two sets in E^N with elements a and b, respectively, where $a = (a_1, a_2, ..., a_N)$ and $b = (b_1, b_2, ..., b_N)$ are N-tuples of elements coordinates.

$$A \oplus B = \left\{ p \in E^N : p = a + b, \quad a \in A \text{ and } b \in B \right\}$$

The binary dilation of A by B is the set of all possible vector sums of pairs of elements, one coming from A and the other from B; the result of the dilation is given by those points p. After this step, we can identify solder regions more clearly.

– *Step 2*: template matching. In this step, the template matching uses the XOR operation to obtain the difference between template sub-image and active sub-image by comparing both images pixel-by-pixel. This operator is used to obtain the defects but still has noise in the result sub-image, so we need to reduce noise from the output.

– *Step 3*: remove noise. The binary erosion operator is used in this step to reduce noise. Binary erosion is an operator of morphology for shrinking the shapes contained in the input image by combining two sets using vector subtraction of set elements. Let A and B be the active image and structuring element, respectively.

$$A \ominus B = \left\{ p \in E^N : p = a + b \ \in A \ \text{for} \ b \in B \right\}$$

The binary erosion of A by B is the set of all elements p, for which $a + b \ \in A$, for every $b \in B$. The result of the erosion is given by those points p, the structure element acquired from the experiment. Using this operator, we can obtain the defects clearly.

Figure 4.9(a) shows grayscale sub-images of the solder joint after preprocessing images are generated. In Figure 4.9(b), solder regions are improved by a dilation operator. Figure 4.9(c) shows the result after template matching obtained from using a XOR operator. Finally, the final output after noise reduction was shown in Figure 4.9(d).

In step 1 and step 2, the morphology causes problems in assigning the size of the structure element for the dilation and erosion operator. We tested and recorded the efficacy of several sizes of the structure elements. Then, we obtained the most appropriate structure element for the dilation and erosion operator.

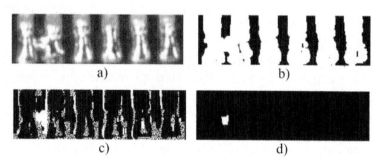

Figure 4.9. *Result images: a) gray sub-image; b) improved solder regions; c) result after template matching; d) result after noise reduction*

4.4.4. *Experimental result*

The chain code method explained in section 4.4.2 is applied in solder joint defect detection in the case of a solder ball bridging another ball and a solder ball not being complete on both sides of the slider and suspension. Its performance is compared to the morphology and template matching method discussed in section 4.4.3. A total of 942 HGA images of size 640 × 480 pixels were prepared by an expert using the optical microscope. The images are acquired by a mechanical positioning tool which positions the camera to take a picture. It produces the same size, position and resolution but may have differences in illumination. This test set consisted of 794 non-defective images, 128 images of a solder ball bridging another ball and 20 images of a solder ball not complete on both sides of slider and suspension.

The two methods use a template image for comparison of the characteristics of a good solder joint image with an active solder joint image. In the literature, Beutel *et al.* [BEU 02] created a mean template image for the classification task. In this research, template images were created from 794 images which are not defective images. Figure 4.10 shows the template image obtained by the mean values.

a)   b)

Figure 4.10. *Template images: a) grayscale image from mean calculation; b) binary image from mean calculation*

4.4.4.1. *Result obtained by the chain code method*

The chain code descriptor explained in section 4.4.2 was applied for the detection of solder joints on HGA images. Table 4.3 shows the result of applying the chain code method to the solder joint images with the defined threshold value of 0.35. In this table, images in order number 1 to 5 are defective solder joint images in the case of *solder ball bridging another ball*, and images in order number 6 to 10 are good solder joint images. It is observed that four samples were incorrectly classified.

Table 4.4 shows the result of applying the chain code method to the solder joint images with the defined threshold value of 0.13. In this table, images in order number 1 to 5 are defective solder joint images in the case of *solder ball not complete on both sides of slider and suspension*, and images in ordered number 6–10 are good solder joint images. As can be observed from Tables 4.3 and 4.4, the chain code method can be used to detect the defect on the solder joint in the case of solder ball bridging as well as the solder ball not complete. However, its effectiveness is dependent on the threshold value.

Number	Grayscale image	Similarity measurement	Result	
			Defective	Non-defective
1		0.4161		×
2		0.2915	✓	
3		0.3268	✓	
4		0.4538		×
5		0.4775		×
6		0.3856		✓
7		0.3962		✓
8		0.4024		✓
9		0.5005		✓
10		0.3332	×	

Table 4.3. *Result obtained by the chain code method applied to some images containing a solder joint defect on HGA in the case of the solder ball bridging another ball. The method uses threshold value = 0.35*

Number	Grayscale image	Similarity measurement	Result	
			Defective	Non-defective
1		0.1263	✓	
2		0.1133	✓	
3		0.1290	✓	
4		0.1226	✓	
5		0.1658		✗
6		0.3332	✗	
7		0.6192		✓
8		0.6704		✓
9		0.7269		✓
10		0.7421		✓

Table 4.4. *Result obtained by the chain code method applied to some images containing a solder joint defect on HGA in the case of the solder ball not being complete on both sides of the slider and suspension. The method uses threshold value = 0.13*

4.4.4.2. *Application of morphology and template matching method*

In order to apply the morphology and template matching method explained in section 4.4.3 for the detection of solder joints on HGA images, the image test set is provided and the process was to follow the steps discussed in Figure 4.8. Figure 4.11 shows the results of applying morphology and template matching method to the HGA images in case of solder ball bridging another ball. Figure 4.12 shows the result of applying the proposed method to the non-defective images. It can be observed that the proposed method was effective to detect this type of defect at 100% accuracy on these samples.

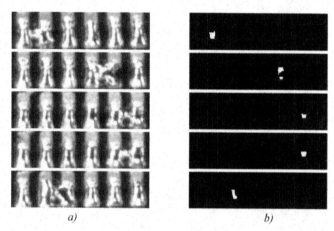

a)   *b)*

Figure 4.11. *Result of applying morphology and template matching for detection of solder joint defect on HGA in case of solder ball bridging another ball: a) grayscale image; b) result image*

We also detect solder joint defect where at least one of solder ball is not complete on both sides of the slider and suspension. These samples are shown in Figure 4.13 (defective samples) and Figure 4.14 (non-defective samples). In the defective samples, it can be seen that the white pixels appeared in the result images. In the decision-making step, these white pixels (both in Figure 4.11(b) and Figure 4.13(b)) were used. If the total number of white pixels in the result image is greater than the defined decision value, the tested HGA image is determined to be a defective sample.

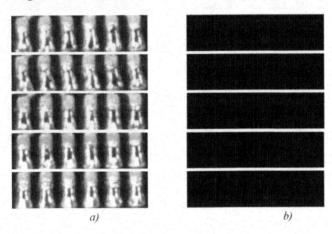

a)   *b)*

Figure 4.12. *Result of applying morphology and template matching to the non-defective images of solder joint on HGA: a) grayscale image; b) result image*

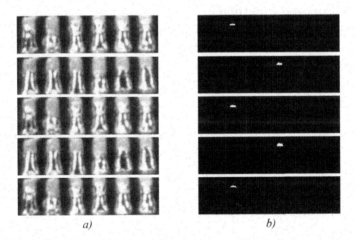

a)   *b)*

Figure 4.13. *Result of applying morphology and template matching for detecting the solder joint defect on HGA in the case of solder ball not complete on both sides of the slider and suspension: a) grayscale image; b) result image*

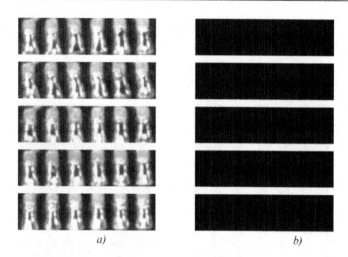

a)   *b)*

Figure 4.14. *Result of applying morphology and template matching to the non-defective images of solder joint on HGA: a) grayscale image; b) result image*

Tables 4.5 and 4.6 summarize the detection results based on the four measurements. The proposed method provides high performance and is better than the chain code method. The proposed method can attain the performance in detecting the solder joint at 99.89% accuracy in case of the solder ball bridging another ball; 99.02% accuracy in case of the solder ball not complete on both sides of slider and suspension; and 100% specificity and precision for detecting the two defects.

Measurements	Morphology and template matching	Chain code discrete Fourier's transform
Sensitivity	0.9987	0.9257
Specificity	1.0000	0.4113
Precision	1.0000	0.9097
Accuracy	0.9989	0.8562

Table 4.5. *Performance evaluation of the morphology and template matching method, and the chain code method, applied for detecting solder joint defect on HGA in case of the solder ball not being complete on both sides of slider and suspension*

Measurements	Morphology and template matching	Chain code discrete Fourier's transform
Sensitivity	0.9899	0.8967
Specificity	1.0000	0.4000
Precision	1.0000	0.9834
Accuracy	0.9902	0.8845

Table 4.6. *Performance evaluation of the morphology and template matching method, and the chain code method, applied for detecting the solder joint defect on HGA in the case of a solder ball bridging another ball*

4.5. Detection of missing solders on HGA

In addition to the defects previously discussed, HGA also introduces missing balls. In this section, an image segmentation algorithm is developed for detection of the missing solder balls on HGA. The detection process is made up of five steps detailed as follows.

4.5.1. *Image acquisition and enhancement*

The images are taken by an automatic two-side view super zoom camera and include 591 images of size 2,400 × 2,000 pixel from top view (Figure 4.15) and 591 images of size 640 × 480 pixel from 45 degree view (Figure 4.15). The HGA images taken from the top view are chosen because they have a better contrast quality than the image taken from the 45 degree view. For each image, the region of interest of size 402 × 27 pixel is obtained by the normalized cross correlation. This region focuses on solder ball areas.

The next step improves the image quality to be suitable for the subsequent operation by adjusting the contrast of the sub-image. In particular, this will reduce the computation complexity of the K-mean clustering with fast grouping elements of the HGA image and the efficiency detection of solder balls.

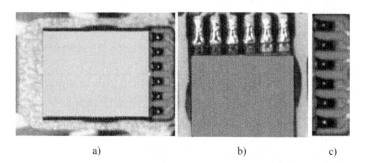

a)   b)   c)

Figure 4.15. *HGA images taken at a) top view; b) 45 degree view; c) the region of interest containing pad area*

4.5.2. *Clustering of image pixels*

This step employs the K-mean algorithm for pixel clustering in order to segment the solder balls from the background image. It is observed from Figure 4.16 that the grayscale values of the sub-image are distributed within 3 regions. This can be conveniently partitioned by the K-mean algorithm.

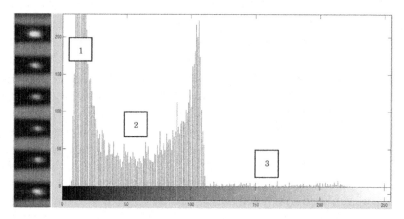

Figure 4.16. *Example of graylevel image in a histogram graph: gray color of solder ball image (left), histogram graph (right)*

From plotting the histogram graph, we can see three groups of histogram bars in which all solder balls on the HGA image have almost the same intensity values. Therefore, we may set K = 3 for the clustering. K-mean is used for grouping the solder ball on HGA image pixels, according to the following cost function.

$$J = \sum_{i=1}^{k} \sum_{j \varepsilon S_i} |X_j - Z_i|^2$$

where J is the summation of difference between the center point of data in groups, k is the number of groups, S_i is the set of pixels in the i-th group, X_j is the data that is in a particular group, and Z_j is the average of all data in the j-th group.

In the K-mean algorithm, three groups of suitable data are chosen and define three center points of data. Then, the distances between each data point and the three center points are calculated. The data group is classified using the shortest distance. The center point of the new data group is calculated and these steps are repeated until the cost function J falls behind a threshold value. As a result, all pixels of the HGA image are quantized though the K-mean clustering, and can be displayed in a three color map.

4.5.3. Decision making

Figure 4.17(a) shows the binary image obtained by segmentation of the solder region after quantization with the 3-class centroids. The binary image can be described by a matrix, $\mathbf{A} = [a_{ij}]_{m \times n}$. This is transposed to $\mathbf{A}^T = [a_{ji}]_{n \times m}$. The summation along the column direction is then taken. This results in a one-dimensional signal which is used as an image feature. It can be observed from Figure 4.17(a) that a non-defective image contains 6 perfectly closed loops. Otherwise, the image is a defective image as shown in Figure 4.17(b).

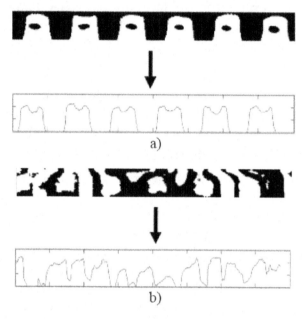

Figure 4.17. *Feature extraction for a) non-defective image and b) defective image*

4.5.4. Inspection result

In the experiment, we tested the defect detection algorithm using 591 images. Figure 4.18 shows the images of defective samples compared to the non-defective samples. The results after image segmentation and feature extraction are shown in Figure 4.19. It can be observed that the features extracted from the defective samples are sufficiently different from the non-defective sample. The number of closed loops can be used for the classification.

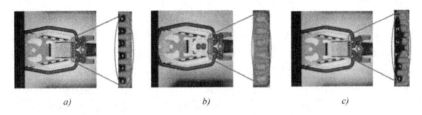

a)   b)   c)

Figure 4.18. *Images of three samples from the test set:
a) non-defective sample; b) defective sample with missing
solder balls; c) defective sample with solder burning*

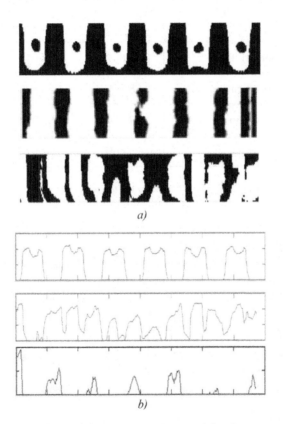

Figure 4.19. *a) Binary images of the three
samples shown in Figure 4.18, segmented by
the K-mean algorithm; b) the corresponding image features*

In the experiment, the image segmentation is also compared with Otsu's method. Table 4.7 shows the statistical analysis of the detection results. The performance of the system that uses K-mean for image segmentation is outperformed by that of the system using Otsu's method. The sensitivity, precision and accuracy are more than 99%.

Measurement	Segmentation methods	
	K-mean	Otsu's method
Sensitivity	99.83%	64.61%
Specification	88.89%	88.89%
Precision	99.83%	99.73%
Accuracy	99.66%	64.97%

Table 4.7. *Performance evaluation on detection of solder balls missing and burning*

The processing speed of the two methods used to detect the solder ball on HGA images were also compared in order to know the processing time of all the images as well as the average processing time for each image. From the experimental results, the K-mean clustering method used 47.56 s for processing all solder balls on HGA images, or 0.08 s for each image. However, Otsu's method used 81.90 s for processing all images, or 0.14 s for each image.

4.6. Conclusion

This chapter presents five methods for automatic visual inspection of HGA defects. First, the vertical edge detection for solder ball or pad burning defect detection provided a very high detection performance. Second, we proposed the morphology and template matching method for detection of solder ball bridging, and compared it with the chain code method. The experimental results show the effectiveness of the proposed method, having an accuracy of 99.02%, a sensitivity of 98.99%, a specification of 100% and a precision of 100%. The proposed method has a higher performance than the chain code method. Third, we also applied the proposed method and the chain code method to detect the defect where at least one solder ball is not complete on both sides of the slider and suspension. The last two methods, K-mean and Otsu's method, are adopted to detect the missing solder balls on HGA.

4.7. Bibliography

[BEU 02] BEUTEL J., FITZPATRICK J.M., HORII S.C., *et al.*, *Handbook of Medical Imaging, Display and PACS*, vol. 3, pp. 221–275, SPIE Press, Washington D.C., 2002.

[DEN 11] DENG C., MA W., YIN Y., "An edge detection approach of image fusion based on improved Sobel operator", *IEEE, 4th International Congress on Image and Signal Processing (CISP)*, pp. 1189–1193, 2011

[GON 02] GONZALEZ R.C., WOODS R., *Digital Image Processing*, Prentice-Hall, New Jersey, 2002.

[HAN 06] HAN J., KAMBER M., *Data Mining: Concepts and Techniques*, Morgan Kaufmann Publishers, Elsevier, San Francisco, CA, 2006.

[IBR 12] IBRAHIM I., IBRAHIM Z., KHALIL K., *et al.*, "An improved defect classification algorithm for six printing defects and its implementation on real printed circuit board images", *International Journal of Innovative Computing, Information and Control*, vol. 8, no. 5(A), pp. 3239–3250, May 2012.

[IEA 12] IEAMSAARD J., TANGDEE B., YAMMEN S., *et al.*, "Solder joint and styrofoam bead detection in HDD using mathematical morphology", *International Computer Science and Engineering Conference (ICSEC)*, pp. 99–104, 2012.

[LEW 95] LEWIS J.P., "Fast template matching", *Vision Interface*, vol. 95, no. 120123, pp. 15–19, 1995.

[MA 10] MA C., YANG L., GAO W., *et al.*, "An improved Sobel algorithm based on median filter", *Proceeding of IEEE, the 2nd International Conference on Mechanical and Electronics Engineering (ICMEE)*, pp. V1-88–V1-92, 2010.

[MUN 12] MUNEESAWANG P., YAMMEN S., FUANGPIAN T., *et al.*, "Morphology-based automatic visual inspection for SJB defect on HGA", *Proceeding of the 4th International Data Storage Technology Conference*, pp. 32–35, 2012.

[MUN 13] MUNEESAWANG P., YAMMEN S., "Automatic visual inspection of hard disk drives", *Proceedings of International Electrical Engineering Congress (iEECON)*, pp. 36–39, 2013.

[PUT 10] PUTERA S.H.I., IBRAHIM Z., "Print circuit board defect detection using mathematical morphology and Matlab image processing tools", *International Conference on Education Technology and Computer (ICETC)*, Shanghai, vol. 5, pp. V5-359–V5-363, 2010.

[SAE 10] SAENTHON A., KAITWANIDVILA S., "Development of new edge detection filter based on genetic algorithm", *The International Journal of Advanced Manufacturing Technology*, vol. 46, nos. 9–12, pp. 1009–1019, 2010.

[SAE 11] SAENTHON A., KAITWANIDVILA S., "Pattern recognition technique for pad inspection using chain-code-descrete Fourier transform and signal correlation", *Proceeding of the International MultiConference of Engineers and Computer Scientists (IMECS)*, pp. 569–572, 2011.

[SHI 09] SHI F.Y., *Image Processing and Mathematical Morphology Fundamentals and Applications*, CRC Press, Taylor & Francis Group, Boca Raton, FL, 2009.

[SON 08] SONKA M., HLAVAC V., BOYLE R., *Image Processing, Analysis and Machine Vision*, Thomson Learning, Toronto, Canada, 2008.

[SOI 99] SOILLE P., *Morphological Image Analysis: Principles and Applications*, Springer-Verlag, New York, 1999.

5

Analysis Methods for Fault Deformation of Solder Bump on the Actuator Arm

Due to the small size of integrated circuit (IC) die components in hard disk drives (HDD), fault deformation of solder bumps is found frequently. This chapter presents the analytical method for the analysis of bump shape changes in the symmetrical and asymmetrical pattern in the production process of IC die packages. Based on different bump alloys, some parameters in the production, such as the temperature used for melting the bump, the height of the bump and the surface tension of bump materials, are investigated. The chapter also presents the finite element method for investigating the stress performance that is related to the fault deformation of solder bumps. The simulation is conducted on the bump positions in both symmetric and asymmetric forms. The experimental results show that the finite element method and analytical method are seen to be suitable for this study.

Chapter written by Somporn RUANGSINCHAIWANICH.

5.1. Introduction

The manufacturing of the actuator arm of HDD in the assembly industry is made up of two manufacturing processes – flip-chip and hook up assemblies. The flip-chip assembly combines different components to flex and the hook up assembly combines flex from the flip-chip assembly to bracket and joint to the arm actuator assembly. Figure 5.1 shows the IC die package which is made up of the preamp, flex and bump. These components are very small and are attached on top of the flex by the flip-chip assembly. In this configuration, solder bumps are important components because they work as connectors to combine the preamp and flex together. The main problem of solder bumps is that they are often improperly melted in the melt process due to many factors [TEE 03, ROL 06, LI 07, CLE 07]. If solder bumps are deformed, the flip-chip is, therefore, faulty.

In order to solve the aforementioned problem, section 5.2 presents a method to analyze factors affecting this deformation. Since it is observed that when a component is heated, its surface tension changes which makes the component melt, the primary focus of this chapter is to analyze the effect of the surface tension of the material on the deformation of solder bumps. Specifically, the analytical method is applied for the analysis of bump shape change in the symmetrical and asymmetrical pattern. Different bump alloys are analyzed. In addition, some parameters of IC die package production, such as the temperature used for melting the bump, the height of the bump and the surface tension of bump materials, are investigated.

Section 5.3 will investigate how the solder bump position will affect the deformation of solder bumps. The analysis method is used to investigate the stress performance, regarding bumps positioned in both symmetric and asymmetric forms, as well as corner/center positions.

a)   b)

Figure 5.1. *Samples of an IC die package: a) focusing on the three components: flex, bump and preamp; b) focusing on the bump position*

5.2. Surface tension analysis

An IC die package is heated by a reflow machine in order to connect bumps with the preamp and flex. If the bumps are melted appropriately as shown in Figure 5.2, the IC die package will be ready for usage. If the bumps are not appropriately melted as shown in Figure 5.3, it might be as a result of many causes, therefore, the IC die package cannot be used.

Figure 5.2. *The changes in acceptable bump process*

The melting process of bumps is very crucial. Before being heated, bumps bear the weight of the preamp on top. However, the shape of bumps will not change because action and reaction force are equal. When bumps are heated, bump shape will change because its surface tension reduces. Therefore, the current work aims to investigate the surface tension, temperature and shape of bumps made from different materials by using analytical method. In particular, the asymmetrical pattern will be used for the analysis of the change of bump shape since the asymmetrical bump shape is commonly found in the real production.

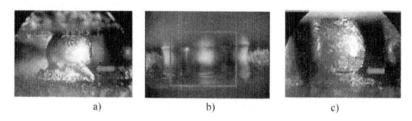

a)   b)   c)

Figure 5.3. *The changes in bumps from a reject process:*
a) non-reflow; b) missing ball; c) fracture

There are many research studies investigating the deformation of solder bumps. Chiang and Yuan [CHI 01] studied the three methods that can predict the solder bump shape, i.e. the geometry-based truncated sphere method, the force-balanced analytical solution and the energy-based algorithm. It was found that all three methods can accurately predict the solder reflow shape in an accurate range. Verges *et al.* [VER 01] studied the relationship between the geometry of the liquid bridge and the residual forces. Liu and Chiang [LIU 03] investigated the effect of force on bumps and the effect of bump position on deformation. The studies of Verges *et al.* [VER 01] focused on tension while the study of Liu and Chiang [LIU 03] focused on compression. When the force on bumps was reversed, it was found that both studies used the same formula. Moser, *et al.* [MOS 07] experimented on different material properties of an alloy, e.g. surface tension and density, and drew a formula from the experimental results. However, most studies tend to investigate the bump shape change in the symmetrical pattern.

5.2.1. *Model analysis*

Table 5.1 shows the parameters of materials A, B, C, D and E, which are different alloys and usually used for making bumps [MOS 07]. Based on a single bump, the study was conducted in [MOS 07] to analyze the relationship of surface tension, temperature and bump shape. It was shown that when temperature is above the melting point, the surface tension of alloy decreases and the bump shape is changed.

In order to study the force on bumps, the following set of conditions can be obtained [VER 01, LIU 03]:

– the molten solder ball is in static equilibrium when the solder solidifies;

– the solder pads on the chip and substrate are circular and are perfectly aligned when the solder solidifier;

– the surface profile of the molten solder ball is axial-symmetric;

– the meridian defining the free surface of the solder joint is assumed to be a circular arc;

– the solder pads are completely covered by solder, but the solder does not spread beyond the pads.

Figure 5.4 shows the free body diagram of a solder ball [LIU 03]. The force on the bump in symmetrical condition can be expressed as:

$$F_h + \left[\gamma \sin\left(\pi - \theta_h \right) \right] \cdot 2\pi R - P_h \pi R_h^2 = 0 \qquad [5.1]$$

Material	Bump alloy	$\gamma = A + BT$ (mN/m)
A	Sn3.8Ag	= 585.1 - 0.0881 T
B	Sn2.76Ag0.46Cu	= 587.0 - 0.0964 T
C	Sn3.13Ag0.74Cu	= 582.1 - 0.0867 T
D	Sn3.13Ag0.48Cu4.02Bi	= 555.3 - 0.0623 T
E	Sn3.55Ag0.5Cu3Bi3Sb	= 561.5 - 0.0880 T

Table 5.1. *Surface tension of bump alloy [MOS 07], where γ is the surface tension (mN / m), and T is the temperature (°C).*

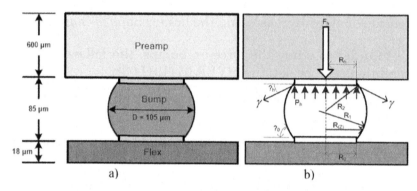

a)   b)

Figure 5.4. *a) Dimension of the IC die package used in the current work and b) free body diagram of solder ball with axial-symmetric discussed in [LIU 03]*

Since the system in the reflow machine is in open air conditions, pressure equals 0. Therefore, equation [5.1] can be expressed as:

$$F_h + \left[\gamma \sin\left(\pi - \theta_h \right) \right] \cdot 2\pi R = 0 \qquad [5.2]$$

where θ_h is the degree, F_h is the weight of the component or force (N), γ is the surface tension (N/m) and R is the radius (μm).

The analysis of the change of bump shape will be investigated in two patterns. These are discussed in the following sections.

5.2.1.1. Symmetrical pattern

In the symmetrical pattern, R_h (upper bump metal diameter) equals R_0 (lower bump metal diameter) [CHI 01]. The relationships of height, radius and surface tension in the symmetrical pattern $(R_h = R_0)$ can be found from the truncated sphere theory, which are:

$$h = 2\sqrt{R^2 - R_h^2} \qquad\qquad [5.3]$$

$$R = \frac{\sqrt{h^4 + 4 \cdot h^2 R_h^2}}{2 \cdot h} \qquad\qquad [5.4]$$

$$V = \frac{\pi \cdot h}{6} \cdot \left[h^2 + 3 \cdot \left(R_h^2 + R_0^2 \right) \right] \qquad\qquad [5.5]$$

5.2.1.2. Asymmetrical pattern

In the asymmetrical pattern, R_h is not equal to R_0. The relationship of height, radius and surface tension in the asymmetrical pattern $(R_h \neq R_0)$ can be expressed as:

$$h = \sqrt{R^2 - R_h^2} + \sqrt{R^2 - R_0^2} \qquad\qquad [5.6]$$

$$R = \frac{\sqrt{h^4 + 2 \cdot h^2 \cdot \left(R_h^2 + R_0^2 \right) + \left(R_h + R_0 \right)^2 \left(R_h - R_0 \right)^2}}{2 \cdot h} \qquad [5.7]$$

$$V = \frac{\pi}{3} \cdot \left[\sqrt{R^2 - R_0^2} \cdot \left(2R^2 + R_0^2 \right) + \sqrt{R^2 - R_h^2} \cdot \left(2R^2 + R_h^2 \right) \right] \quad [5.8]$$

where R is the radius (µm), R_h is the lower bump metal radius (µm), R_0 is the upper bump metal radius (µm), h is the height (µm) and V is the volume (µm³).

5.2.2. Simulation

This study investigated the surface tension of the alloy and the temperature level of bumps in the symmetrical and asymmetrical patterns. Figures 5.5 and 5.6 show the changes of bump shapes in the symmetrical and asymmetrical patterns by using the analytical method. However, in the manufacturing process, bumps are usually melted in the asymmetrical pattern. Figure 5.7 shows the sample of the acceptable melted bumps. It shows that the bottom of the bump is melted more than the top because flux is applied at the bottom of the bump, which can conduct heat very well.

Figure 5.8 shows the radius of bumps in the symmetrical and asymmetrical patterns. It is apparent that the variation of height by radius of the symmetrical pattern is similar to linearity, however, in reality, in the production process of the IC die package, the asymmetrical pattern is commonly found. The radiuses from the symmetrical analytical method are longer than those from the asymmetrical analytical method.

Figure 5.9 shows the changes of surface tension at the same temperature level in the symmetrical and asymmetrical patterns by using the analytical method. Materials A, B, C, D and E as described in Table 5.1 were analyzed. The results show that material C has the highest surface tension and material D has the lowest surface tension at any height of bump. Figure 5.10 shows the analysis of temperature required for the change of bump height from 85 to 75 µm in the symmetrical and asymmetrical patterns. The results show that material C needed the highest temperature in order to change bump shape.

Figure 5.11(a) compares the surface tension of different materials at the height of 75 µm in the symmetrical and asymmetrical patterns. The result shows that the surface tension of material C is the highest and the surface tension of material D is the lowest. Figure 5.11(b) shows that at the height of 75 µm, material C needs less heat than other alloys during the changing process while material D needs more heat than other alloys. When comparing Figure 5.11(a) with 5.11(b), it appears that the surface tension of analyzed material and temperature of bump shape change is in an inverse relationship which is a common characteristic of other materials.

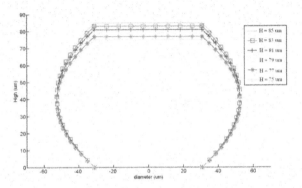

Figure 5.5. *Change of bump shapes in the symmetrical pattern*

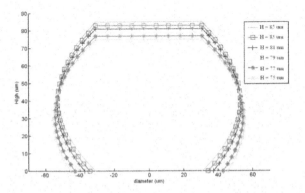

Figure 5.6. *Change of bump shapes in the asymmetrical pattern*

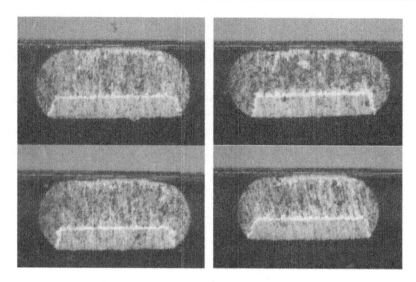

Figure 5.7. *The melted solder bumps in the actual IC die package*

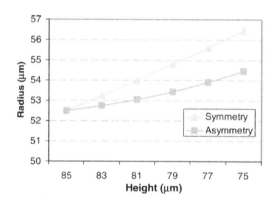

Figure 5.8. *Height versus radius of the analytical method*

5.3. Analysis of stress performance at different configurations of solder bump positions

This section investigates the effect of the position of solder bumps to the stress performance using the finite element method (FEM). When solder bumps are heated from the reflow process, bumps at different positions will deform differently. In the manufacturing process of HDD, there are many solder bumps positioned asymmetrically. Therefore, solder bumps will have much different stress at different positions, which results in a high possibility of fault deformation.

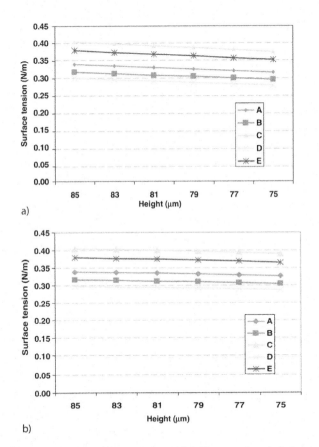

a)

b)

Figure 5.9. *Surface tension of different materials in a) the symmetrical pattern and b) the asymmetrical pattern*

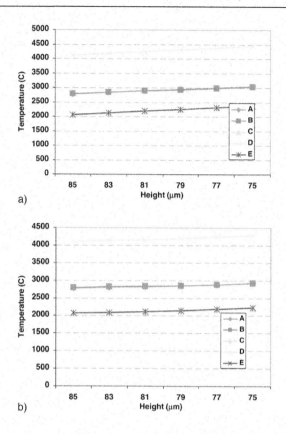

Figure 5.10. *Temperature of different materials in a) the symmetrical pattern and b) the asymmetrical pattern*

To date, various applications of FEM have been conducted for the analysis of solder bumps [TEE 03, ROL 06, LI 07]. Tee *et al.* [TEE 03] studied the FEM analysis of solder bump design. Several parameters of solder bump performance were studied, for example, small maximum solder ball diameter, short thermal cycle temperature range and large solder mask opening. They found that the FEM was greatly useful for solder bump analysis and package and board design. Furthermore, Rolling *et al.* [ROL 06] studied the material parameters for creep experiments on real solders by FEM modeling. ANASYS was also used to model for investigating material characteristics. Different shapes of solder bumps and materials on mechanical behavior were compared. The results showed that the bump outline shape must be considered in creep experiments and results of the experiment and simulation were similar. Li and Wang [LI 07] also investigated the thermo-fatigue life evaluation of SnAgCu solder joints by FEM. The solder bump life model predicated according to accumulated creep strain was shown to have a higher value than the model predicated according to accumulated creep strain energy density.

In this section, the FEM is used to investigate the stress performance which is related to fault deformation of solder bumps. Particularly, solder bump position will be investigated as to how it affects the deformation of solder bumps.

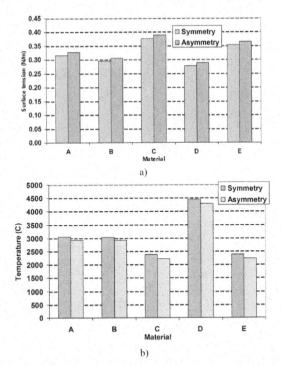

Figure 5.11. *a) Surface tension of different materials at height of 75 μm and b) temperature of different materials at height of 75 μm*

5.3.1. *Analysis model*

5.3.1.1. *Force analysis*

Figure 5.12 shows the parameters used in force analysis in solid circumstances. The position of force, P_i, on solder bumps can be expressed as:

$$P_i = (W / n) + (M_y / I_y) \cdot x + (M_x / I_x) \cdot y \qquad [5.9]$$

where W is the weight of the preamp, n is the number of solder bumps, and M_x and M_y are the moments of the X-axis and Y-axis. These are defined as:

$$M_y = W \cdot e_x \qquad [5.10]$$

$$M_x = W \cdot e_y \qquad [5.11]$$

where e_x and e_y are the distance of force and center of gravity of preamp, and

$$I_y = \Sigma x_i^2 \qquad [5.12]$$

$$I_x = \Sigma y_i^2 \qquad [5.13]$$

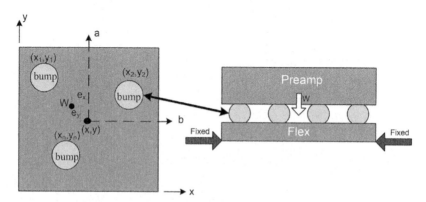

Figure 5.12. *Parameters and positioning*

5.3.1.2. *Stress and strain analysis*

Stress and strain are represented by the following column matrices as:

$$\boldsymbol{\sigma} = \begin{bmatrix} \sigma_x & \sigma_y & \sigma_z & \tau_x & \tau_y & \tau_z \end{bmatrix}^T \text{ and}$$

$$\boldsymbol{\varepsilon} = \begin{bmatrix} \varepsilon_x & \varepsilon_y & \varepsilon_z & \gamma_x & \gamma_y & \gamma_z \end{bmatrix}^T \tag{5.14}$$

The stress/strain relationships for an isotropic material are given by:

$$\boldsymbol{\sigma} = \mathbf{D}\boldsymbol{\varepsilon} \tag{5.15}$$

where $\boldsymbol{\sigma}$ and $\boldsymbol{\varepsilon}$ are defined by equation [5.14], and the constitutive matrix $\mathbf{D}$ is now given by:

$$\mathbf{D} = \frac{E}{(1+v)(1-v)} \begin{bmatrix} 1-v & v & v & 0 & 0 & 0 \\ & 1-v & v & 0 & 0 & 0 \\ & & 1-v & 0 & 0 & 0 \\ & & & \dfrac{1-2v}{2} & 0 & 0 \\ & & & & \dfrac{1-2v}{2} & 0 \\ & & & & & \dfrac{1-2v}{2} \end{bmatrix} \tag{5.16}$$

where v is Poisson's ratio and E is Young's modulus.

5.3.2. *Design and analysis using FEM*

The simulation was conducted by the ANSYS program. The preamp and have flex the size of 0.48×0.48 mm^2. Forces on the preamp equal the weight of preamp. There are five configurations: 1-bump geometry model, 2-bump geometry model, 3-bump geometry model, 4-bump geometry model and 16-bump geometry model. Material properties for all five models are shown in Table 5.2.

	Material		
Property	Flex	Preamp	SnAgCu
Young's modulus (MPa)	1.30E+5	1.07E+5	4.5E+4
Poisson's ratio	0.33	0.28	0.38
Density (kg/mm³)	8.3E-6	2.33E-6	7.44E-6
Thermal expansion (1/°C)	1.8E-05	2.60E-06	1.76E-5
Thermal conductivity (W/mm °C)	0.401	0.149	7.32E-2
Specific heat (J/kg °C)	385	700	226
Melting point (°C)	1,084.62	1,414	217

Table 5.2. *Properties of material*

For the 1-bump geometry model, a solder bump was positioned at the center. For the 2-bump, 3-bump and 4-bump geometry models, solder bumps were positioned symmetrically. For the 16-bump geometry model, all bumps were positioned symmetrically.

Figure 5.13 shows the stress distribution inside solder bumps of 1-bump, 2-bump, 3-bump and 4-bump geometry models. The results of stress from the simulation are shown in Figure 5.14. The results show that stress of the 1-bump model is the highest. Stress of the 2-bump model is lower than that of the 1-bump model and is equally distributed. Stress of the 3-bump model is also lower than those of the first two models, but it is not equally distributed. Stress of the B3 bump is higher than those of the B1 and B2 bumps because it is separated from the other two bumps. Stress of the 4-bump model is also lower than those of the first two models and is equally distributed.

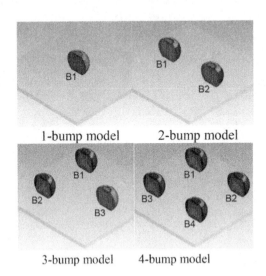

1-bump model   2-bump model

3-bump model   4-bump model

Figure 5.13. *Von Mises equivalent stress in solder bumps with constant geometry boundary conditions*

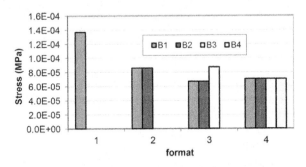

Figure 5.14. *Comparison stress level of models*

Solder bumps of the 16-bump geometry model were divided into four symmetrical sets, i.e. set A, set B, set C and set D as shown in Figure 5.15(a). First, the simulation result of each set was presented separately. For example, stress distribution inside solder bumps of set B was presented as shown in Figure 5.15(b). Stress values of each bump in set B were unequally distributed as shown in Figure 5.15(c).

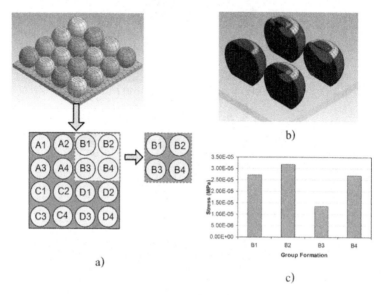

Figure 5.15. *a) 16-bump geometry model, b) Von Mises equivalent stress in solder bumps of set B and c) comparison stress level of set B*

Figure 5.16 shows the stress results of all four sets. The stress of each set is unequally distributed, in which it is difficult to recognize any significant results. However, Figure 5.15(c) shows that the stress of B2 is the highest while the stress of B3 is the lowest.

Therefore, solder bumps of the 16-bump model were relabeled to X, Y and Z as shown in Figure 5.17. X refers to bumps positioned at the corners. Z refers to bumps positioned at the center of geometry. Y refers to all other bumps.

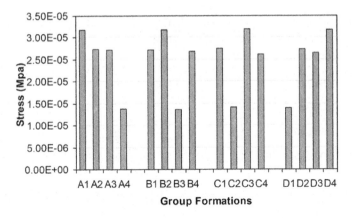

Figure 5.16. *Comparison stress level of the 16-bump model*

Stress performances of solder bumps were grouped according to their labels as shown in Figure 5.18. All solder bumps labeled X show the highest stress. All solder bumps labeled Y show the medium stress. Finally, all solder bumps labeled Z show the lowest stress.

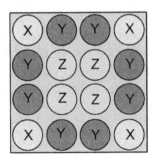

Figure 5.17. *The new labeled 16-bump model*

5.4. Experimental result

The IC die package with the solder bump position shown in Figure 5.19 was tested. The stress of bumps in the studied IC package was analyzed by the FEM program. Figure 5.19(b) shows the deformed bumps from FEM analysis. It can be observed that the level of deformation was higher in the area where there were fewer bumps (as indicated by the arrow).

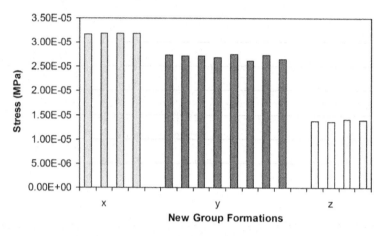

Figure 5.18. *Comparison stress level of new labeled groups*

Figure 5.20(a) shows the rejected IC packages that bump deformation caused bump bridging in many areas, especially the area where there were fewer bumps. The bump deformation may make the preamp unbalanced and slightly lifted during the reflow process, which makes the bumps on the other side of the package partly melted as shown in Figure 5.20(b).

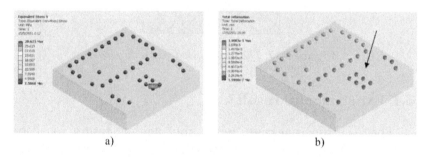

Figure 5.19. *a) Stress of bumps from FEM and
b) deformation of bumps from FEM*

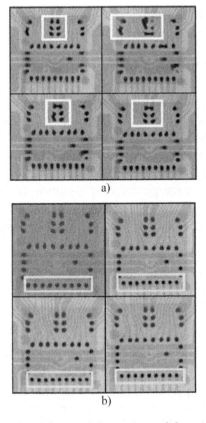

Figure 5.20. *a) Bump deformations of the rejected IC packages and b) unmelted bumps of the rejected IC packages*

5.5. Conclusion

This chapter presents the analysis methods regarding solder bump shape and position within the fault deformation during manufacturing process. Analysis of bump shape change is possibly done using the analytical method. The advantage of this method is that bump shape is gradually changed and can easily be observed. In addition, it shows the temperature of bump shape changes. Finally, the model of bump shape change in the asymmetrical pattern is proposed. The results of the analytical method of the asymmetrical pattern are reasonable when comparing with those of the symmetrical pattern.

The FEM simulation of this study shows the significant results that solder bumps at different positions have different stresses. Therefore, when solder bumps are heated from the reflow process, bumps at different positions will deform differently. Two or four solder bump models that are symmetrically positioned will have a similar stress level. However, in the manufacturing process of HDD, there are many solder bumps positioned asymmetrically. Therefore, solder bumps will have much different stress at different positions, which results in a high possibility of fault deformation.

5.6. Bibliography

[CHI 01] CHIANG K.N., YUAN C.A., "An overview of solder bump shape prediction algorithms with validations", *IEEE Transactions on Advanced Packaging*, vol. 24, no. 2, pp. 158–162, May 2001.

[CLE 07] CLECH J.P., "Review and analysis of lead-free solder material properties", BRADLEY E., HANDWERKER C.A., BATH J., *et al.*, (eds.), *Lead-Free Electronics: iNEMI Projects Lead to Successful Manufacturing*, John Wiley & Sons, Inc., Hoboken, NJ, USA, 2007.

[LI 07] LI X., WANG Z., "Thermo-fatigue life evaluation of SnAgCu solder joint in flip chip assemblies", *Journal of Materials Processing Technology*, vol. 183, no. 1, pp. 6–12, 2007.

[LIU 03] LIU C.M., CHIANG K.N., "Solder bumps layout design and reliability enhancement of wafer level packaging", *International Conference on Electronic Packaging Technology Proceedings (ICEPT) 2003*, pp. 50–64, 2003.

[MOS 07] MOSER Z., GASIOR W., BUKAT K., *et al.*, "Pb-free solders: part III, Wettability testing of Sn-Ag-Cu-Bi alloys with Sb additions", *Journal of Phase Equilibria and Diffusion*, vol. 28, no. 5, pp. 433–438, 2007.

[RÖL 06] RÖLLIG M., WIESE S., WOLTER K.J., "Extraction of materials for creep experiments on real solder-joint by FEM analysis", *7th Conference Proceedings on Thermal, Mechanical and Multiphysics Simulation and Experiments in Microelectronics and Micro-Systems, EuroSim 2006*, pp. 1–9, 2006.

[TEE 03] TEE T.Y., LIM M., PAN S., *et al.*, "Design analysis of TFBGA with customized solder joint fatigue model", *5th Electronic Materials and Packaging Conference (EMAP) Conference Proc.*, Singapore, pp. 309–315, 2003.

[VER 01] VERGES M.A., LARSON M.C., BACOU R., "Force and shape of liquid bridges between circular pads", *Proceeding of the Experimental Mechanics*, vol. 41, no. 4, pp. 351–357, 2001.

6

Artificial Intelligence Techniques for Quality Control of Hard Disk Drive Components

This chapter presents the theoretical aspect concerning the application of artificial intelligence (AI) techniques to control the quality of hard disk drive (HDD) components. The application of AI in quality control (QC) is discussed first. Subsequently, three examples, inclusive of the case of using artificial neural networks (ANN) for multipanel lamination process modeling, HDD actuator arm control chart pattern recognition with AI and finally machine clustering with AI, are given.

6.1. Introduction

QC is a very important function in the industry as it is a process to ensure that the product manufactured meets the specifications and the requirements of the customer. The concept of quality management was first introduced in the early 1900s. Then, the control of quality had its emphasis on

Chapter written by Wimalin LAOSIRITAWORN.

separating defective products through inspection. However, the focus of quality management has changed over time from quality inspection to statistical process control (SPC), quality assurance and total quality management. Nowadays, there is a need for more advanced QC techniques as product characteristics have become more complex, calling for higher production accuracy with shorter production lead time.

QC of HDD components is very challenging as HDD component production involves very high technology. The complexity of production also arises from the large number of machines, diverse kinds of equipment and nonlinear work flow. HDD consists of four main components: electronics, head subassemblies, media and motors [GOU 00]. Head production, for example, is highly automated and complex as regards the fabrication of wafers. Media production, similar to heads production, is subject to high technology. Therefore, there exists a need for more advanced QC methods in order to deal with the nature of this industry.

The era of AI, one of the fields in science and engineering, began soon after World War II [RUS 10], but it was not until the 1960s and 1970s that the firm foundations for knowledge representation and problem solving were laid down. AI is a multidisciplinary field that is concerned with making computers think or act humanly and rationally. AI applications in engineering began in the 1980s [SRI 06]. Since then, AI tools, for example knowledge-based systems, fuzzy logic, inductive learning, neural network and genetic algorithm, have been applied to solve various engineering problems [PHA 99]. The use of AI in the manufacturing industry is concerned with the design, planning, production and system-level activities [TET 97].

As AI has learning ability and being capable of dealing with complex problems, it is an ideal tool to deal with the complex nature of QC problems in HDD manufacturing. The possible uses of AI for the purpose of QC will be discussed. Three case studies were given in this chapter to demonstrate the actual application of AI in a HDD component factory. The first case is the flexible printed circuit (FPC) production modeling with AI. The second case is the control chart pattern recognition using AI in HDD actuator production. The third case demonstrates machine clustering of HDD actuator production in order to determine order for quality inspection.

The rest of this chapter is organized as follows: section 6.2 describes general guidelines of how AI could be applied to QC task. This section also includes review of some key literatures. Section 6.3 provides detailed case studies of AI applications in QC of various HDD components. Finally, a conclusion is given in section 6.4.

6.2. Artificial intelligence tasks in quality control

AI tasks in QC can be classified into three groups: classification and prediction, clustering and time series analysis.

6.2.1. *Classification and prediction*

Classification and prediction are the two forms of supervised learning tasks where models describing data class or future data trends are extracted. Classification is used for predicting discrete or unordered output variables, while the term "prediction" is used for continuous output variables.

The common AI techniques used for classification and prediction include, for example, decision tree classifiers, ANNs, support vector machines (SVMs), rule-based classifiers and Bayesian classifiers. Other approaches are k-nearest-neighbor classifiers, case-based reasoning, genetic algorithms and fuzzy logic. Regression-based models are usually used for the task of prediction; however, techniques like ANN and SVM are also designed to perform such a task.

AI could be used to classify and predict variables, which can help to improve product QC in various ways. A few examples of AI application are as follows:

6.2.1.1. *Classifying quality characteristic*

Quality inspection is usually performed after the critical manufacturing process to test if the quality characteristic passes the specification. This is to prevent the defective product from going through the next process. However, if defects occur, the defective parts are subject to either rework or becoming scrap, which, either way, costs money. The quality of the part depends very much on the setting of the machine. In some cases, it is possible that the detection of the possible defect will take place before it actually happens on account of reading some indication during the production process. This allows adjustments to be made to prevent the product characteristic from going out of specification.

The drilling process, one of the most widely used processes in the industry, makes for an excellent example of this application. The research work in [FER 11] applied the classification algorithm to improve QC in the drilling process in the aeronautic industry. Burr generation is the major problem in the drilling process performed on the wings of aeroplanes. After drilling, visual inspection and manual burr elimination have to be performed to ensure drilling quality before riveting. In this work, predictive variables related to the spindle signal were used to predict the class of the outcome to be either "admissible burr" or "non-admissible burr". Various classifiers, including classification trees, induction rules, distance-based techniques and probability-based techniques, were used. The result reveals that almost all the models provide high accuracy in predicting the burr class.

6.2.1.2. *Process modeling*

Process modeling is a task where process parameters such as process setting or in-process measurement are used to predict the process response. Once the model is constructed, it can be used to study the process by changing inputs and observing how that affects the output. It can also be used with other quality improvement techniques such as the design of the experiment. By performing experiments on the process model, the optimum parameter setting can be determined with minimum process disruption.

The research work in [SUK 05] applied neural networks to the model superplastic forming (SPF) process. Input parameters such as the hot separation initial drop pressure, hot separation time, start SPF temperature, average SPF temperature and number of gas pulses were used to predict the finished geometry of the product. The model can be used for the prediction, improvement and optimization of the process.

6.2.2. *Cluster analysis*

Cluster analysis is a form of unsupervised learning. A cluster is a group of objects that are similar to one another within the same cluster but dissimilar to those in other groups. The objective of cluster analysis is to group objects that have similar properties under the same category. A number of AI clustering algorithms are available: for instance, the expectation–maximization (EM) algorithm, *k*-means clustering algorithm, growing self-organizing map (GSOM), etc.

One possible use of cluster analysis is as a technique to differentiate between good and defective products. The research work in [KAR 08] applied the GSOM algorithm in the complex manufacturing environment of wafer fabrication in Motorola, USA, which involved hundreds of process control measures, process steps and QC data. Grouping into clusters, according to the quality measured, helps to monitor the process more easily.

6.2.3. *Time series analysis*

Time series analysis is a sequence of values obtained over a period of time. The apparent use of time series analysis in the QC area is through the use of control charts. The basic principle of a control chart is to graphically display quality characteristics and to detect if the process is in-control (only chance causes are present) [MON 13]. Detecting whether a non-random pattern exists is traditionally done through decision rules. However, there have been reports that these rules have the tendency to produce false alarms. With the ability to detect a pattern, AI is the ideal tool for control chart pattern recognition.

Various AI tools have been used for recognizing patterns in control charts: for example ANN [LAO 13, GUH 99], SVM [LIN 11], decision tree [WAN 08] and *k*-nearest neighbor (kNN) [HE 07]. According to a survey [HAC 12], ANN is the most popular.

To sum up, AI has a number of powerful tools that are capable of dealing with complex and nonlinear problems. This makes AI a very suitable tool to be used in HDD component production. The next section provides some applications of AI, specifically, QC in various HDD component production plants.

6.3. AI applications in HDD component quality control

This section provides some examples of the application of AI in HDD component QC. The first case is from a printed circuit board manufacturing plant. The company was experiencing a high rate of defects in the multipanel lamination process. ANN was applied to model the multipanel lamination machine in order to find the optimum setting that could bring down the rate of defects. The second and third cases were from the manufacturer of the actuator arm. In the second case, ANN was used to recognize the pattern in the control chart, while in the third case, a clustering algorithm was used to group the machines to ensure that the machines that were categorized in the higher risk group were inspected earlier than the machines in the lower risk group. The details of the application are as given in the following section.

6.3.1. *Multipanel lamination process modeling using ANN*

The case considered is that of a manufacturer of printed circuit boards as a component for HDDs. The company was encountering the problem of high and excessive rates of the adhesive squeeze out defect due to the improper setting of the multipanel lamination machine. The 2^k experimental design with center point was used to optimize the setting. However, the results showed nonlinearity in the system; therefore, a more advanced design-like response surface had to be used. Instead of conducting more response surface experiments, ANN was trained with the 2^k experiment to predict the response for the central composite design (CCD).

The optimization results obtained using ANN proved to be better, compared to the results from the 2^k experiments. The details of this application are as follows.

6.3.1.1. *Flexible printed circuit production*

The product used in this case study was the FPC which is an ultrathin and flexible version of the printed circuit board. FPC is made from screen-printed copper circuit on polyimide film. It consists of three main components: head area, dynamic area and static area, as shown in Figure 6.1.

FPC production started just recently, yet its demand has been high and expanding rapidly. As the production is in its initial stage, it has been found to suffer from high rates of defects. The highest defect percentage belongs to the excessive adhesive squeeze out defect. It contributed to 4.95% of the entire production.

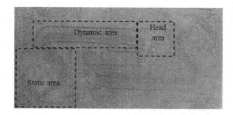

Figure 6.1. *The flexible printed circuit product*

Figure 6.2 shows two common types of the excessive adhesive squeeze out defect. The first type is where the glue overflow occurs at the edge of the film. The second type, which is considered very serious, is where the overflow occurs at the copper pad, as the copper pad provides electrical connectivity to the circuit. Preliminary studies suggested that the aforementioned types of defect occurred in the multipanel lamination machine. The quality of the lamination process depends on various factors. To optimize these factors, ANN was trained by using data collected from 2^3 experimental designs, as described in the next section.

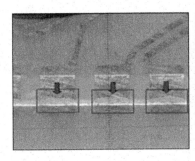

Figure 6.2. *The excessive adhesive squeeze out defect: a) glue overflow at the edge of the film and b) glue overflow at the copper pad*

6.3.1.2. *2³ experimental design for multipanel lamination machine*

The company applied the design of the experiment technique in order to optimize these settings [LAO 12]. The three factors considered were the prebake time, lamination pressure and type of film. The setting of these factors is summarized in Table 6.1.

Factor	Description	Level Setting		
		Low	Center point	High
A	Time (in minutes) used to preheat film before lamination procedure	0	20	40
B	Pressure (in Klb) used in lamination process	310	370	430
C	Type of lamination film	Dahlar	None	Sekisui

Table 6.1. *Factors affecting multipanel lamination process and setting for 2³ experimental design with center point*

As there are two factors (factor A and factor B) at low, high and center point levels and one factor (factor C) that does not have a center point, 22 experiments were generated with Minitab software, as presented in Table 6.2. The response in this experiment was taken as the defect percentage. The experiments were carried out according to the design, and the results are shown in Table 6.2.

Order	A	B	C	% defect
1	0	310	Dahlar	21.53
2	40	310	Dahlar	2.78
3	0	430	Dahlar	29.51
4	40	430	Dahlar	3.82
5	0	310	Sekisui	0
6	40	310	Sekisui	0
7	0	430	Sekisui	0.35
8	40	430	Sekisui	0
9	0	310	Dahlar	19.79
10	40	310	Dahlar	3.47
11	0	430	Dahlar	30.56
12	40	430	Dahlar	4.17
13	0	310	Sekisui	0
14	40	310	Sekisui	0
15	0	430	Sekisui	1.04
16	40	430	Sekisui	0
17	20	370	Dahlar	5.9
18	20	370	Sekisui	0
19	20	370	Dahlar	7.64
20	20	370	Sekisui	0
21	20	370	Dahlar	6.6
22	20	370	Sekisui	0

Table 6.2. 2^k *experiment with center point for lamination process*

The optimum condition found was at 40 min of prebake time, 430 Klb of lamination pressure and with the Sekisui film. This setting predicted a defect rate of 1.08%. However,

Analysis of Variance (ANOVA) analysis confirmed the significance of curvature; therefore, more experiments need to be conducted using other experimental designs such as response surface in order to be able to fit higher order models. In this work, instead of conducting more experiments, data from Table 6.2 were used to model ANN to predict the response for more advanced experimental designs.

6.3.1.3. ANN modeling of multipanel lamination process

ANN is a form of AI that simulates the way the human brain processes information. Artificial neurons are connected together to mimic biological neurons in the human brain. The strength of the connection is quantified by a number called the "weight". There are many types of ANN. In this work, multilayer perceptrons trained with backpropagation algorithm were used. In this type of network, neurons are located in the input layer, the hidden layer and the output layer (Figure 6.3).

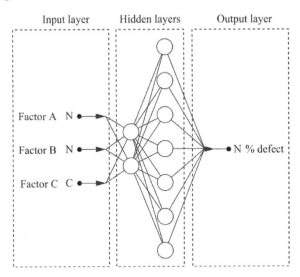

Figure 6.3. *The ANN model of the multipanel lamination process consists of three neurons in the input layer, two neurons in the first hidden layer, seven neurons in the second hidden layer and one neuron in the output layer*

The number of neurons in the input layer is determined by the number of input factors. In this work, three neurons were used to represent each input. Factor A and factor B have numerical values. These values were scaled into the same range before being input into ANN, using the following formula:

$$SF = \frac{SR_{max} - SR_{min}}{X_{max} - X_{min}} \qquad [6.1]$$

$$X_p = SR_{min} + (X - X_{min}) \times SF \qquad [6.2]$$

where X is the actual value of a considered numeric column, X_{min} is the minimum actual value of the column, X_{max} is the maximum actual value of the column, SR_{min} is the lowerscaling range limit, SR_{max} is the upperscaling range limit, SF is the scaling factor and X_p is the preprocessed value.

Factor C is categorical and needs to be coded into numerics. In this case, as there are two possible categories for factor C (either Dahlar or Sekisui), one neuron was used, and each Dahlar and each Sekisui were represented by −1 and 1, respectively. The number of neurons in the hidden layers was determined by exhaustive search for up to two hidden layers and up to eight neurons in each layer. The best architecture found had two neurons and seven neurons in the first hidden layer and second hidden layer, respectively.

Next, the backpropagation training algorithm [DAY 90] was applied for network training. First, for each neuron, the weighted sum (S_j) of the training sample was calculated and the result, S_j, was passed through the logistic transfer function $g(x)$ to produce the output for that neuron:

$$S_j = \sum_i a_i w_{ij} \qquad [6.3]$$

$$g(x) = \frac{1}{1+e^{-x}} \qquad [6.4]$$

where a_i is the activation level of unit i and w_{ij} is the weight from unit i to unit j. After that, the error is calculated to adjust the weight for each neuron in the output layer (equation [6.5]) and the hidden layer (equation [6.6]):

$$\delta_j = (t_j - a_j)g'(S_j) \qquad [6.5]$$

$$\delta_j = \left[\sum_k \delta_k w_{kj} \right] g'(S_j) \qquad [6.6]$$

In these equations, t_j is the target value for unit j, a_j is the output value for unit j, $g'(x)$ is the derivative of the logistic function $g(x)$ and S_j is the weighted sum of inputs to j. Then, the weight adjustment is calculated as $\Delta w_{ji} = \eta \delta_j a_i$, where η is the learning rate. These forward and backward processes repeat with new input vectors until the stopping criteria are met.

The data from Table 6.2 were divided into three sets for training, validating and testing at the ratio of 68%:16%:16%. The training data were used to adjust the weight in the training process. The validating data were also used in between the training to prevent overfitting. The testing data were used after the training was completed to test the network accuracy with the unseen input. The trained ANN had a testing mean absolute error (MAE) of 0.008032 and a correlation coefficient of 0.977. As the MAE value was low and the correlation coefficient very close to 1, it can be concluded that the ANN model has high accuracy. The details regarding ANN training can be found in [LAO 15].

6.3.1.4. *ANN prediction of response surface experiments*

The fully trained ANN was used to predict response surface experiments, by using CCD. Their design and their predicted ANN response are presented in Table 6.3. Two response surfaces were fitted separately for Dahlar and Sekisui. The response surface η is defined by $\eta = f(x_1, x_2)$, where x_1 is the prebake time and x_2 is the lamination pressure. A second-order model is defined by:

$$y = \beta_0 + \sum_{j=1}^{k} \beta_j x_j + \sum_{j=1}^{k} \beta_{jj} x_j^2 + \sum \sum_{i<j} \beta_{ij} x_i x_j + \varepsilon \qquad [6.7]$$

where k is the number of variables, β_j represents the coefficients of the linear parameter, β_{jj} represents the coefficients of the quadratic parameter, β_{ij} represents the coefficients of the interaction parameters and ε is the residual associated with the experiments.

The ANOVA analysis showed that x_1, x_2 and their interactions are significant at 95% confidence. Minitab's response analysis was used to find the optimum setting, and it was found that the Sekisui film type should be used with a prebake time of 36.77 min and lamination pressure of 310.51 Klb. This new setting had a predicted defect rate at 0.0009%, which is much lower than the optimum found previously.

This case study has demonstrated how ANN can be used to model the HDD component production process. ANN has proved to be a useful tool capable of producing high-accuracy models. The predicted response from ANN has led to better setting of process parameters, which produces lower defect rates.

6.3.2. Control chart pattern recognition with AI in actuator production

This is a case study applying ANN, kNN and rule induction in control chart pattern recognition in metal frames for actuator production. AI techniques were trained to recognize upward/downward shifts, upward/downward trends and cycles.

Standard order	Natural variables		Coded variables		Predicted responses from ANN	
	Prebake time (ξ_1)	Lamination pressure (ξ_2)	Prebake time (x_1)	Lamination pressure (x_2)	y_1 (Dahlar)	y_2 (Sekisui)
1	5.8579	327.574	−1.00000	−1.00000	17.1160	0.246720
2	34.1421	327.574	1.00000	−1.00000	3.9170	0.059984
3	5.8579	412.426	−1.00000	1.00000	26.8429	0.262879
4	34.1421	412.426	1.00000	1.00000	4.6086	0.124765
5	0.0000	370.000	−1.41421	0.00000	26.8490	0.262654
6	40.0000	370.000	1.41421	0.00000	3.9376	0.059925
7	20.0000	310.000	0.00000	−1.41421	4.5899	0.125474
8	20.0000	430.000	0.00000	1.41421	17.0066	0.246762
9	20.0000	370.000	0.00000	0.00000	7.2094	0.204501
10	20.0000	370.000	0.00000	0.00000	7.2094	0.204501
11	20.0000	370.000.	0.00000	0.00000	7.2094	0.204501
12	20.0000	370.000	0.00000	0.00000	7.2094	0.204501
13	20.0000	370.000	0.00000	0.00000	7.2094	0.204501

Table 6.3. *Central composite design and response predicted from ANN*

6.3.2.1. *Control chart of metal frame for actuator*

This is a case from a manufacturer of metal frames for actuators (Figure 6.4). Both $\bar{x}$ and R control chart (average and range control chart) and $\bar{x}$ and S control chart (average and standard deviation control chart) were used to monitor the borehole diameter of the actuator arm. Decision rules were used to detect the non-random pattern. For example, an out-of-control situation occurs when one or more points fall beyond the control limit, nine consecutive points are on the one side of the center line and six points are steadily on the increase or decrease. However, recent research suggests that decision rules have a tendency to produce false alarms. As a result, AI tools were used to recognize the pattern in the control chart. Three products were used in this case study, but for the sake of safeguarding confidentiality, these products will be called products X, Y and Z.

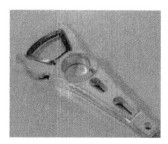

Figure 6.4. *The metal frame for actuator*

6.3.2.2. *Pattern generation*

The patterns covered in this case study were cycle, upward trend, downward trend, upward shift and downward shift (Figure 6.5).

Let $d(t)$ be the pattern, where t is the time index. The formulas used to generate the patterns $d(t)$ for AI training are as follows:

– Shift pattern: $d(t) = us$, where u is a variable for position shift ($u = 0$ before a shift and $u = 1$ after a shift). s represents the shift magnitude; in this work, s was set in the range of $-0.2\sigma \leq +2.5\sigma$, where σ is the standard deviation.

– Trend pattern: $d(t) = dt$, where d is the slope of the trend that varies in the range of $-0.22\sigma \leq +0.22\sigma$.

– Cycle pattern: $d(t) = a\ sin(2\pi t/\Omega)$, where a is the amplitude of the cycle in the range of $1\sigma \leq 2.5\sigma$, and Ω is the period of the cycle.

Figure 6.5 is an example of non-random pattern simulation and the graph of normal data with no pattern added. The x-axis is the number of each of the 36 data entries, and y-axis is the borehole diameters. In order to respect the company's confidentiality, the scales of measurement are not provided in the graph.

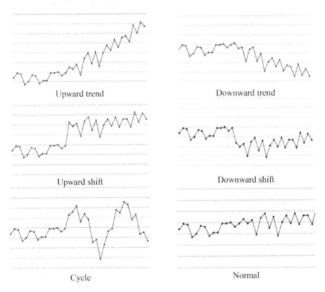

Figure 6.5. *The examples of the patterns generated for AI training*

6.3.2.3. AI tools

ANN, kNN and rule induction were compared.

ANN is the most widely used AI tool for control chart pattern recognition. In this work, multilayer perceptrons trained with backpropagation algorithm were used. A training method that is very similar to the previous case (section 6.3.1.3) was used. The main difference is in the ANN architecture. The input layers to ANN have n values of the consecutive data point called "window size", where n equals 6, 9 and 12 input data. Four output nodes were used to represent each of the output categories. The appropriate numbers of hidden layers and hidden nodes were determined through exhaustive search.

kNN is one of the popular algorithms for classification that use the "instance-based learning" method. In instance-based learning, the training data are memorized and new records are classified by comparing them to the most similar records. Suppose the training samples are described by the attribute n; a kNN classifies new records by searching the pattern space of the k training samples to find the ones closest to the unknown record. In this work, Euclidean distance, which is the most common measure of similarity, was used. The Euclidean distance between two inputs represented in n-dimensional space by $X_1 = (x_{11}, x_{12},...,x_{1n})$ and $X_2 = (x_{21}, x_{22},...,x_{2n})$ is denoted by $d(X_1, X_2) = \sqrt{\sum_{i=1}^{n}(x_{1i} - x_{2i})^2}$. All input data are normalized to be in the range of [0, 1].

Rule induction is one of the AI techniques where rules are extracted from a set of observations. Rule learners are adapted from decision tree learning that grows a complex tree, which overfits the data, following which pruning of the algorithm is carried out to simplify the tree, using repeated incremental pruning to produce error reduction (RIPPER). RIPPER consists of two phases: growing phase and pruning phase. In the growing phase, rules are greedily added to the rule set until all positive examples are covered. Let p be the number of positive examples covered by this rule (true positives) and n is the number of negative examples covered by this rule (false negatives). Thereafter, in the pruning phase, the pruning matrix $p/(p+n)$ is used until there are no positive examples left or until the error rate is not greater than 50%.

6.3.2.4. Pattern recognition results

The results of the three AI techniques were compared based on the percentage of records correctly classified, which was calculated by dividing the number of correctly classified records by the number of total data and multiplying by 100. As demonstrated in Figure 6.6, model accuracy depends very much on the window size. For product X, the highest accuracy achieved was at 91.73% from ANN at a window size of 12. For product Y, the highest accuracy belonged to kNN with a window size of 9 at 96.99%, and for product Z, kNN with a window size of 12 gave the highest accuracy at 98.57%. To sum up, kNN provided the highest accuracy for all the products. The effect of the window size is less conclusive: a window size of 6 was found to have the lowest accuracy in all the cases, but the window size that provided the highest accuracy was either 9 or 12, depending on the type of classifier.

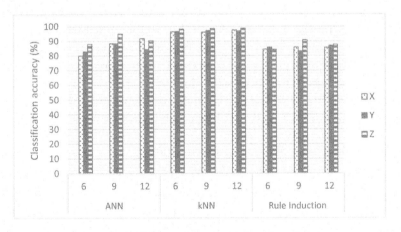

Figure 6.6. *The comparison of the AI models in terms of percentage of correctly classified records*

In conclusion, this case is the comparative study of AI tools for pattern chart recognition in hard disk actuator arm production. All three AI techniques used provided high accuracy. However, of all the three methods, kNN is the AI technique that provided the highest accuracy.

6.3.3. *Machine clustering using AI technique*

The last case study is from a manufacturer of metal frames for actuators (the same company as in the previous case). In this factory, more than 300 computer numerical control (CNC) machines are used to fabricate the actuator. During production, random samples are taken from each CNC to be inspected at the QC department. If the samples show a tendency to be out of specification, then it means that the machine that was producing those samples would have to be adjusted or shut down. In this factory, there are more than 120 machines in operation each day, and six samples were taken for every machine in each shift. However, the samples were not inspected right away due to the large amount of samples waiting for inspection. The QC department used the first-come-first-serve policy, so there is a possibility that the machine that was producing the defective metal frames would be inspected later and the damage caused could be significant. This research applied the clustering algorithm to group the machines according to their tendency to produce defective pieces so that the machines that had a higher risk could be inspected earlier. The details of this case study can be found in [LAO 10].

6.3.3.1. *Machine clustering methodology*

Data collection. The first step is data collection in which inspection data for the previous three months were collected. Four methods were used for quality inspection: namely, coordinate measuring machine (CMM), air gauge, dismicro and manual measurement. Apart from the inspection data, production-related data such as lot number, machine number, production date and production shift were also collected.

Machine clustering. The inspection data collected were used to cluster the machines into three groups: high risk, medium risk and low risk. Three algorithms, namely k-means clustering, EM clustering and TwoStep clustering, were used and the results compared with each other to identify the algorithm that provided the best clustering results.

Machine scoring. For each cluster, simple additive weight (SAW) was used to score each machine to identify the order in which each machine would be inspected. SAW is the simplest and the most widely used multiple attribute decision-making method. First, each alternative is given a weight. The sum of all the weights must be equal to one. Then, each alternative is assessed with regard to each of the attributes. The overall score of an alternative is given as follows:

$$P_i = \left[\sum_{j=1}^{M} w_i (m_{ij})_{normal} \Big/ \sum_{j=1}^{M} w_j \right] \qquad [6.8]$$

where $(m_{ij})_{normal}$ is the normalized value of m_{ij} (score of machine i with respect to the jth criteria), w_i is the weight of criteria i and P_i is the overall score of the machine.

6.3.3.2. *Algorithm for the computer numerical control machine clustering*

k-means clustering. The basic idea of *k*-means is to discover the *k* cluster such that the records within each cluster are similar to each other and distinct from the records in the other clusters. The algorithm *k*-means starts with the random selection of *k* objects to be used as the center of the cluster. Then, the distance between each of the objects to the center of the cluster is calculated and the object is assigned to the cluster that is the most similar. After that, the new mean for each cluster is calculated, and the process is repeated the same way until the criterion function converges. Square-error criterion, as given in the following equation [HAN 06], was used in this research.

$$E = \sum_{i=1}^{k} \sum_{p \in C_i} |p - m_i|^2 \qquad [6.9]$$

where E is the sum of the square error values for all the objects, p is the data point and m_i is the mean of cluster C_i.

EM clustering. The EM algorithm expands k-means by – instead of assigning objects to clusters, like in the k-means algorithm – assigning objects to each cluster according to the weight that characterizes its membership probability. The algorithm is described in [HAN 06]. EM clustering is begun by randomly selecting k objects to represent the cluster mean and by making a guess of the other parameter vector. Then, interactively, the clusters are refined, based on two steps: the expectation (E) step and the maximization (M) step.

In the E step, object x_i is assigned to cluster C_k with the probability:

$$P(x_i \in C_k) = p(C_k \mid x_i) = \frac{p(C_k)p(x_i \mid C_k)}{p(x_i)} \qquad [6.10]$$

where $p(x_i \mid C_k) = N(m_k, E_k(x_i))$ follows the normal distribution around mean m_k, with expectation E_k.

After that, in the M step, the model parameters are reestimated using probability estimation, as discussed previously. For instance:

$$m_k = \frac{1}{n} \sum_{i=1}^{n} \frac{x_i P(x_i \in C_k)}{\sum_j P(x_i \in C_j)} \qquad [6.11]$$

TwoStep clustering. This algorithm uses the likelihood distance measure which assumes the independence of the variables in the cluster. First, the algorithm passes through the data and compares the variables to classify them into subclusters. Then, the subclusters are merged into larger clusters, using a hierarchical clustering method. The advantages of this algorithm are that it determines the optimum number of clusters and removes outliers automatically.

6.3.3.3. *Clustering results*

Statistical analysis was performed, and from the 45 inspection items, only 22 significant items were used with the three clustering algorithms. For the purpose of preserving confidentiality, the description of the inspection item cannot be given as that would reveal the actual dimensions of the product. Hence, the inspection item will be referred to as parameter A up to parameter V. Table 6.4 shows the mean and the standard deviation of each parameter.

The three clustering algorithms described in the preceding text were used for the analysis. F and p-value were used to measure the variability of each parameter (Table 6.4). It was observed that the two-step algorithm has the lowest p-value compared to the other two methods, which means that the two-step algorithm is the one capable of differentiating between the clusters the best. Figure 6.7 shows the box plot of the mean of some significant parameters for the two-step algorithm's three clusters. The box plot shows good distinction between the means of the different clusters. Therefore, the cluster of the machine based on two steps will be used in the next step.

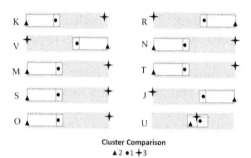

Figure 6.7. *The box plot of the mean of some significant parameters of the clusters from the two-step algorithm*

| Parameter | Mean | Std. dev. | Clustering results | | | | | |
| | | | EM | | K-means | | Two step | |
			F	p-value	F	p-value	F	p-value
A	6.253	0.037	1,250.2	0.00000	1,248.25	0.0000	1,210.2	0.00000
B	6.253	0.038	1,396.1	0.00000	1,417.12	0.0000	1,298.4	0.00000
C	2.670	0.001	7.615	0.00100	7.617	0.0010	7.449	0.00082
D	2.670	0.001	8.467	0.00000	8.467	0.0000	8.589	0.00029
E	1.166	0.003	6.462	0.00200	6.462	0.0020	6.519	0.00192
F	−1.150	0.001	11.119	0.00000	11.329	0.0000	11.496	0.00002
G	−1.150	0.001	22.46	0.00000	22.406	0.0000	24.318	0.00000
H	1.165	0.003	6.875	0.00100	6.897	0.0010	6.926	0.00132
I	21.880	0.005	3.465	0.03400	3.489	0.0330	4.261	0.01582
J	8.100	8.775	4,473.4	0.00000	4,476.83	0.0000	3,962.7	0.00000
K	5.780	0.314	4,507.5	0.00000	4507.54	0.0000	4,070.0	0.00000
L	21.878	0.005	3.112	0.05000	3.104	0.0480	3.018	0.02918
M	−2.017	4.516	4,476.8	0.00000	4,486.80	0.0000	3,972.8	0.00000
N	−15.998	7.550	4,479.4	0.00000	4,477.35	0.0000	3,966.8	0.00000
O	−2.013	4.515	4,490.6	0.00000	4,488.65	0.0000	3,971.6	0.00000
P	3.903	2.350	4,473.2	0.00000	4,466.29	0.0000	3,949.1	0.00000
Q	7.152	0.95	4,499.2	0.00000	4,493.29	0.0000	3,968.4	0.00000
R	−3.246	12.164	4,492.0	0.00000	4,481.78	0.0000	3,967.3	0.00000
S	11.714	3.030	4,433.8	0.00000	4,483.95	0.0000	3,972.5	0.00000
T	3.254	3.302	4,480.4	0.00000	4,478.46	0.0000	3,966.0	0.00000
U	−4.582	1.130	4,475.0	0.00000	4,477.99	0.0000	3,957.0	0.00000
V	5.781	0.314	4,473.1	0.00000	4,478.68	0.0000	4,048.6	0.00000

Table 6.4. *Central composite design and response predicted from ANN*

6.3.3.4. *Machine scoring*

SAW was used on the three clusters. The weight of each variable for each of the clusters was determined by the production engineer. Thereafter, the score was calculated for each machine. This score was used to determine the inspection order. The machines with low scores needed to be inspected before those with high scores. In order to test the effectiveness of the new method, the time interval between the arrival of a part in the QC room and the discovery of the defect was recorded (Figure 6.8).

From Figure 6.8, it can be seen that the defect occurred twice with machine numbers 141 and 139. With the proposed method, both the defects could be discovered earlier than with the current method. Such early detection prevents more than 5,000 parts from becoming defective.

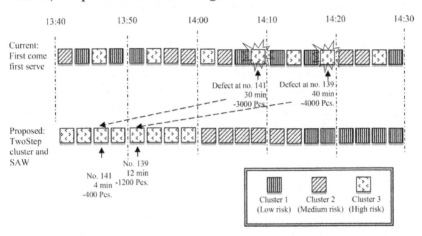

Figure 6.8. *The comparison between the defect detection time intervals of the current method and the proposed method*

6.4. Conclusion

This chapter focused on the application of AI tools in the QC of HDD components. The application of AI in the task of

QC was discussed first to provide a general idea of the topic. The application is classified into three groups: classification and prediction, clustering and time series analysis and was described in detail.

Three examples were given. The first case demonstrated the application of ANN in the modeling of the multipanel lamination process using the data obtained from the 2^3 experimental design. The model was used to predict the response for a more advanced design of the experiment technique, the response surface, which would bring about improvement in the optimization results. The second case study applied three AI techniques for control chart pattern recognition in metal frames produced for actuators. The third case applied clustering algorithms to cluster machines into groups in order to calculate their scores. The scores were used to establish the inspection order so that the machines with higher risk are inspected earlier.

From all the examples, it can be concluded that AI tools have demonstrated highly promising results in the field of QC of HDD components where the process is complex and usually nonlinear. The use of AI, however, is not limited to HDD components; AI can be applied to any manufacturing process that is similar in nature.

6.5. Bibliography

[DAY 90] DAYHOFF J.E., *Neural Network Architectures: An Introduction*, Van Nostrand Reinhold, New York, 1990.

[FER 11] FERREIRO S., SIERRA B., IRIGOIEN I., *et al.*, "Data mining for quality control: burr detection in the drilling process", *Computers & Industrial Engineering*, vol. 60, no. 4, pp. 801–810, 2011.

[GOU 00] GOUREVITCH P., BOHN R., MCKENDRICK D., "Globalization of production: insights from the hard disk drive industry", *World Development*, vol. 28, no. 2, pp. 301–317, 2000.

[GUH 99] GUH R.S., ZORRIASSATINE F., TANNOCK J.D.T., *et al.*, "On-line control chart pattern detection and discrimination – a neural network approach", *Artificial Intelligence in Engineering*, vol. 13, no. 4, pp. 413–425, 1999.

[HAC 12] HACHICHA W., GHORBEL A., "A survey of control-chart pattern-recognition literature (1991–2010) based on a new conceptual classification scheme", *Computers & Industrial Engineering*, vol. 63, no. 1, pp. 204–222, 2012.

[HAN 06] HAN J., KAMBER M., *Data Mining Concepts and Techniques*, Elsevier, San Francisco, CA, 2006.

[HE 07] HE Q.P., JIN W., "Fault detection using the k-nearest neighbor rule for semiconductor manufacturing processes", *IEEE Transactions on Semiconductor Manufacturing*, vol. 20, no. 4, pp. 345–354, 2007.

[KAR 08] KARIM M.A., RUSS G., ISLAM A., "Detection of faulty products using data mining", *Proceedings of the 11th International Conference on Computer and Information Technology (ICCIT 2008)*, Bangladesh, pp. 101–107, 24–27 December 2008.

[LAO 10] LAOSIRITAWORN W., HOLIMCHAYACHOTIKUL P., "Metal frame for actuator manufacturing process improvement using data mining techniques", *Chiang Mai Journal of Science*, vol. 37, no. 3, pp. 421–428, 2010.

[LAO 12] LAOSIRITAWORN W.S., AOONCHAN P., "Multi-panel lamination process optimization with design of experiment", *Proceedings of the World Congress on Engineering and Computer Science*, San Francisco, CA, 24–26 October 2012

[LAO 13] LAOSIRITAWORN W.S., BUNJONGJIT T., "Classification techniques for control chart pattern recognition: a case of metal frame for actuator production", *Chiang Mai Journal of Science*, vol. 40, no. 4, pp. 701–712, 2013.

[LAO 15] LAOSIRITAWORN W.S., "Improving multi-panel lamination process optimization using response surface methodology and neural network", *Advances in Intelligent Systems and Computing*, vol. 1089, pp. 221–226, 2015.

[LIN 11] LIN S.-Y., GUH R.-S., SHIUE Y.-R., "Effective recognition of control chart patterns in autocorrelated data using a support vector machine based approach", *Computers & Industrial Engineering*, vol. 61, no. 4, pp. 1123–1134, 2011.

[MON 13] MONTGOMERY D.C., *Statistical Quality Control,* John Wiley & Sons, Inc., 2013.

[PHA 99] PHAM D.T., PHAM T.N., "Artificial intelligence in engineering", *International Journal of Machine Tools and Manufacture*, vol. 39, no. 6, pp. 937–949, 1999.

[RUS 10] RUSSELL S., NORVIG P., *Artificial Intelligence: A Modern Approach*, Pearson Education, Inc., NJ, 2010.

[SRI 06] SRIRAM R.D., "Artificial intelligence in engineering: personal reflections", *Advanced Engineering Informatics,* vol. 20 no. 1, pp. 3–5, 2006.

[SUK 05] SUKTHOMYA W., TANNOCK J., "The training of neural networks to model manufacturing processes", *Journal of Intelligent Manufacturing*, vol. 16, no. 1, pp. 39–51, 2005.

[TET 97] TETI R., KUMARA S.R.T., "Intelligent computing methods for manufacturing systems", *CIRP Annals – Manufacturing Technology*, vol. 46, no. 2, pp. 629–652, 1997.

[WAN 08] WANG C.-H., GUO R.-S., CHIANG M.-H., *et al.*, "Decision tree based control chart pattern recognition", *International Journal of Production Research,* vol. 46, no. 17, pp. 4889–4901, 2008.

7

Borehole Diameter Inspection for Hard Disk Drive Pivot Arms Using Hough Transform in Panorama Images

One of the processes in the quality control section in the hard disk drive (HDD) industry is to measure the dimensions of the HDD components. An automated dimension inspection with high-resolution visualization is needed. A microscope is used for this purpose. However, some of the HDD components, e.g., borehole of a pivot arm, etc., are not covered 100% by one field of view of a microscope. Hence, a system that can reconstruct the whole part using panorama image construction from image sequences is required. Then, the system accordingly measures the diameter of a reconstructed borehole using the Hough transform (HT).

7.1. Introduction

The dimension measurement of a HDD component is an important process in the HDD industry, which is one of the

Chapter written by Sansanee Auephanwiriyakul, Patison Palee, Orathai Suttijak and Nipon Theera-Umpon.

most prolific industries in Thailand. In this chapter, we focus on borehole (a hole at the center of a pivot arm) dimension inspection. Currently, there are several pieces of measuring equipment such as an air gauge and pin gauge utilized in borehole dimension measurement. These human-operated pieces of equipment are used to measure a large number of pivot arms. Hence, measurement errors may occur from human fatigue. Although a smart scope is used in some factories, it is very expensive and some measurement errors still occur. To compare with the smart scope, a dimension inspection system with high-resolution visualization using a microscope is needed. Unfortunately, for an image with adequate resolution, the whole borehole cannot be covered by one field of view of a microscope. Hence, reconstruction of an entire borehole image from several parts of the borehole image sequences is required. After that, a dimension inspection is performed.

There are several methods in panorama construction or image mosaicing, e.g. [PIR 05, ZOM 06, GAR 01a, BRO 03, BRO 05] and [PHA 12]. However, the provided borehole image sequences are low-contrast images and there is noise in the images. Hence, this chapter discusses a feature-based panorama construction method following our work in [PAL 08]. There are also several research works on the automatic measurement of objects e.g. [YI 00, KHA 05, HUA 06, KOS 01, LEI 04, LEI 05] and [GRI 92]. However, in this chapter, we discuss a dimension measurement using the HT following our work in [SUT 08].

In this chapter, we discuss an automated dimension inspection system for a borehole in pivot arms. This system is operated on graylevel images. The color images from a microscope are converted to graylevel images using luminance (Y) component [GON 08]. We discuss a panoramic image construction method in section 7.2 followed by the HT in section 7.3. Finally, some of experiment results are presented in section 7.4.

7.2. Panorama image construction

There are four steps in constructing a borehole panoramic image [PAL 08] from image sequences as shown in Figure 7.1, i.e. (1) enhancing and finding interesting points, (2) correspondence evaluation, (3) outlier removal and (4) constructing the panoramic image.

In order to make the process of finding the interesting points easier, we put a round piece of paper with the background into the borehole (as shown in Figure 7.1) during the measurement process. Then, a Gaussian image pyramid with standard deviation $\sigma_P = 1.0$ and sampling rate $s = 2$ is used to convolve with each image sequence. The multi-scale Harris corners [BRO 05] are used to select interesting points. The Harris corners are computed from:

$$H_r = \begin{bmatrix} I_x^2 & I_x I_y \\ I_x I_y & I_y^2 \end{bmatrix}, \qquad\qquad [7.1]$$

where I_x^2, $I_x I_y$ and I_y^2 are calculated from the gradient operator of input image I. We can calculate the corner strength function from the equation of harmonic mean of eigenvalues (λ_1, λ_2) as:

$$f_{HM} = \frac{|H_r|}{\text{trace}\{H_r\}} = \frac{\lambda_1 \lambda_2}{\lambda_1 + \lambda_2}. \qquad\qquad [7.2]$$

An interesting point is selected when it has the corner strength f_{HM} more than its 8 neighbors and above the threshold value of 500. We then use the adaptive non-maximal suppression (ANMS) [BRO 05] to make the interesting points nicely distributed throughout the images, as shown in [PAL 08]. An example of this step is shown in Figure 7.2.

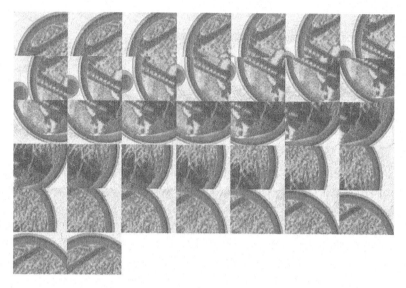

Figure 7.1. *Borehole image sequences with background*

Figure 7.2. *An example of interesting points (white dots) selected by corner strength with ANMS*

Then, for the correspondence evaluation, we need to find the best match. Block-matching is used to perform coarse matching [GAR 01a, GAR 01b]. The block-matching uses an $n \times n$ window I centered at each interesting point $p(x, y)$ in the present image I_m to compare with an $n \times n$ window I' centered at an interesting point $p'(x, y)$ in the next image I'_m. The correspondence between 2 windows is computed by:

$$corr(p, p') = \frac{\sum_{i=1}^{n}\sum_{j=1}^{n}\left[I(x+i, y+j) - \overline{I(x,y)}\right]\left[I'(x'+i, y'+j) - \overline{I'(x',y')}\right]}{n^2\sqrt{\sigma^2(I) \cdot \sigma^2(I')}}, \quad [7.3]$$

where $\overline{I(x,y)}$ and $\overline{I'(x',y')}$ are average values of the intensity in the $n \times n$ window in I_m and I'_m, respectively. $\sigma^2(I)$ is the variance of the image I_m in the $n \times n$ window, i.e.

$$\sigma^2(I) = \sqrt{\frac{\sum_{i=1}^{n}\sum_{j=1}^{n}\left[I(x,y)\right]^2}{n^2} - \overline{I(x,y)}^2}. \quad [7.4]$$

A set of texture operators, i.e. contrast 3×3, contrast 5×5, contrast 7×7, L3L3 standard deviation, E3E3 positive average, E3E3 negative average, L5S5 positive average, E5L5 standard deviation, E5S5 negative average [GAR 01a, GAR 01b, LEO 06], are utilized to determine the most similarity of the 10 candidate points selected from equation [7.3]. The outputs of these texture operators are computed from each interesting point in I_m and their candidate points. The Euclidean distance is calculated between each interesting point texture vector and the texture vectors of the 10 candidate points. The minimum one is the best match.

At the outlier removal step, we need to get rid of the false matching that may occur because of the selected correspondence pairs. We utilize the majority voting filter that selects the city block distance along the x-axis and y-axis. This method chooses a group of the corresponding pairs that are most similar in the city block distance sense and gets rid of other pairs. As shown in [PAL 08], this method is better than other outlier removal methods. The output of this step in shown in Figure 7.3. The black dots represent the interesting points in the current image whereas the white dots represent that in the next image. Therefore, the black lines represent the remaining corresponding pairs after the outlier removal. As we have prior knowledge that the consecutive images are related by the translation only, we expect to have a group of black lines that have the same length and direction in the good matching.

Figure 7.3. *Outlier removal by majority voting filter*

In the final step, the distances along the *x*-axis and *y*-axis from the majority voting filter are used for the panorama image construction by translation only. An example of the borehole panorama construction is shown in Figure 7.4. Now, we are ready for the dimension estimation step.

Figure 7.4. *An example of borehole panorama construction*

7.3. Dimension estimation

The constructed borehole panorama image as shown in Figure 7.4 has an ellipse shape not a circular shape. Hence we utilize the nearest neighbor graylevel interpolation with backward mapping [CAS 96] as shown in Figure 7.5.

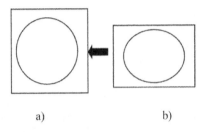

a)   b)

Figure 7.5. *Backward mapping: a) input image and b) output image*

Let I_{input} be an input image and I_{output} an output image. The mapping is as follows:

$$I_{Output}(x,y) = I_{Input}(x \times a_x, y \times b_y) \qquad [7.5]$$

where a_x and b_y are the scaling factors in the x and y directions, respectively. In our experiment, we manually select a_x and b_y at 103.89 and 90.63 pixels, respectively. An example of this step is shown in Figure 7.6.

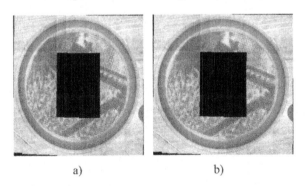

a)   b)

Figure 7.6. *Borehole panorama image: a) before and b) after shape correction*

We then use a median filter [GON 08] with a 5 × 5 window to reduce noise in the image. We use the Canny edge operator [GON 08] to find the edge. Readers can review all the details of this step in [SUT 08]. Then finally the HT for circle detection is performed in three-dimensional (3D) parameter space (a, b, r). The circular equation is:

$$(x-a)^2 + (y-b)^2 = r^2 \qquad [7.6]$$

where (x, y) is a pixel coordinate. The parametric equations for a circle in the polar coordinate are:

$$x = a + r\cos\theta, \qquad [7.7]$$

$$y = b + r\sin\theta. \qquad [7.8]$$

This method [SUT 08] attempts to make a circle that is optimized with a set of points that are the edges in an image by using the accumulator array $M(a, b)$ by calculating a and b along the line where $0 < \theta < 360$. The local maximum in the accumulator array is the center of the circle in the image. Since the unknown parameters are a, b and r, we initialize the range of r for the HT method. In our experiment, r is set to vary from 920 to 980 pixels since the microscope is magnified to 40 times. The parameter set (a, b, r) that produces the maximum accumulator array $M(a, b, r)$ is selected to be the result of the HT.

7.4. Experiment result

The performance of both borehole panorama image construction [PAL 08] and HT in swage hole dimension inspection [SUT 08] are efficient. Hence, we implement borehole dimension inspection here. The data set is collected from 30 boreholes. There are two sides of the hole to be measured, i.e. the side with a serial number (C-side) and the opposite side from C (Off C-side). For each side, 40 small parts of a borehole are captured from a microscope with 40 times magnification. A panorama image is constructed from each side. We compare our estimation to the diameters provided from an air gauge because it is considered a standard instrument. We also compare our results with the values from a smart scope since it is used regularly in a factory.

The data set consists of 3 subsets: (1) 10 boreholes from a computer numerical control (CNC) machine, (2) 10 boreholes before plating, and (3) 10 boreholes after plating. We found that only with the Off C-side of data set 1 could a borehole panorama image be constructed completely. There are 18 out of 600 times that our system could not construct borehole images. This might be because there are not enough interesting points to stitch two images together as shown in Figure 7.7.

Figure 7.7. *An example of unsuccessful panorama image construction because there are a small number of interesting points*

Tables 7.1 and 7.2 show the diameter estimation of 1 borehole in C-side and Off C-side, respectively, from 10 rounds of measurement. We can see from Tables 7.1 and 7.2 that both the air gauge and smart scope do not have the same diameter value for all 10 rounds. The diameter estimation from the smart scope is different from that of the air gauge with the average of 3.5865 and 4.3180 µm for C-side and Off C-side, respectively. Our system produces errors on the average when comparing with the air gauge for C-side and Off C-side around 15.0568 µm and 12.372 µm, respectively. Whereas, the errors on the average when comparing with the smart scope for C-side and Off C-side are around 17.7391 µm and 10.9828 µm, respectively.

	Air gauge diameter (µm)	Smart scope diameter (µm)	Our estimated diameter (µm)	Error of smart scope comparing with air gauge (µm)	Error of our result comparing with	
					air gauge (µm)	smart scope (µm)
1	11,148.568	11,153.089	11,167.320	4.5210	18.7520	14.2310
2	11,149.076	11,152.810	11,131.890	3.7340	17.1860	20.9200
3	11,149.330	11,152.886	11,131.890	3.5560	17.4400	20.9960
4	11,149.330	11,152.759	11,143.700	3.4290	5.6300	9.0590
5	11,149.076	11,152.734	11,120.080	3.6580	28.9960	32.6540
6	11,149.330	11,152.480	11,143.700	3.1500	5.6300	8.7800
7	11,148.822	11,152.556	11,120.080	3.7340	28.7420	32.4760
8	11,149.076	11,152.530	11,143.700	3.4540	5.3760	8.8300
9	11,149.076	11,152.378	11,131.890	3.3020	17.1860	20.4880
10	11,149.330	11,152.657	11,143.700	3.3270	5.6300	8.9570
Average	11,149.101	11,152.688	11,137.795	3.5865	15.0568	17.7391
Standard deviation	0.2526	0.2121	13.9182	0.3807	9.2514	9.3827

Table 7.1. *Example of a C-side borehole diameter estimation in 10 rounds*

	Air gauge diameter (μm)	Smart scope diameter (μm)	Our estimated diameter (μm)	Error of smart scope comparing with air gauge (μm)	Error of our result comparing with	
					air gauge (μm)	smart scope (μm)
1	11,148.568	11,152.886	11,164.030	4.3180	15.4620	11.1440
2	11,148.822	11,153.140	11,164.030	4.3180	15.2080	10.8900
3	11,148.568	11,152.632	11,140.320	4.0640	8.2480	12.3120
4	11,148.314	11,153.140	11,152.170	4.8260	3.8560	0.9700
5	11,148.822	11,152.886	11,175.890	4.0640	27.0680	23.0040
6	11,148.822	11,153.140	11,128.460	4.3180	20.3620	24.6800
7	11,148.822	11,152.886	11,128.460	4.0640	20.3620	24.4260
8	11,148.822	11,152.632	11,152.170	3.8100	3.3480	0.4620
9	11,148.568	11,153.140	11,152.170	4.5720	3.6020	0.9700
10	11,148.314	11,153.140	11,152.170	4.8260	3.8560	0.9700
Average	11,148.644	11,152.962	11,150.987	4.3180	12.1372	10.9828
Standard deviation	0.2091	0.2091	15.2560	0.3387	8.6992	10.1439

Table 7.2. *Example of an off C-side borehole diameter estimation in 10 rounds*

Although the average errors are not as small as the smart scope error when comparing with an air gauge, there are some rounds in Off C-side that show our result is better than that from the smart scope. Table 7.3 shows the average smart scope error comparing with the air gauge and that of our system comparing with the air gauge of all data sets. However, we compare the result for only 582 complete panorama image constructions because of the reason mentioned earlier. From the table, we can see that the average diameter error of all data sets on both sides computed from the smart scope comparing with the air gauge is 10.2441 µm, whereas those computed from our system comparing with the air gauge and the smart scope are 20.0299 µm and 20.2877 µm, respectively. The reason for the higher error from our system might be that the panoramic image construction is not good for a mismatched edge for example as shown in Figure 7.8 or there is reflection from the light source. These problems can cause an error in the edge detection step, and ultimately causes an error in the diameter estimation.

Data set	Diameter average error (µm)					
	Smart scope comparing with an air gauge		Our system comparing with an air gauge		Our system comparing with a smart scope	
	C-Side	Off C-Side	C-Side	Off C-Side	C-Side	Off C-Side
1	6.2282	13.3477	15.7967	18.5360	15.7351	20.6607
2	6.1701	15.7375	20.3635	19.7564	21.1717	21.9385
3	8.6663	11.3148	27.6379	18.0891	24.8245	17.3596
Average error	7.0215	13.4667	21.2660	18.7939	20.5771	19.9862
Average error of all boreholes	10.2441		20.0299		20.2817	

Table 7.3. *Errors of diameter of all boreholes*

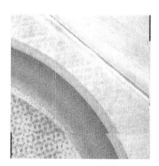

Figure 7.8. *An example of unsuccessful panorama image construction because of mismatched stitching images*

7.5. Conclusion

In this chapter, we have discussed a borehole panoramic image construction method. The HT is applied to detect and estimate the diameter of a circle. The experiment results are also shown. From the result, we can see that our method for panorama image construction is efficient. The HT performs quite satisfactorily in estimating the diameter. However, there are some problems occurring in construction of a borehole panorama image because there are not enough interesting points. This causes an incorrect edge detection and ultimately causes the error in the diameter estimation.

7.6. Acknowledgment

This work was supported by the Hard Disk Drive Institute (HDDI) and the National Electronics and Computer Technology Center (NECTEC). We would like to thank Lanna Thai Electronic Components (LTEC) Ltd. for the valuable information and we are very grateful for their cooperation during this research.

7.7. Bibliography

[BRO 03] BROWN M., LOWE D.G., "Recognising panoramas", *IEEE International Conference on Computer Vision*, pp. 1218–1225, October 2003.

[BRO 05] BROWN M., SZELISKI R., WINDER S., "Multi-image matching using multi-scale oriented patches", *IEEE Computer Society Conference on Computer Vision and Pattern Recognition*, pp. 510–517, June 2005.

[CAS 96] CASTLEMAN K.R., *Digital Image Processing*, Prentice Hall Inc., Upper Saddle River, New Jersey, USA, 1996.

[GAR 01a] GARCIA R., CUFI X., BATLLE J., "Detection of matchings in a sequence of underwater images through texture analysis", *IEEE International Conference on Image Processing*, vol. 1, pp. 361–364, October 2001.

[GAR 01b] GARCIA R., BATLLE J., CUFI X., "A system to evaluate the accuracy of a visual mosaicing methodology", *MTS/IEEE Conference and Exhibition on OCEANS*, vol. 4, pp. 2570–2576, November 2001.

[GRI 92] GRIFFIN P.M., VILLALBOS J.R., "Process capability of automated visual inspection systems", *IEEE Transactions on Systems, Man, and Cybernetics*, vol. 22, no. 3, pp. 441–448, 1992.

[GON 08] GONZALEZ R.C., WOODS R.E., *Digital Image Processing (Third Edition)*, Pearson Education, Inc., Upper Saddle River, New Jersey, USA, 2008.

[HUA 06] HUANG C.K., WANG L.G., TANG H.C., *et al.*, "Automatic laser inspection of outer diameter run-out and taper of micro-drills", *Journal of Materials Processing Technology*, vol. 171, no. 2, pp. 306–313, 2006.

[KHA 05] KHAN U.S., IQBAL J., KHAN M.A., "Automated inspection system using machine vision," *Proceedings of the 34th Applied Imagery and Pattern Recognition Workshop*, pp. 212–217, December 2005.

[KOS 01] KOSMOPOULOS D., VARVARIGOU T., "Automated inspection of gaps on the automobile production line through stereo vision and specular reflection", *Computers in Industry*, vol. 46, no. 1, pp. 49–63, 2001.

[LEI 04] LEI L., "A machine vision system for inspecting bearing-diameter", *Proceedings of the 5th World Congress on Intelligent Control and Automation*, Hangzhou, P.R. China, pp. 3904–3906, 2004.

[LEI 05] LEI L., ZHOU X., PAN M., "Automated vision inspection system for the size measurement of workpieces", *Conference on Instrumentation and Measurement Technology*, Ottawa, Canada, pp. 872–877, 2005.

[LEO 06] LEONE A., DISTANTE C., MASTROLIA A., *et al.*, "A fully automated approach for underwater mosaicing", *IEEE Conference on OCEANS*, pp. 1–6, September 2006.

[PAL 08] PALEE P., AUEPHANWIRIYAKUL S., THEERA-UMPON N., "An automated panorama image construction for dimension inspection", *KKU Research Journal*, vol. 13, no. 3, pp. 457–463, April 2008.

[PHA 12] PHAM T.Q., COX P., "Multi-hypothesis projection-based shift estimation for sweeping panorama reconstruction", *IEEE International Conference on Multimedia and Expo*, pp. 97–102, July 2012.

[PIR 05] PIRES B.E., AGUIAR P.M.Q., "Featureless global alignment of multiple images", *IEEE International Conference on Image Processing*, vol. 1, pp. 57–60, September 2005.

[SUT 08] SUTTIJAK O., AUEPHANWIRIYAKUL S., THEERA-UMPON N., "Swage hole diameter inspection using Hough transform", *KKU Research Journal*, vol. 13, no. 3, pp. 464–470, April 2008.

[YI 00] YI Y., LI Z., LI X., *et al.*, "Laser measurement for slight deformation of a large-scale structure," *Proceedings of SPIE on Optical Measurement and Nondestructive Testing: Techniques and Applications*, vol. 4221, pp. 239–242, 2000.

[ZOM 06] ZOMET A., LEVIN A., PELEG S., *et al.*, "Seamless image stitching by minimizing false edges", *IEEE Transactions on Image Processing*, vol. 15, pp. 969–977, April 2006.

8

Electrostatic Discharge Inspection Technologies

Electrostatic discharge (ESD) events are serious hazards in hard disk drive (HDD) manufacturing assembly lines. This chapter provides current technologies for visualizing invisible ESD events including ESD sensitivity tests of automated product manufacturing equipment, monitoring of ESD prevention equipment and ESD event localization technologies which are a key requirement for proactive ESD prevention and enhanced ESD control capability.

8.1. Introduction

The ESD technology roadmap insists that ESD has become a problem in electronics industries since the late 1970s [ESD 13]. The ESD events were causing device failures, manufacturing yield losses and system interference. To avoid this phenomenon, devices were designed to improve robustness, and manufacturing processes were designed to improve the device handling capability. The ANSI/ESD

Chapter written by Nattha JINDAPETCH, Kittikhun THONGPULL, Sayan PLONG-NGOOLUAM and Pornchai RAKPONGSIRI.

S20.20-2007 [ESD 07] standard constitutes the requirements that are necessary to design, establish, implement and maintain the ESD control program for activities that manufacture, process, assemble, install, package, label, service, test, and inspect electronic parts, assemblies and equipment. Based on the historical experience of both military and commercial organizations, this standard covers the ESD control program requirements and offers guidance for setting up a program for handling ESD sensitive items. This standard also follows ESD association, U.S. military and American National Standards Institute (ANSI) approved standards for material properties and test methods.

The above control program is a static ESD control program that aims to prevent ESD events. All metallic components, automatic equipment and operators are well grounded. All work stations are equipped with ionizers to balance the static charges on the insulative devices or carriers. These pieces of ESD prevention equipment must be periodically tested to assure their correct functionality. However, ESD events can randomly occur anywhere. In this case, online ESD monitoring systems can locate such random ESD events.

This chapter provides the details of ESD sensitivity tests of automated product manufacturing equipment, monitoring of ESD prevention equipment and ESD event localization technologies.

8.2. ESD sensitivity test technologies

To improve the device robustness or process handling capability, both device engineers and circuit designers must be able to identify the key parameters that help them develop the device capabilities and classify the level of the control needed for the environment that they are using, manufacturing and shipping. In order to identify the electrostatic device sensitivity level, it is best to know the human body model (HBM) and charged device model (CDM) sensitivity levels for all devices which will be handled. Since a discharge can also be conducted from a charged conductive object such as a metallic tool, automatic equipment or fixture that directly contacts to the electrostatic discharge sensitive (ESDS) device, the machine model (MM) is also considered.

8.2.1. Human body model testing

The most common cessation of electrostatic damage is the direct transferring of the electrostatic charges through an equivalent series resistor from the human body or from a charged material into the ESDS device. When a human walks across a floor, electrostatic charges will accumulate on the body. Then, the simple contact of a finger to the leads of an ESDS device or assembly allows the body to discharge and cause device damage.

The model used to simulate this event is called HBM. This model is the oldest and most commonly used model for classifying device sensitivity to ESD. The model represents the discharge from the fingertip to the device. It is modeled by a 100 pF capacitor which is discharged by a switching component and a 1.5 kΩ series resistor to the component. This model was developed by the U.S. military for investigating explosions of gas mixtures in mines in the 19th Century. This model was adopted by the military in MIL-STD-883 Method 3015 [US 91] and is referenced in the ANSI/ESDA/JEDEC JS-001-2012 joint standard for electrostatic discharge sensitivity testing-HBM [ESD 12]. This joint standard replaces the previous ANSI/ESD STM5.1-2007 and JESD22-A114F standards.

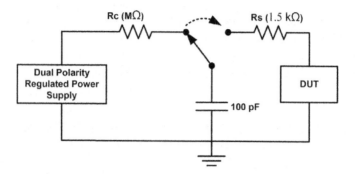

Figure 8.1. *Typical human body model (HBM) circuit*

A typical HBM circuit is presented in Figure 8.1. In general, the HBM sensitivity testing is performed by the automated test systems. The device is placed in the test system and contacted through a relay matrix. Then, the testing is started by the desired output voltage of the regulated power supply to charge the capacitor. The switch is then released to discharge the 100 pF capacitor to the device under test (DUT) via the series resistor (1.5 kΩ). The increase of the desired regulated output voltage and the firing is repeated until the DUT is determined to have failed, providing it does not meet the datasheet parameters using parametric and its functional testing.

8.2.2. Charged device model testing

The discharge of stored charges from an ESDS device can be a cause of device damage. A device might be charged from sliding, rubbing, electric field induced or directly charged from an electrical source due to this device being floated from the grounded path. These events can be a cause of stored charges onto the ESDE devices. If such devices are contacting the metallic base, fixture or another lower potential conductive surfaces, a rapid discharge event can occur from the devices to these conductive objects. This event is called CDM and may create more destruction than the HBM. The peak current from such a CDM event can reach several tens of amperes.

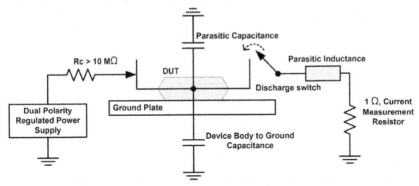

Figure 8.2. *Typical charged device model circuit*

Figure 8.2 is an illustration of a typical CDM test circuit according to the ANSI/ESD S5.3.1-2009 standard test method for electrostatic discharge sensitivity testing CDM component level [ESD 09a]. The test method involves placing a DUT on the ground plate with its leads pointing up for charging by a dual polarity regulated power supply and then discharging the DUT to ground via a current measurement resistor.

8.2.3. *Machine model testing*

MM simulates a worst case of the HBM. It consists of a 200 pF capacitor that is directly discharged into the DUT without a series resistor. The rapid current discharges from the metallic contacts to the grounded device. These metallic parts may be a charged circuit board assembly, the charged cables or handles/arms of automatic testers or device handlers.

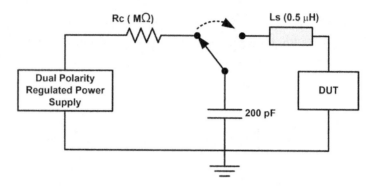

Figure 8.3. *Typical machine model circuit*

The ANSI/ESD STM5.2-2009 standard test method is constituted for electrostatic discharge sensitivity testing of the MM [ESD 09b]. The test procedure is similar to HBM testing. The test apparatus are also similar except slightly different at the test head. The MM does not have a 1.5 kΩ series resistor, but it is replaced by a series inductor as shown in Figure 8.3. This series inductor is the dominance parasitic element that shapes the oscillating waveform of the MM. This series inductor is known through the specification of various waveform parameters such as peak currents, rise times and the oscillating waveform period.

8.3. Monitoring of ESD prevention equipment

ANSI/ESD S20.20-2007 [ESD 07] is the guidance of ESD control program for the protection of electrical and electronic parts, assemblies and equipment. The fundamental ESD control principles on this handbook suggest the basic requirement as follows:

– All conductors including personnel must be connected to ground or a virtual grounding. This connection makes an equipotential balance between all items or personnel. This method can protect the discharge event as long as all items are stated at the same potential.

– An ionization system is required if necessary non-conductors in the environment have been triboelectrically charged, because of which they cannot lose their electrostatic charges by the ground connection.

– Transportation of ESDS items outside an ESD protected area (EPA) requires enclosure in packaging that has an ESD shielding property, although the type of material depends on the situation and destination.

The technical report handbook [ESD 08] provides a collection of technical data and test results to support ANSI/ESD S20.20-2007 ESD control program. It focuses on providing the guidance that can be used for developing, implementing and monitoring an ESD control program in accordance with the ANSI/ESD S20.20-2007 standard [ESD 07].

8.3.1. *Grounding and equipotential bonding systems*

Grounding and equipotential bonding systems are used to reduce the chance of damage or interference from ESD. The report in [ESD 08] mentions that ESDS can be protected by wiring ground paths to all ESD protective materials and personnel to have the same electrical potential. All conductors and personnel must be electrically connected to a known ground so that an equipotential balance between all items and personnel can be assured. As long as all items in the system are at the ground potential, ESD protection can be maintained.

However, the non-conductors in an EPA cannot lose their electrostatic charges by connection to ground. Therefore, all personnel must be electrically connected to the grounding or the equipotential bonding system when handling ESDS items. The use of a garment to achieve personnel grounding will be electrically conductive from one sleeve. The wrist strap system will be provided at ESD protective workstations with connection to ground for seating operation. For standing operations, personnel will be grounded via a wrist strap system or by a flooring footwear system. In addition, ground contacting also requires for flooring, shoes, casters and wheels [ESD 07, ESD 08].

There are some monitoring systems to visualize the failure of these grounding and equipotential bonding systems. Siew and Doo [SIE 98] used resistance comparison circuits which compare the grounding resistances to earth ground. The ESD protection failure is indicated when the resistance comparison circuits detect that the grounding resistance is greater than the maximum acceptable ESD protection resistance. A more advanced monitoring circuit for ESD protective device includes an oscillating unit, a signal processing unit and a comparator [LIU 14]. A test method and data that assist the end user in selecting the most suitable wrist strap monitoring technology for today's HDD heads has been reported in [SAL 03].

8.3.2. *Ionization*

Since all insulators cannot lose their charges by the grounding method, an ionization technique is widely used to neutralize these electrostatic charges [ESD 08, JIN 12]. The electrostatic charges that present on the objects in the workstation will be neutralized by the attracting of opposite polarity charges from the air. However, this technique cannot be replaced instead of the grounding method in all conditions. It is used when it is impossible to properly apply a ground connection and the electrostatic static control program that becomes a necessary part of preventing ESD and electrical overstress (EOS) damage for ESDS devices. In addition, ionization also keys other hidden issues such as:

– the malfunction of equipment due to an electromagnetic interference (EMI);

– product handling problems caused by the presence of static charge;

– a contamination due to electrostatic attraction and the bonding of a particulate to critical product surfaces;

– a Brownian motion of an airborne particle in some processes such as spraying;

– an injury to personnel caused by static discharge.

The static discharge performance of all air ionization devices should be evaluated using the ANSI/ESD STM3.1-2006 standard [ESD 06]. This standard describes the ionizer's performance in two categories: offset voltage and discharge or decay time. The offset voltage is the apparent voltage caused by accumulated charges that were collected by the exposed conductive surface. The specified capacitance of the surface is 20 pF which has a surface area of 6×6 square inches. The discharge time or decay time is the period that the ionizer neutralized the charge on the standard conductive plate until the voltage on that plate reached the specified end-voltage after the such plate had been charged by the specific start-voltage. The test method requires a charged plate monitor (CPM) as shown in Figure 8.4.

A non-contact voltmeter is used to measure the appeared voltage on the conductive plate with zero current drainage. The direct current (DC) voltage power supply is used to charge this plate for the start-voltage when performing the decay time test. The timer is started hereof, and will then be stopped if the remained voltage at the plate reaches the desired end-voltage. The ANSI/ESD STM3.1-2006 standard [ESD 06] recommends +/–1,000 V for the start-voltage and +/–100 V for the end-voltage.

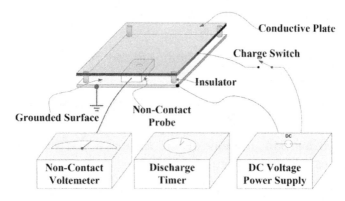

Figure 8.4. *ANSI / ESD STM3.1-2006 charged plate monitor apparatus*

In decay time testing, a CPM is placed in the ionized environment under an ionizer. The CPM acts as the current and the fields and the ionized air of a DC ionizer acts as a linear resistor. Therefore, the ionized air resistor and the CPM capacitor construct the general solution of the Resistor Capacitor (RC) time constant as shown in Figure 8.5. This solution approaches the low-voltage decay time analyzer by the method described in [JIN 12]. This low-voltage decay time analyzer is constructed using a simple induced charge meter, pulse generator circuit and a microcontroller which connects to the monitoring system network via a built-in Ethernet peripheral. The induced charge meter contains a charged plate and an ultra-high input impedance amplifier with a fixed capacitor. The ionized air generated from the ionizer is modeled as a resistor. Therefore, the decay time is calculated from this RC discharge time. Then, the microcontroller performs the correlation to the standard decay time. This is a convenient way for evaluation of ionizers. The experimental results in [JIN 12] indicate the capability of the prototype unit for the decay time ionizer measurement described in ANSI/ESD STM3.1-2006 [ESD 06] and comparable to the conventional equipment. The basic functions are met by the standard test method requirements. This decay time analyzer is smaller in size because the design does not require a high-voltage power supply. In addition, this decay time analyzer can be further monitored and controlled via the monitoring system network so that it effectively reduces the ionizer test time that may be waste in a routine work if there are more than 100 ionizers to be checked.

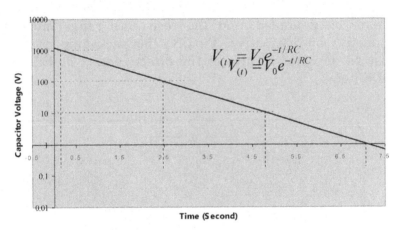

Figure 8.5. *RC discharge characteristic*

8.3.3. *Packaging*

An ESD protective packaging is necessary to store, transport and protect ESDS electronic items. The protection of ESDS devices from ESD is provided by packaging materials such as shielding bags or corrugated boxes. At the inside, the EPA packaging should be low charging and dissipative. On the outside, the EPA packaging has to be constructed as an ESD shielding. Thus, the purpose of the

ESD protective packaging is to protect the ESD/EOS damage for ESDS products when it is shipped to a customer or stored. In addition, it is also used for the product handling in the internal facility transportation.

The main functions of these packaging and material handling products are to limit the possible impact of ESD from triboelectric charge generation and to protect a direct discharge event and in some cases electrostatic field induction. The first requirement is that the material properties need a consideration to have a low charging material when it is contacted to the ESDS items. The second requirement is that the ESD protective packaging must be able to be grounded, and the resistance range must be conductive or dissipative. Finally, the packaging property must be designed to protect the direct contact or ESDs to ESDS items.

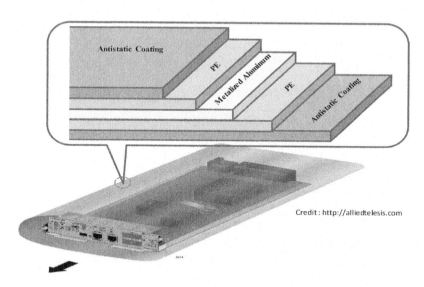

Credit: http://alliedtelesis.com

Figure 8.6. *An ESD protective packaging by a metalized shielding bag*

Many materials are available to provide all three properties: triboelectric charging, resistance and discharge shielding. The inside of these packaging materials have a low charging layer, as well as an outer layer with a surface resistance conductive or dissipative range. Figure 8.6 illustrates an example of a metalized shielding bag that is made up of multilayer thin films. The antistatic layer is used to prevent the triboelectric charge from contacting the inner and the outer side at all. The polyethylene (PE) layers are a transparency dielectric material that provides the flexibility and robustness in mechanical properties. Finally, the metalized aluminum layer is an electrical shield to make the bag as "faraday cage" for providing a discharge shielding property.

8.4. ESD event localization technologies

Since ESD events can occur anywhere and anytime, the static test methodologies and static control methods are not sufficient and waste man-hours. Although ESD protection is well controlled, any triboelectric charging which occurs when products are in contact and in motion on the conveyer of the manufacturing assembly line can cause an ESD event. ESD events are very short time intervals, usually 10 ns or less. Their discharge energy can suddenly heat HDD heads. Such random events are detected very difficultly by static test equipment.

Online monitoring of ESD events is an effective solution. The ESD events generate EMI which is broadband electromagnetic radiation in 10 MHz–2 GHz frequency range. Therefore, the EMI can be received by the appropriate antennas. The EMI signal strength and its arrival time at the antennas can be calculated to get the distance between the antenna and the ESD event. In this section, there are various ways to locate the position of the ESD events as the following details.

8.4.1. *EMI locators*

The monitoring system consists of a sensing part to detect the underlying events and a communication part to forward the events to the base station. The base station should contain a graphic user interface (GUI) and database software. The 3M™ EM Aware ESD monitor [3M 10] shown in Figure 8.7 provides this feature. It is an EMI detector that can measure HBM, MM and CDM with sensitivity of 1–1,000 V, and can report ESD event magnitude and count. Therefore, the 3M™ EM Aware ESD monitor can perform being a stand-alone ESD monitor by being installed near the suspicious area. In addition, it also provides a conventional 4-20 mA analog output and an RJ45 connector to interface to the data acquisition systems or facility monitoring systems (FMSs). However, the monitoring system that uses only one 3M™ EM Aware ESD monitor cannot locate the exact position of the ESD events because the antenna can receive the EMI signal from every direction.

Figure 8.7. *3M™ EM Aware ESD monitor [3M 10]*

EMI signal strength indicates the distance from the ESD source to the EMI detector antenna. Figure 8.8 shows an EMI signal strength-based localization system [THO 10]. The 4-20 mA analog output of each EMI detector, which is the ESD magnitude, namely, the EMI signal strength, is read by a data acquisition device and forwarded to a personal computer. Figure 8.9 shows that the EMI signal strength at four EMI detectors is correlated with the distances from the ESD source [THO 10, THO 11, WIL 91]. The ESD event is located by a set of three EMI detectors, or by the four EMI detectors for more accuracy [THO 13]. From a study result, the EMI signal strength-based localization system works well in the area less than 1.5×1.5 m^2 because EMI signals are easily attenuated by the environment [THO 13].

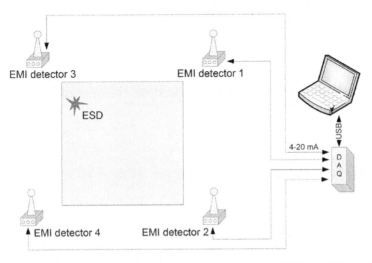

Figure 8.8. *An EMI signal strength-based system [THO 10, THO 11]*

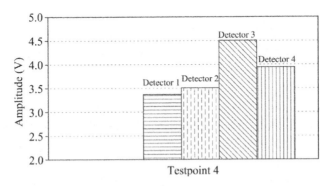

Figure 8.9. *Signal strength received by the four EMI detectors [THO 10]*

8.4.2. High-speed oscilloscope-based ESD event localization systems

Using three EMI detectors and the arrival time at each EMI detector antenna can locate where the ESD event occurs. This method does need a multichannel storage digital oscilloscope with bandwidth of more than 1 GHz to measure the arrival times of three antennas as shown in Figure 8.10 [STE 99]. When an ESD event occurs, the EMI will arrive at the closer antenna before the others. The arrival times are then translated into the distances between the ESD event and three fixed location EMI detectors. Finally, the ESD event position can be calculated from the trilateration method, the bounding-box method or the global positioning system (GPS).

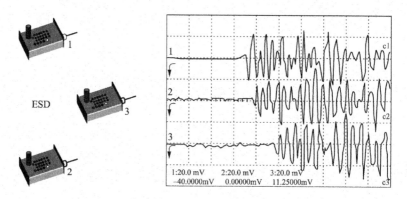

Figure 8.10. *Arrival time measurement of EMI from an ESD event [STE 99]*

A more robust ESD event localization system is made by using four antennas such as the ESD event locator system (EELS) [LIN 98] shown in Figure 8.11. The four antennas construct a 3D Cartesian coordinate system with one antenna at its origin and the other three on the known positive x-, y- and z-axis, respectively. The (x, y, z) coordinate is obtained from an inverse GPS method. The ESD event location and its strength are automatically displayed on the personal computer monitor. However, this system has some strict requirements such as all antennas having the same characteristics and the same-length cables connected to the inputs of the digital oscilloscope with a sampling rate of at least 5 Gigasamples per second.

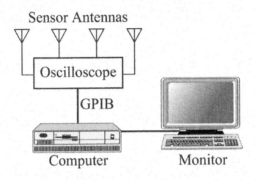

Figure 8.11. *An ESD event locator system (EELS) [LIN 98]*

8.4.3. RFID localization systems

Radio-frequency identification (RFID) technology provides low cost and reliable object localization applications. Figure 8.12 illustrates a simple RFID localization system composed of RFID tags, RFID readers, a computer and a server. Each RFID tag contains necessary information of the product it is attached to. The tags may contain a processing unit and sensors to acquire the inspecting events such as ESD events in manufacturing lines. The inspected events are then written into the corresponding tags. The RFID readers read the information from the tags in coverage area and forward to the computer via an Ethernet, a universal serial bus (USB), serial links (such as UART in RS232/RS485) or wireless communications. The collected information is then annually reported or stored in the database server.

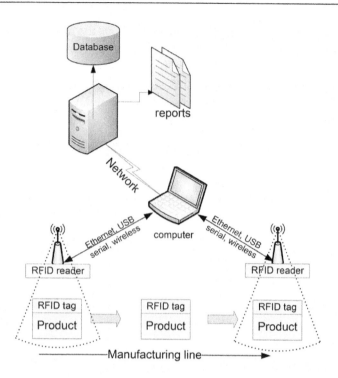

Figure 8.12. *A simple RFID system*

The RFID localization systems can be implemented in various ways, depending on the selection of tags, readers and their roles. The tags can be passive tags, semi-active tags or active tags. The readers can be passive readers or active readers. The locations are determined by means of tag localization or reader localization. The localization systems may track stationary or mobile objects. With regard to tag types, the RFID localization systems are categorized into passive RFID localization systems and active RFID localization systems. With regard to the roles of tags and readers, the RFID localization systems are categorized into tag localization systems and reader localization systems. Moreover, the algorithms to improve RFID localization systems still be an open-end research topic.

Passive RFID tags are small, cheap and battery-less, but need more sophisticated and expensive RFID readers. Read-only tags assigned with permanent identity and location information limit their usage only to reader localization systems in which the mobile readers calculate their positions from the fixed location tags. Such read-only tags cannot support sensing conditions from the environment. When applied in ESD event localization applications, the readers of such read-only tags should contain an ESD event sensor, a microcontroller and a memory to store locations when ESD events are detected. This limitation was solved when a high-function RFID tag shown in Figure 8.13 was introduced by Powercast Corporation and Vanguard ID [SWE 14]. To preserve the battery-less advantage of passive RFID tags, the radio frequency (RF) power-harvesting technology is used to power a microcontroller and built-in sensors. Therefore, the tags can be attached to mobile objects or products conveyed along the manufacturing line to perform a tag localization system, and send the sensing data to the fixed readers in the coverage inspection range of up to 8 m.

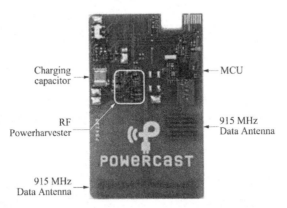

Figure 8.13. *A high-function passive tag with RF power-harvesting technology from Powercast Corporation and Vanguard ID [SWE 14]*

Semi-active and active RFID tags need battery and expensive, but have longer range up to 100 m and need simpler readers. In active RFID localization systems, some active RFID tags are used as reference locations for localizing the mobile tags so that the system accuracy can be satisfied with few expensive readers. Moreover, due to the long effective sensing distance, active RFID tags have potential to be distributed in 3-D environments, especially ESD event localization.

The RFID localization system cost increases when the accuracy and precision are required to be higher. In passive RFID localization systems, increasing the density of tag distribution is a simple way to improve the accuracy and precision. However, more tags come up with higher system cost and the interference between neighbor tags is still a big problem to be solved.

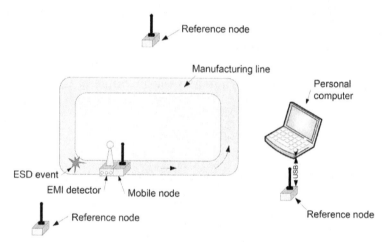

Figure 8.14. *A wireless sensor network (WSN)-based localization system [THO 11]*

8.4.4. WSN-based localization systems

Wireless sensor network (WSN)-based monitoring systems gain the advantages of low cost and easy installation. Figure 8.14 shows a WSN-based localization system

[THO 11, THO 13] that uses only one EMI detector and four wireless sensor nodes in a coverage area. A wireless sensor node is composed of a microcontroller, sensors and an RF transceiver module. The wireless sensor nodes are much cheaper than the EMI detectors. We can easily find a $40 wireless sensor node, whereas the price of one EMI detector is about $1000–$9000 depending on the model [QSO 14].

The WSN-based localization systems also gain the goodness from the received signal strength indicator (RSSI) information that can be easily read from the register of most RF transceivers and does not require additional and expensive hardware. In the system of Figure 8.14, only EMI detector is equipped to a mobile wireless sensor node that moves along the manufacturing line. The other three reference wireless sensor nodes are installed at the known positions. One of them acts as a base station and is connected to a personal computer running monitoring software. Once an ESD event is detected by the EMI detector, the mobile wireless sensor node reads the ESD magnitude via the 4-20 mA interface and broadcasts this event to the three reference nodes. At this moment, the RSSI information observed by the three reference nodes is forwarded to the base station. The RSSI information from each reference node can be translated into the distance from the mobile node. Then, three distances from the reference nodes are calculated to locate the mobile node by using the trilateration method, the bounding-box method and so on. The ESD event is located by the location of the mobile wireless sensor node.

The RSSI-based localization has potential to cover large inspection areas using a small number of wireless sensor nodes. However, the RSSI signal fluctuates over time due to multipath propagation from the reflections of this signal to walls and machines in the real manufacturing environment. Many methods have been devised to smoothen RSSI signals for the more accuracy localization. This still be an active research topic.

8.4.5. *Hybrid localization systems*

The localization systems gain more robustness from mixed technologies. Figure 8.15 shows a hybrid localization system that provides the accuracy and reliability from RFID-based localization and the larger coverage area and flexibility of WSN-based localization [KNU 10]. A ZigBee module and sensors are integrated into a semi-active RFID tag that moves along the manufacturing line to detect the ESD events and other environmental parameters. Sensing parameters, as well as their locations, are collected by the wireless access points (WAPs) and forwarded to the base station via wireless networks. In addition to a ZigBee standard, the wireless networking standard may be the IEEE 802.15.4 standard or the IEEE 802.11 standard, or a mixed standard. This hybrid localization system allows more coverage areas or inspection zones, and every zone can communicate with each other in the same manner as WSNs.

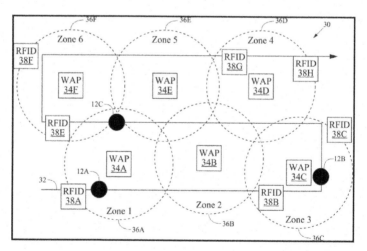

Figure 8.15. *An RFID-WSN hybrid localization system [KNU 10]*

8.5. Conclusion

This chapter has overviewed the current technologies for visualizing invisible ESD events that cause damage to ESD sensitive devices in HDD manufacturing assembly lines. The details include ESD sensitivity tests of automated product manufacturing equipment, monitoring of ESD prevention equipment and ESD event localization technologies. These technologies have a great potential to support proactive ESD prevention and enhance ESD control capability.

8.6. Bibliography

[ESD 06] ESD Association, ANSI/ESD STM 3.1-2006: For protection of electrostatic discharge susceptible items-ionization, July 2006.

[ESD 07] ESD Association, ANSI/ESD S20.20-2007: Development of an electrostatic discharge control program for protection of electrical and electronic parts, assemblies and equipment, March 2007.

[ESD 08] ESD Association, ESD TR 20 20–2008: Handbook for the development of an electrostatic discharge control program for the protection of electronic parts, assemblies and equipment, April 2008.

[ESD 09a] ESD Association, ANSI/ESD S5.3.1-2009: Electrostatic discharge sensitivity testing-charged device model (CDM)-component level, December 2009.

[ESD 09b] ESD Association, ANSI/ESD STM5.2-2009: Electrostatic discharge sensitivity testing-machine model, December 2009.

[ESD 12] ESD Association, ANSI/ESDA/JEDEC JS-001-2012: Joint standard for electrostatic discharge sensitivity testing-human body model (HBM)-component level, April 2012.

[ESD 13] ESD Association, Electrostatic discharge (ESD) technology roadmap–revised March 2013, March 2013.

[JIN 12] JINDAPETCH N., PLONG-NGOOLUAM S., THONGPULL K., et al., "A low-voltage decay time analyzer for monitoring ionizers", Journal of Electrostatics, vol. 70, no. 6, pp. 489–498, December 2012.

[KNU 10] KNUDSON O.B., JOHNSON J.M., RASMUSSEN T.W., et al., Detection and tracking of environmental parameters, United States Patent Application Publication, no. US 2010/0051692 A1, March 2010.

[LIN 98] LIN D.L., DECHIARO L.F., JON M., "A robust ESD event locator system with event characterization", Journal of Electrostatics, vol. 44, no. 3/4, pp. 159–175, September 1998.

[LIU 14] LIU C., Monitoring circuit and system for ESD protection device, United States Patent Application, no. 20140176153, June 2014.

[QSO 14] QSOURCE Inc., ESD event & EMI field detectors, October 2014. Available at http://www.qsource.com/c-892-esd-event-emi-field-detectors.aspx.

[SAL 03] SALISBURY J.M., STUCKERT G.A., OSWALD N.R., et al., "Wrist strap monitor testing for use with the latest MR head technologies", Electrical Overstress/Electrostatic Discharge (EOS/ESD) Symposium, pp. 1–5, 2003.

[SIE 98] SIEW A., DOO L.S., ESD protection continuous monitoring device, United States Patent, no. 5835327, November 1998.

[STE 99] STEINMAN A., BERNIER J., BOEHM D., et al., "Test methodologies for detecting ESD events in automated processing equipment", Electrical Overstress/Electrostatic Discharge (EOS/ESD) Symposium, pp. 168–177, 1999.

[SWE 14] SWEDBERG C., "High function passive UHF tag supports built-in sensors, display screen", RFID Journal online news. Available at http://www.rfidjournal.com/articles/view?11699, April 2014.

[THO 10] THONGPULL K., JINDAPETCH N., TEERAPABKAJORNDET W., "An electrostatic discharge event localization system using electromagnetic interference strength", Khon Kaen University (KKU) Research Journal, vol. 15, no. 78, pp. 738–750, August 2010.

[THO 11] THONGPULL K., JINDAPETCH N., A wireless electrostatic discharge event locator system, Thailand Petty Patent no. 7158, 2011.

[THO 13] THONGPULL K., JINDAPETCH N., TEERAPABKAJORNDET W., "Wireless ESD event locator systems in hard disk drive manufacturing environments", *IEEE Transactions on Industrial Electronics*, vol. 60, no. 11, pp. 5252–5259, 2013.

[US 91] US Department of Defense, MIL-STD-883D, Test Methods and Procedures for Microelectronics: Method 3015.7 Electrostatic Discharge Sensitivity Classification, 1991.

[WIL 91] WILSON P.F., MA M.T., "Fields radiated by electrostatic discharges", *IEEE Transactions on Electromagnetic Compatibility*, vol. 33, no. 1, pp. 10–18, February 1991.

[3M 10] 3M Electronic Solutions Division, Static Control Products and Services Catalog, 2010.

9

Inspection of Styrofoam Beads on Adapter of Hard Disk Drives

In manufacturing, the hard disk drives (HDDs) to be tested are inserted into the adapters of the HDD testing apparatus in a test process. In a conventional operator, each adapter is checked by using operator's eyes which often make errors. This chapter presents the practical application of the morphological template-base method and several image processing algorithms to check the availability of adapters. The proposed method consists of image subtraction, thresholding, morphological operation and logical operation. This application is then followed by a model of a decision system in which a computer decides "success" or "failure" while monitoring each adapter via a digital camera. The proposed method shows superior sensitivity and accuracy for detecting styrofoam beads attached inside adapter slots of the HDD testing apparatus.

9.1. Introduction

HDDs are produced by several processes included: mechanical assembly, servo write, function test, burn-in test.

Chapter written by Suchart YAMMEN.

They are then put through a final test process to confirm whether an HDD is normally settled with defect processing. Each HDD is typically tested by using an HDD testing apparatus that contains 240 slots of the adapters shown in Figure 9.1. Before testing each HDD, an operator is required to check the availability of 240 adapters by using his eyes to confirm whether all slots of the adapters have styrofoam beads attached inside adapter slots or not. If there are styrofoam beads in the adapter, the connection between the HDD and a test computer will have a problem that prevents the testing signal and the HDD cannot be tested. These styrofoam beads come out of an anti-static box, where HDDs are contained to prevent electrostatic discharge while transferring all HDDs to the testing apparatus. As is generally known, the operator takes about half an hour to check all adapter slots per testing apparatus with his eyes. However, human errors occur frequently in cases when the inspector continuously works long hours. This error results in the loss of quality of the HDD products, and makes customers lack product confidence and trust.

To solve or reduce this human error, an automatic system development in visual inspection technology for detecting the styrofoam beads is presented in this chapter. Section 9.2 covers the *morphological template-based method* to detect the styrofoam beads inside slots of adapters from the images. The method consists of four image processing techniques: image subtraction, thresholding, morphological operation and logical operation. Then, section 9.3 presents a model of a decision system deciding 'success' or 'failure' in terms of the adapter availability while monitoring each adapter via a digital camera. Section 9.4 demonstrates the use of the morphological template-based method in the detection application, and then discusses the application. Finally, section 9.5 concludes with a comparison to the original method.

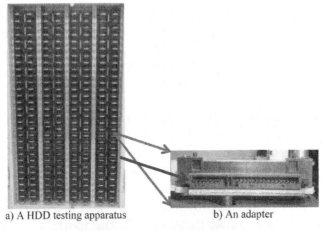

a) A HDD testing apparatus   b) An adapter

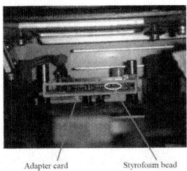

Adapter card   Styrofoam bead

c) Styrofoam bead attached to the adapter card.

Figure 9.1. *Example of 240 slots of the adapters in the HDD testing apparatus. For a color version of this figure, see www.iste.co.uk / muneesawang / visualinspect.zip*

9.2. Morphological template-based method

Since the proposed method is composed of several image processing algorithms, the review of research works that employed these algorithms is now in order. Recently, researchers have developed an automatic system for detection in various fields. For example, Zuwairie *et al.* [ZUW 08] proposed a noise elimination procedure of printed circuit board. The process consists of separating negative images and positive images by using image subtraction. Then, converting into a binary image and combining the noise using the XOR logic operator. This method is well suited for small and medium scale printed circuit board (PCB) manufacturers.

Aisha *et al.* [AIS 10] proposed a method of detection and classification of vehicles based on image processing via an aerial camera. The detecting process involved use of a sobel operator to detect an edge and converting the edge into a binary image. Then, the morphology method is used to remove noise. Proper vehicle classification is achieved at the rate of more than 85%. In this work, the morphology method is applied to reduce noise.

Ruihua *et al.* [RUI 09] proposed a method to describe the overlapping phenomenon among the cells in the mice macrophage images. This begins with using Otsu method for image segmentation. Subsequently, morphological image processing was used to remove noise. Then, the watershed algorithm based on a distance transform is carried out to segment the image of macrophages, which are cells of mice. In this work, the Otsu method is applied to convert grayscale images into binary images.

Putera *et al.* [PUT 10] proposed the defect inspection of the PCB by using morphology approach to segment in preparing the images for defect detection and classification.

In this chapter, an automatic algorithm for detecting styrofoam beads in an adapter card image is developed by using image processing techniques. The proposed technique involves the transforming of a test image into two images; a negative image and a positive image by using the image subtraction operator and the threshold operator [GON 02]. In this step, an obtained zero image is ignored because the corresponding pixels between the template image and test image are no different.

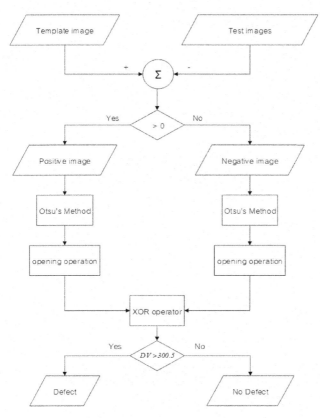

Figure 9.2. *Proposed methods*

Next, each of the two grayscale negative and positive images is converted into a binary image by using the Otsu method [NOB 79]. Then, noises in the two binary images are reduced by using an opening operator [SOI 03]. Finally, the defects in both positive and negative binary images are combined by using XOR operator to identify the styrofoam beads. For detecting styrofoam beads in an adapter card image, the overall detection algorithm is illustrated in Figure 9.2.

9.2.1. *Image subtraction*

In the first step, image subtraction is often applied. Consider image differences of the form:

$$g[n_r, n_c] = f[n_r, n_c] - h[n_r, n_c] \qquad\qquad [9.1]$$

The $h[n_r, n_c]$ sequence is the template, which is an image of a region of an adapter card without any styrofoam beads as shown in Figure 9.3.

Figure 9.3. *Template image*

The $f[n_r, n_c]$ sequence is a test image of a region of an adapter card while taking a series of images captured by an intensity digital camera as shown in Figure 9.4.

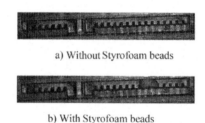

a) Without Styrofoam beads

b) With Styrofoam beads

Figure 9.4. *Two test images*

The net effect of subtracting the template from each sample test image is the areas that are different between $f[n_r, n_c]$ and $h[n_r, n_c]$ appearing in the $g[n_r, n_c]$ output image. The output image is used to generate three types of images: a zero image, a negative image and a positive image. The styrofoam bead in the output image is actually the combination of styrofoam bead in both negative and positive grayscale images. For examples, both positive and negative grayscale images without styrofoam beads are shown in Figures 9.5(a) and (b), respectively. Both positive and negative grayscale images with styrofoam beads are also shown in Figures 9.6(a) and (b), respectively. A zero image does not affect the output image.

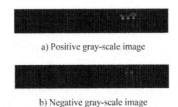

a) Positive gray-scale image

b) Negative gray-scale image

Figure 9.5. *Positive or negative grayscale image without styrofoam beads*

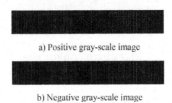

a) Positive gray-scale image

b) Negative gray-scale image

Figure 9.6. *Positive or negative grayscale image with styrofoam beads*

9.2.2. Otsu method

In the second step, the Otsu method is applied to select an automatic threshold value, and to convert both positive and negative grayscale images into positive and negative binary images. This threshold value is selected by maximizing the variance of the two groups of the graylevel values.

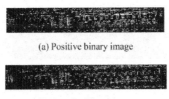

(a) Positive binary image

(b) Negative binary image

Figure 9.7. *Positive or negative binary images without styrofoam beads obtained from the Otsu method*

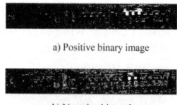

a) Positive binary image

b) Negative binary image

Figure 9.8. *Binary images with styrofoam beads obtained from using the Otsu method*

9.2.3. *Morphological operation*

In the third step, the mathematical morphology is applied to remove areas, which are not interested (noise) from the test adapter card image without destroying both size and shape of styrofoam beads. The used operator is opening, which is erosion followed by dilation.

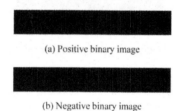

(a) Positive binary image

(b) Negative binary image

Figure 9.9. *Binary images without styrofoam beads obtained from using the opening operator*

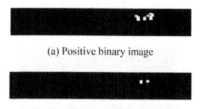

(a) Positive binary image

(b) Negative binary image

Figure 9.10. *Binary images with styrofoam beads obtained from using the opening operator*

9.2.4. *Logical operation*

In the fourth step, logical operators are often applied to combine negative and positive binary images by using the XOR operator. This leads to identifying styrofoam beads in the adapter card image; for example, Figure 9.11 shows the binary image obtained by using the XOR operator to the adapter card image with styrofoam beads while Figure 9.12 shows the binary image obtained by using the XOR operator to the adapter card image without styrofoam beads.

Figure 9.11. *Binary image with styrofoam beads obtained from using the XOR operator*

Figure 9.12. *Binary image without styrofoam beads obtained from using the XOR operator*

9.3. Decision model

In the fifth step, decision value (*DV*) is calculated to classify the adapter card image with styrofoam beads and without styrofoam beads. The DV is the average between the maximum number of white pixels in the adapter card image without styrofoam beads and the minimum number of white pixels in the adapter card image with styrofoam beads. If the number of white pixels in the test adapter card image is greater than the DV, the test image will have some styrofoam beads. If not, the test image will not have any styrofoam beads.

Performance evaluation measurement involves, with the evaluation of the detection efficiency, how well the proposed method does. To verify how well the proposed method detects the styrofoam beads, four measures are involved: sensitivity, specification, precision and accuracy [SON 08] are used to provide the efficiency of the detection process.

9.4. Application

In the experimental results, the 265 test adapter card images consist of 65 grayscale images without styrofoam beads and 200 grayscale images with styrofoam beads. After the proposed method described in section 9.2, which was applied for detecting styrofoam beads in 265 test images, the proposed method can correctly detect styrofoam beads in the 65 adapter card images. Furthermore, the proposed method can correctly classify the 200 adapter card images without styrofoam beads. The results show that the four values of the sensitivity, specificity, accuracy and precision are all equal to one, as shown in Table 9.1.

	Automatic inspection result
Sensitivity	1.00
specificity	1.00
Precision	1.00
Accuracy	1.00

Table 9.1. *Performance evaluation*

9.5. Conclusion

In this chapter, the automatic proposed algorithm for detecting styrofoam beads in the adapter card image is developed by using the image subtraction, the Otsu method, mathematical morphology and the XOR operator. From experimental results to the 65 grayscale images without styrofoam beads and 200 grayscale images with styrofoam beads, it shows that the proposed algorithm provides perfectly good result for detecting styrofoam beads. This result is verified with four values of the sensitivity, specificity, accuracy and precision. Therefore, all values are one.

9.6. Bibliography

[AIS 10] AISHA A., IBRAHIM M.H., "Vehicle detection using morphological image processing technique", *Proceedings of International Conference on Multimedia Computing and Information Technology* (MCIT), pp. 65–68, 2010.

[DEE 08] DEEPAK K.K., SUNEETA A., SHANKAR N., "Normalized cross-correlation based fingerprint matching", *Proceedings of the 5th International Conference on Computer Graphics Imaging and Visualization* (CGIV), pp. 229–232, 2008.

[FEN 06] FENG Z., QINGMING H., WEN G., "Image matching by normalized cross-correlation", *Proceedings of the International Conference on Acoustics, Speech and Signal Processing*, (ICASSP), vol. 2, pp. 729–732, 2006.

[FEN 10] FENG Z., SHUNYOUNG Z., WENLING X., "A line labeling and region growing based algorithm for binary image connected component labeling", *Proceedings of the 2nd Pacific-Asia Conference on Circuits, Communications and System* (PACCS), pp. 487–490, 2010.

[GON 02] GONZALEZ R.C., WOODS R.E., *Digital Image Processing*, Prentice Hall, Upper Saddle River, N.J., 2nd edition, p. 794, 2002.

[HAN 06] HAN J., KAMBER M., *Data Mining: Concepts and Techniques*, Morgan Kaufmann, Elsevier, Amsterdam, Boston, San Francisco, CA, 2nd ed., 2006.

[LIA 10] LIANG P., ZHIWEI X., JIGUANG D., "Fast normalized cross-correlation image matching based on multiscale edge information", *Proceedings of the International Conference on Computer Application and System Modeling* (ICCASM 2010), pp. 507–511, 2010.

[LIU 91] LIU J., LI W., TIAN Y., "Automatic thresholding of gray-level pictures using two-dimensional Otsu method", *Proceedings of China 1991 International Conference on Circuits and Systems*, vol. 1, pp. 325–327, 1991.

[NOB 79] NOBU Y.O., "A threshold selection method from gray-level histograms", *IEEE Transactions on Systems, Man and Cybernetics*, vol. 9, no. 1, pp. 62–66, 1979.

[PUT 10] PUTERA S.H.I., IBRAHIM Z., "Printed circuit board defect detection using mathematical morphology and MATLAB image processing tools", *Proceedings of International Conference on Education Technology and Computer* (ICETC 2010), pp. 359–363, 2010.

[RUI 09] RUIHUA X., PING W., WU Z., *et al.*, "A novel overlapping mice macrophages images segmentation method", *Proceedings of International Conference on Image Analysis and Signal Processing* (IASP 2009), pp. 40–43, 2009.

[SIM 08] SIM K.S., KHO Y.Y., TSO C.P., "Application of contrast enhancement bilateral closing top-hat Otsu thresholding (CEBICTOT) technique on crack images", *Proceedings of 7th IEEE International Conference on Cybernetic Intelligent Systems* (CIS 2008), pp. 350–353, 2008.

[SOI 03] SOILLE P., *Morphological Image Analysis: Principles and Applications*, 2nd ed., Springer, Berlin, New York, p. 392, 2003.

[SON 08] SONKA M., HLAVAC V., BOYLE R., "Image processing, analysis, and machine vision", *3rd ed., Thompson Engineering*, Toronto, p. 850, 2008.

[WEI 09] WEI W., GONG S., "Research on Unstructured Road Detection Algorithm Based on the Machine Vision", *Proceedings of Asia-Pacific Conference on Information Processing*, pp. 1–4, 2009.

[ZUW 08] ZUWAIRIE I., NOOR K.K., ISMAIL I., *et al.*, "A noise elimination procedure for printed circuit board inspection system", *Proceedings of International Conference on Modeling & Simulation* (AICMS 08), pp. 332–337, 2008.

10

Inspection of Defect on Magnetic Disk Surface and Quality of the Glue Dispenser Route

The scratching of magnetic disks in hard disk drives (HDDs) often causes errors in the processing of read/write data. An effective monitoring system for scratch detection that can be used during the manufacturing of HDDs is required. A scratch is often caused by the crashing together of the disk and the read/write head during the operation of the disk drive. In addition, the contamination during the manufacturing of the drive is also another cause of a scratch. For these problems, the scratch detection must be monitored by advanced visual inspection techniques such as: atomic force microscopy (AFM), scanning electron microscope (SEM), Candela, read/write error, microscope and laser Doppler effect. These techniques are also described. In addition, the visual inspection of the route of the glue dispenser for the manufacturing of the top cover of the HDD during the assembly process is also explained by developing computer vision and back-propagation neural network (BPNN) techniques.

Chapter written by Anan KRUESUBTHAWORN.

10.1. Introduction

The areal density in HDDs has been doubling in terms of capacity every year, which has led to a reduction in the dimensions of components and an increase in the features of the drives. One of the most important components of any HDD is the magnetic disk or media that typically has a carbon "overcoat" which is less than 50 Å in thickness and covered with about 10 Å of lubricant to protect the media from sliding contact or scratches from the recording head. A scratch is a notch on the surface of the disk caused by faulty mechanical handling. A ding is a "hole" on the disk surface caused by a faulty head stack that bumps against the media surface. A glove mark is a group of powder particles that are transferred from a clean room glove to the media surface by erroneous handling by a human operator. Particle contamination is defined as excessive random dust particles resting on the media surface [KUM 10]. Figure 10.1 illustrates the four types of defects on the disk surface that are commonly found on the HDD media [CHO 12b]. The flying height between the recording head and media is only about 3–5 nm. Therefore a scratch on the media must be closely monitored during the HDD assembly processes.

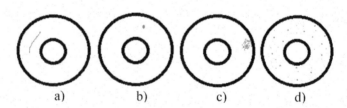

Figure 10.1. *Surface defects on HDD media: a) scratch, b) ding, c) glove mark and d) particle contamination [CHO 12b]*

This chapter attempts to highlight the computer vision technologies used in the HDD industry to inspect the defects on media surfaces and the quality of the glue dispenser route. The visual inspection methods for detecting defects on the surface of the media use AFM [MAT 00], SEM [JAC 01, SHI 11], laser scanning [ISH 01], optical scanning [ZHO 05], read/write error [DIE 01] and laser Doppler heterodyne interference system [ZHU 12]. In addition, the inspection methodology of route quality of the glue dispenser is applied by using the computer vision and the BPNN technique is explained [TIN 08, TIN 07].

10.2. Computer vision technologies for scratch detection on media surfaces

The computer vision technologies, used to detect a scratch on media surfaces, are described in detail in the following. The first instrument for scratch detection methodology is AFM which is a scanning probe microscope. The probe is designed to measure the material properties, such as height, friction and magnetism. To acquire an image, the probe is used to scan a small area of the sample, measuring the material properties simultaneously. AFM can also provide three-dimensional (3D) profiles of the surface at nano-level, by measuring forces between a sharp probe (<10 nm) and the surface at very short distances (0.2–10 nm) depending on the probe size. AFM can then be used to measure a scratch at nanoscale. In addition, the size of the scratch is also displayed by the AFM. Examples of AFM images on magnetic media are shown in Figure 10.2. The disadvantages of this method are that it takes a long time to examine the surface properly even though the sample area is very small [GUD 11] and also scratch detection on a magnetic recording disk has to be identified before evaluation [GRE 06]. In addition, the AFM machine is a destructive technique on the disk and so it is impossible to use the disk after the detection process.

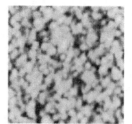

a) The 0.1 µm scratch size

b) The surface of the magnetic
recording disk size 0.5 µm x0.5 µm.

Figure 10.2. *Scratch images on the magnetic recording
disk from AFM [MAT 00, FUR 08]*

The second method to detect scratches on a magnetic recording disk is by using an SEM machine which uses high-energy electrons to generate an image. Figure 10.3 illustrates the work process systems of an SEM machine. The image taken from the SEM is shown in Figure 10.4. The detection system is used to scan the surface by the use of internal field emissions to inject electronic charge carriers into the surface. Then, the results are processed and shown in photographs and 3D images. This method is one of the high-technology measurement methods used for the detection of scratches. The SEM method can also be used to detect the size of a scratch as well as the AFM method.

The advantage of SEM over traditional microscopes is the large depth of field, which allows more of a sample to be in focus at one time and a higher resolution that enables much higher levels of magnification to be employed. These advantages are made possible because the degree of magnification can be controlled by using electromagnets. Thus, SEM is one of the most useful instruments for scratch detection.

The use of SEM also has its disadvantages and these include: the inspection cost of using SEM is very expensive and so the cost of the scratch inspection procedure is also very high. The sample must be cut before testing by the SEM machine and, thus, the disk must be destroyed. Hence, it is not often used in the process of detecting scratches on the magnetic recording disk.

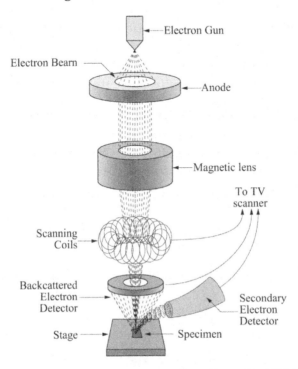

Figure 10.3. *The working processes of standard SEM [SCH 14]*

Figure 10.4. *The SEM image of scratch on the magnetic disk [JAC 01]*

The next methodology of scratch detection is an optical detection that can be used to detect scratches on a surface and can display the geometry of the scratch in terms of width, depth and height as shown in Figure 10.5. This methodology uses an optical laser lens to focus a laser beam on a scratch area during a rotation of a disk. When the laser light is reflected by the scratch, the beam will spread to another lens called a condenser lens. The beam is refocused and sent to the receiver and put in for processing of the signal. Finally, images of the depth, width and length are shown. This system is based on the fundamental principles of reflection of light which state that the beam of light that is reflected from a flat and from a scratched surface is different. This difference is detected by a receiver (photodetector). The components and processes of the transmission shafts and beams are very complicated due to high-precision tools. Hence, the components of the system and the working process were more sophisticated [ISH 01].

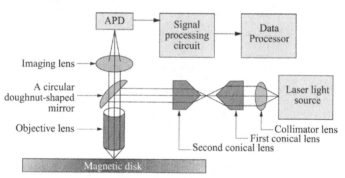

Figure 10.5. *The optical detection system designed by Ishiguro [ISH 01]*

Like the previous methods, this system can only show the scratch dimensions, however, the precise location of a scratch is also necessary for the HDD manufacturers as well. The methodology to identify and specify a scratch position in HDD industries is achieved by using a read/write error. The key processes of scratch detection using this method are shown in Figure 10.6. The test processes are to randomly select a magnetic disk from the HDD assembly process and a signal is then written into a magnetic disk. Finally, the signal is read back from the same position on the disk. If the signal can be read, this means there is no scratch at the position. In contrast, if there is no read back signal at the position, it may indicate the presence of a scratch. After that, the scratch position is marked by writing a signal around the scratch area. The main concepts of scratch detection and the image of the mark signal from SEM are illustrated in Figure 10.7. Finally, the disk is sent to the next stage in the process which might use AFM or another system to capture and display the image of the scratch.

Recently, the performance and efficiency of the reader/writer has increased by the installation of a heating source into the head of the reader/writer. The introduction of a heating element helps the reading/writing and is called heat-assisted magnetic recording technology, as shown in Figure 10.8. The element and functionality of this technology consist of a slider, which is used for reading and writing data, flying over a rotating magnetic disk. A head element placed on a suspension and a heater is incorporated into the slider. The current is applied to the heater to protrude the slider. This is a thermal expansion to adjust a clearance or flying height between the head and the disk. This technology can be applied to detect a scratch on a magnetic disk as well. A test procedure is that the head is moved inside the disk surface and a heater power is set. Then, the temperature of the disk is measured and is set as the initial temperature. After that, the head is moved outside the media surface. To detect a scratch, a different heat power is applied to the disc surface with the same test procedure. If the temperature is changed from the initial temperature, it means that there is a defect or scratch at the area. The change of the temperature is dependant on the size of the defect [DIE 01].

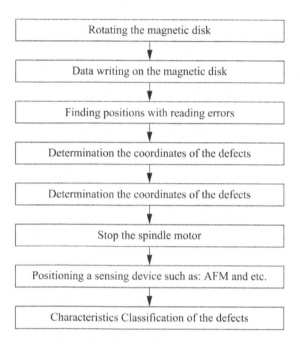

Figure 10.6. *The read / write error processes of scratch detection [DIE 01]*

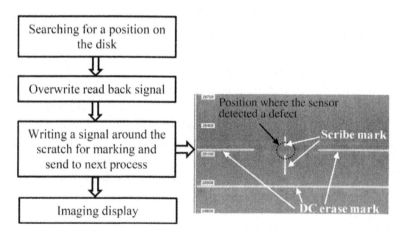

Figure 10.7. *The process of searching for a scratch [GRE 06]*

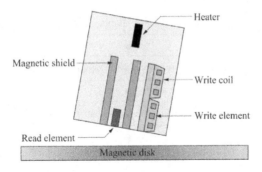

Figure 10.8. *Scratch detection on the disk using the heat on the read/write processes [YOS 08]*

The next process is to display an image of the scratch after the scratch position has been identified by using the previously described process. This process is used to determine the cause of the scratch by using machines which depend on the resolution of the scratches. A low-power microscope is used for low-resolution inspection to detect a scratch on the disk. Then, the disk is sent to an automated inspection instrument to evaluate a defective surface on the disk. The instrument that is used is called an optical surface analyzer (OSA). For the smaller scratches, the Candela is used to determine the scratch after using the digital signal processing. The laser is applied nearby the scratch point and then the scratch becomes visible and can be identified by the Candela machine. After that, the disk is sent for further inspection by using a high-power microscope. The characteristic, size and position of the scratch are displayed, and the root cause of the scratch can be identified. If the size of the scratch is at the nano-scale, the disk must be inspected by AFM. These processes are depicted in Figure 10.9. All methods use an industrial instrument and machine to investigate the scratch on the surface of a magnetic disk. The disadvantages of any of these detection methods are: (1) the random nature of the inspection, (2) the need for an expensive machine and equipment, and (3) the time that is taken to complete this inspection or evaluation.

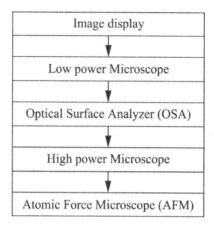

Figure 10.9. *The processing of scratch detection according to the resolution of the scratches [GRE 06]*

The next method of scratch inspection on the disk surface uses an infrared camera which is used to study the heat distribution inside the hard drive [EDD 09, KWE 11, TOD 09]. It is also used for measuring the temperature distribution in the components of the hard drive as shown in Figure 10.10. The heat dissipation in the HDD can be observed from the thermal image. In order to show the temperature of the image accurately, the emissivity of the material which describes the efficiency radiation of infrared energy from the material must be known and set up correctly. However, thermal imaging cameras cannot detect the emissivity of objects in order to calculate the true temperature. The cameras can only calculate the "apparent" temperature of objects. The apparent temperature of an object is a function of both its temperature and emissivity. The apparent temperature of an object might be substantially different from its true temperature. To obtain the true temperature, the emissivity of objects must be known by using black electrical tape method. Then, the true temperature of objects can be precisely calculated.

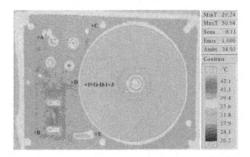

Figure 10.10. *Thermal image of hard disk drive [KWE 11]. For a color version of this figure, see www.iste.co.uk / muneesawang / visualinspect.zip*

The characteristics of thermal imaging are divided into two types – passive and active thermography. Passive thermography is a thermal imaging technique without an external heat source [CAS 12]. The temperature of the object must be sufficiently different when compared to the ambient temperature, in addition the camera sensor must be capable of capturing the temperature as shown in Figure 10.11.

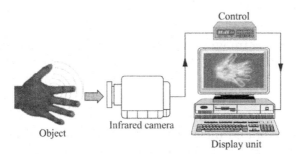

Figure 10.11. *The imaging of passive thermography [CAS 12]. For a color version of this figure, see www.iste.co.uk / muneesawang / visualinspect.zip*

Active thermography is used to capture a heated image that is stimulated by heating or cooling to the interested object [CAS 12]. This method is used to increase the different temperatures of both the defective and good surfaces on the objects. The stimulators are hot air and light which can be applied to the object by transmission or reflection. Active thermography imaging measurement is shown in Figure 10.12.

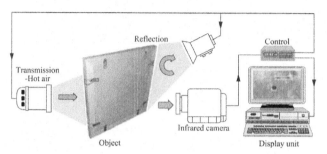

Figure 10.12. *The measurement process of active thermography imaging [CAS 12]. For a color version of this figure, see www.iste.co.uk / muneesawang / visualinspect.zip*

The characteristics of an active thermography image could be classified by heat transfer to an object of interest in several ways. The most popular testing technique consists of two methods which are pulsed and lock-in thermography. Pulsed thermography involves the heating of an object, and then the observation of that object as it cools. The testing methodology is that thermal imaging cameras are used to record the image of the object while the heat is applied. The heat sources are heat guns, flash lamps and bulbs, as shown in Figure 10.13. The advantages of this method are that it is easy to set up an experiment and the entire process is very quick. However, if the heat is applied incorrectly, then the results obtained from the testing might be incomplete or erroneous.

Lock-in thermography is a continuous heating technique. The changes of increased temperatures on the object are recorded and captured while applying a heat as shown in Figure 10.14. The infrared camera is also used to capture the thermal image and is connected to a control unit and personal computer to display the captured images. The advantage of this method is to obtain the size of the object. However, this method is not sensitive to the inconsistency heating power.

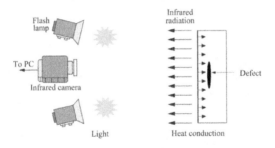

Figure 10.13. *Captured method of a thermal image by pulsed thermography [EHS 12]*

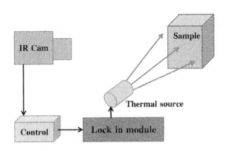

Figure 10.14. *Experiment setup of thermal imaging by using lock-in thermography method [EHS 12]*

The next method to detect a scratch on the surface of a magnetic disk is by using a compact disc (CD) pick-up head. This method is a methodology that has been developed to improve the existing tools and procedures used in the HDD industry. This is because the HDD industries needed to consider both the length of time that machines and equipment are in use and the damage that is caused during the investigation and evaluation process. However, the tools cannot be developed because the tools are always used in manufacturing processes. Hence, the new method for a scratch detection on the magnetic disk using the CD pick-up head was proposed by Ferrari *et al.* [FER 10]. This is because the optical disk is used to record data onto an optical disk which can store the up to gigabytes of data by using a light recording system. This technique can then be used to detect a scratch on a magnetic disk surface. The read/write system made up of laser light, prisms, optical lenses and the photodetector of the CD pick-up head is used as a new testing tool for scratch detection on the magnetic disk surface. The CD pick-up head system is shown in Figure 10.15.

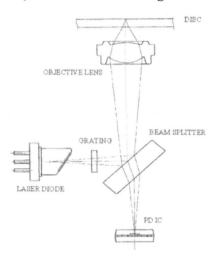

Figure 10.15. *CD pick-up head system [KSM 07]*

In order to measure the oscillation amplitude and average defect size on the surface of a magnetic disk during the rotation of the disk, an optical microscope is used in reflection mode. The laser Doppler heterodyne interference system was developed to evaluate the capability of this dynamic system inside an HDD. In the experiment, the laser Doppler technique was used to detect the oscillation amplitude and defect of the surface of the disk during rotation as shown in Figure 10.16. The light source of the system is a He–Ne laser, which is used to evaluate the performances of the HDD. The smaller diameter of the collimated beam is recommended for increasing energy density for the reflection mode. The diameter of the incident laser light source is around 5 μm. The loss in back optical path to the detector must also be considered. To improve the lateral resolution for the dynamic inspection, the laser Doppler interference technique is proposed [ZHU 12]. The light passing through the interference is reflected back from the sample surface. After this, it is collected by the objective lens and detected by the high-sensitivity photodetector. Then, the signal is converted from an analog to a digital signal, and the data are processed using an oscilloscope and the custom software.

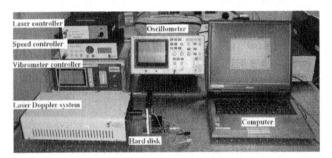

Figure 10.16. *The measurement system of the laser Doppler technique [ZHU 12]*

The surface testing system for an HDD is evaluated by an optical microscope such as the Axioskop 2 MAT; see Figure 10.16. The scratch sizes vary between 10 and 100 µm as shown in Figure 10.17. The two types of surface defect in an HDD are shown in Figure 10.17. These two types of defect are: (1) defects caused by the oxidation of the ambient environment, and (2) defects which are caused by the dust in the air. The area of the defect is very small for an optical microscope to obtain clear images and the thickness of the defect. The non-contact detection method is thus used to measure the thickness of the defects. This is conducted by using the laser Doppler technique. The oscilloscope working on the basis of laser Doppler effects could be calibrated by using the relationship between the voltage and time. The sinusoidal wave is applied to the laser Doppler system to determine the relationship between oscillation amplitude and defects on the surface of the HDD, and this is used to convert the voltage to amplitude. The calculations of the relationship between voltage and amplitude can be calculated as the following procedures of equations [10.1] and [10.2]. The surface properties of the disk can be measured by using the relationship between the applied voltage and the vibration shift [ZHU 12].

$$V_0 = \frac{vibration\ velocity}{voltage} \qquad\qquad [10.1]$$

where V_0 is the output voltage obtained from oscilloscope.

The corresponding vibration shift is calculated by:

$$A = \frac{V_0}{2\pi f} \qquad\qquad [10.2]$$

where f is the frequency of the applied sinusoidal wave and A is the amplitude of the corresponding vibration shift.

The laser Doppler technique can be used for detecting the oscillation amplitude and defects in high-speed rotation of the HDD. The differences in amplitudes are caused by the defects located on the disk, and the thickness of the defect is calculated by the different amplitudes of the output signal. The amplitudes of the output signal are different because the thicknesses of the defects are varied. The average thicknesses of these defects are in the range of 1–5 μm.

Chow et al. [CHO 12a] presented the improvement of the low-cost image acquisition instrumentation for surface inspection on magnetic disks by using dependency of optical wavelength. The images of the defects are improved by comparing the optical properties of the disk between the good and bad surfaces. The information obtained from the spectral transmittance or reflectance to/from the object is called spectral imaging. The imaging can be acquired by varying the different wavelengths of light [WIL 90]. The proposed instrument is thus designed to maximize the contrast of defective and non-defective surfaces by using the spectral imaging theorem. In addition, Chow *et al.* proposed an instrument to employ the spectral imaging methodology and the image acquisition instrument system to acquire the images of the disk surface with higher contrast between the surface defects and background. This could improve the accuracy of the detection with their simple and fast software and thus could also improve the evaluation time [CHO 12a].

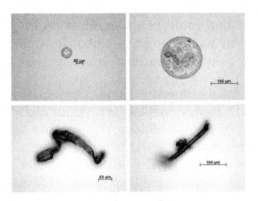

Figure 10.17. *Example images of HDD surface taken by the optical microscope [ZHU 12]. For a color version of this figure, see www.iste.co.uk / muneesawang / visualinspect.zip*

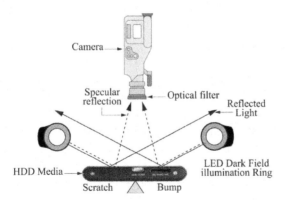

Figure 10.18. *Illustration of the media image acquisition system [CHO 12b]*

For specifications of the image acquisition system, the contrast between the surface of the disk and the background caused by the effects of the different wavelengths of the light sources is shown in Figure 10.18, which illustrates the designed and built instrument with compatibility to a class of 100 clean rooms in HDD manufacturing process. This is the requirement for media inspection in the clean room. The camera specifications consist of the Nikon D90 DSLR camera and a Tamron lens with 17–50 mm f/2.8 zoom at the focal length of 50 mm. The smallest defect level of this image acquisition system could be as small as 36.19 μm which had been detected by measuring the lowest level of detail at high magnification using conventional image processing tools.

For light source specifications, the specular reflections from the HDD media surface are eliminated by using the dark-field lighting methodology. The reason for this is that the media surface of the HDD is highly polished, and thus is extremely reflective [HEP 96]. The other illumination methods could cause excessive light reflection from the surface and would obstruct the detection of the defects on the disk and would prevent them from being accurately marked. The VAOL-5GWY4 is used as the light source with a high-intensity white light-emitting diode (LED) which is selected based on its long lifespan, low cost and broad spectral characteristics [CHO 12b].

The optical band-pass filters were successfully used in conjunction with spectral imaging, and these filters detach the information acquired from each wavelength of the light. The thin film Fabry–Perot interferometer allows for the 10 nm transmission bandwidth of the light and rejects unwanted radiation. 23 optical filters ranging from 440 to 660 nm wavelength spectra with 10 nm step intervals are employed. To detect clusters on HDD media, a definition of a cluster was an occurrence of either extremely similar or completely identical elements in close spatial proximity.

Clustering was the method used to group these elements together [CHO 12b].

10.3. Inspection of glue dispenser route

Ting *et al.* designed the glue dispenser route inspection machine for the assembly of the top covers of HDD [TIN 08, TIN 07]. They applied computer vision and BPNN techniques to the system. The machine consists of three main procedures which are computer vision, positioning and inspection. The real-time inspection system combines image processing binarization and morphological image processing. The Sobel operator, the parallel thinning algorithm, feature extraction and pattern recognition techniques are used to investigate the defects of glue routing including gap, deformation, offset, contamination and opened cover of an HDD.

For the positioning of the defect, this is one of the most important functions before route dispensing and assembly. The accuracy of the position is necessary to ensure the correct position of glue shooting. Otherwise, it could cause serious failures. A cross symbol marked on the defect that is to be glued is used to check the positions of the glued object. If the position is not accurate, the precise location needs to be readjusted until the glue can be dispensed in the correct position. After the positioning processes of the dispenser are completed, the glue shooting begins. In the meantime, the computer vision process is started. The images from the computer vision of the defective area and of a perfect glue track are shown in Figures 10.19(a–h). Serious failures such as broken glue or scrape are investigated to check the numbers of failures/problems. The neural network methodology is also used to detect and analyze other failures. The flowchart of applied computer vision and neural network to inspection system and the detail of each procedure are shown in Figure 10.20 [TIN 08].

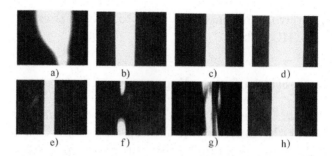

Figure 10.19. *Original image of the glue track [TIN 08]:
a) deformation, b) left-offset, c) right-offset, d) thickness,
e) thinness, f) broken glue (gap), g) scrape and h) normal*

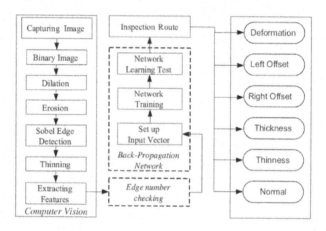

Figure 10.20. *Flowchart of computer vision and BPN inspection [TIN 08]*

The eight images in Figures 10.19(a–h) are acquired from a charge-coupled device (CCD) and image capture card which has the image frame of 640 × 480 pixels, image scale of 104 pixels/mm and a calculated field of view (FOV) of 6.15(H) × 4.62(V) mm. The motion images are simultaneously captured and processed while glue shooting. The configuration of the machine is shown in Figure 10.21. In order to have the same manipulating condition in the dispensing process, the dispensing valve and the CCD camera are used in the same frame. The image of the object is captured under moving conditions and obscured boundaries. This can cause errors during the inspection. Therefore, it is suggested to embark on morphological image processing of the binary image before edge detection [DAV 04, CHI 05]. Sobel edge detection is used for feature extraction in order to search the edge of the track [GON 92]. In addition, the mask detector for the Sobel edge is employed to detect the outer curvature of the face in image processing [TIN 07]. A coloring technique segmentation method to detect the true edges in the digital color image by using the Sobel edge detector is approached by Chittooru et al. [CHI 05]. The recognition system which is used to analyze the effects of varying resolution on recognition is developed by Anjum and Javed [ANJ 05]. Then, the four partial dark-field images of each plate were obtained. After that, the reference coordinate system of each image is determined for construction of a rigid-body transformation from predefined template images. The defective route of each image is identified by using two binary templates. The checking edge number can detect the serious failures such as broken glue (gap), bubble or scrape directly. The soft failures which are left-offset, right-offset, deformed track and thick or thin track are inspected by using the BPNN technique [TIN 08].

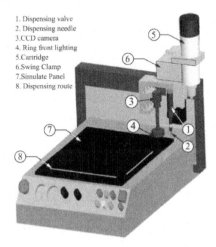

Figure 10.21. *Image of the glue dispenser system [TIN 08]*

The automated visual inspection system is also proposed and developed by Rajchawongis and Kaewtrakulpong [RAJ 11] as shown in Figure 10.22. The system is made up of three main parts which are material handling, user interface and processing units. The functions of the material handling system are loading, unloading and the handling of components for the visual inspection system, which consists of two cameras and a light source. The user interface is used to interact between operator and machine, and is used to control the operation of the machine, the setting of the parameters, the inspection of individual components and the status of the machine.

The processing unit is used for image acquisition and processing. The two Basler scA1000-fm monochrome cameras are used to achieve 0.5 mm resolution with an alignment error of less than 0.2°. To suppress reflections from the metal surface of the disk, the lighting is installed so as to acquire a partial dark-field imaging [HOR 06]. Each camera has a FOV which can be calculated from equation [10.3] [KUM 10] and is shown in Figure 10.23.

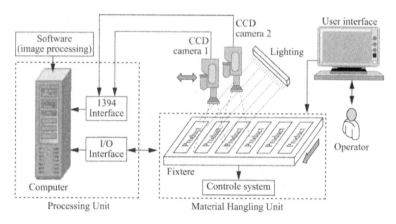

Figure 10.22. *Blue route quality inspection [RAJ 11]*

Field of view = (D_p + L_v)(1 + P_a)   [10.3]

where D_p is the required FOV, L_v is the maximum variation in part location and orientation, and P_a is the allowance for camera pointing as a percentage.

Therefore, each plate has four partial images. A set of the partial images is shown in Figure 10.24. The image processing algorithm for inspection consisted of three main parts which are reference coordinate determination, glue route segment and defect classification. The block diagram of this algorithm is illustrated in Figure 10.25 [HOR 06].

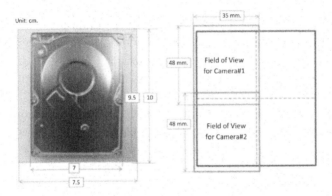

Figure 10.23. *Field of view of each camera [HOR 06]*

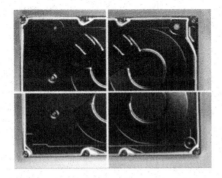

Figure 10.24. *Sample partial images of the same plate [HOR 06]*

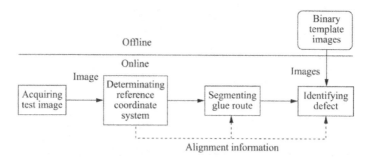

Figure 10.25. *Block diagram of image processing*
for glue route quality inspection [HOR 06]

10.4. Conclusion

In summary, there are many methodologies to detect a scratch on media, i.e. AFM, SEM, Candela, read/write error, microscope and laser Doppler effect, etc. The selection method of scratch detection depends on the detail of scratch and time consumed by the detection process. Thus, the scratch detection method on media must be considered carefully. For the dispenser route inspection, these techniques applied the computer vision and the BPNN techniques to classify a glue route defect.

10.5. Bibliography

[ANJ 05] ANJUM M.A., JAVED M.Y., "Face recognition vs image resolution", *IEEE 1st International Conference on Information and Communication Technologies*, Karachi, Pakistan, pp. 109–112, 2005.

[BOR 12] BORAZJANI E., Inverse heat conduction approach for infrared non-destructive testing of single and multi-layer materials, Master Thesis in Mechanical Engineering, University of Ottawa, 2012.

[CAS 11] CASTANED C.I., BENDADA A., MALDAGUE X., "Infrared vision applications for the nondestructive testing of materials", *5th Pan American Conference for NDT*, Cancun, Mexico, 2-6 October 2011.

[CHI 05] CHIANG Y.Y., KNOBLOCK C.A., CHEN C.C., "Automatic extraction of road intersections from raster maps", *13th Annual ACM International Workshop Geographic Information Systems*, Bremen, Germany, pp. 267–276, 2005.

[CHO 12a] CHOW Z.S., OOI M.P., KUANG Y.C., *et al.*, "Low-cost automatic visual inspection system for media in hard disk drive mass production", *The IEEE Instrumentation and Measurement Technology Conference*, Graz, pp. 234–239, 2012.

[CHO 12b] CHOW Z.S., OOI M.P., KUANG Y.C., *et al.*, "Automated visual inspection system for mass production of hard disk drive media", *International Symposium on Robotics and Intelligent Sensors*, pp. 450–457, 2012.

[DAV 04] DAVIES E.R., *Machine Vision: Theory, Algorithms, Practicalities,* Morgan Kaufmann, San Francisco, CA, 2004.

[DIE 01] DIETZEL A., FLEISCHMANN F., KRAYSE F., Detection and characterization of defects on surfaces of magnetic disks, United US Patent, 6292316 B1, 2001.

[EDD 09] EDDIE NG Y.K., DANIEL LIM H.M., GAO F., "Monitoring and characterising of hard disk drive thermal sources", *Heat Transfer Engineering*, vol. 30, no. 8, pp. 649–660, 2009.

[FER 10] FERRARI J.A., FRINS E., AYUBI G., *et al.*, "Application of DVD/CD pickup optics to microscopy and fringe projection", *The American Journal of Physics*, vol. 78, no. 6, pp. 603–607, 2010.

[FUR 08] FURUKAWA M., XU J., SHIMIZU Y., *et al.*, "Scratch-induced demagnetization of perpendicular magnetic disk", *IEEE Transactions on Magnetics*, vol. 44, no. 11, pp. 3633–3636, 2008.

[GON 92] GONZALEZ R., WOODS R., *Digital Image Processing*, Addison-Wesley, Reading, MA, 1992.

[GRE 06] GREEN P.M., HELF G.W., Method for hard disk drive flip disk diagnostics, US Patent, 7064539 B2, 2006.

[GUD 11] GUDURU R., *In situ* AFM imaging of nanoparticle – cellular membrane interaction for a drug delivery study, Florida International University, p. 422, 2011.

[HEP 96] HEPPLEWHITE L., STONHAM T.J., GLOVER R.J., "Automated visual inspection of magnetic disk media", *The Third IEEE International Conference on Electronics, Circuits, and Systems (ICECS)*, Rodos, Greece, pp. 732–735, 1996.

[HOR 06] HORNBERG A., *Handbook of Machine Vision*, Wiley-VCH, 2006.

[ISH 01] ISHIGURO T., NAKAJIMA H., Optical system for detecting surface defects; a disk tester and a disk method, US Patent, 6330059 B1, 2001.

[JAC 01] JACK W.H., TSAI NATHANSON M., KIMBALL R., *et al.*, "Non-destructive defect detection scheme using Kerr-channel optical surface analyzer", *IEEE Transactions on Magnetics*, vol. 37, no. 4, pp. 1957–1959, 2001.

[KSM 07] The specification of drive unit Model: KSM-213 CCM, 2007. Available at http://elektrotanya.com/files/forum/2010/12/KSS213C_LASER_HEAD_SM_[ET].pdf.

[KUM 10] KUMAR D.P., KANNAN K., "A roadmap for designing an automated visual inspection system", *International Journal of Computer Applications*, vol. 1, no. 19, pp. 34–37, 2010.

[KWE 11] KWEE Y., KEE W., LIU S., "Heat source analysis of hard disk drives with different wall conditions using infrared system", *Engineering*, vol. 3, pp. 22–31, 2011.

[MAT 00] MATE C.M., YEN B.K., MILLER D.C., *et al.*, "New methodologies for measuring film thickness, coverage, and topography", *IEEE Transactions on Magnetics*, vol. 36, no. 1, pp. 110–114, 2000.

[RAJ 11] RAJCHAWONG W., KAEWTRAKULPONG P., "Automated vision-based system for inspecting glue route quality in hard disk drive top cover assembly", *IAPR Conference on Machine Vision Applications*, Nara, Japan, pp. 279–282, 13–15 June 2011.

[SCH 14] SCHWEITZER J., Scanning electron microscope, 2014. Available at http://www.purdue.edu/ehps/rem/rs/sem.htm.

[SHI 11] SHIMIZU Y., XU J., KOHIRA H., *et al.*, "Nano-scale defect mapping on a magnetic disk surface using a contact sensor", *IEEE Transactions on Magnetics*, vol. 47, no. 10, pp. 3426–3432, 2011.

[TIN 07] TING Y., CHEN C.-H., FENG H.-Y., *et al.*, "Apply computer vision and neural network to glue dispenser route inspection", *Proceedings of the 2007 IEEE International Conference on Mechatronics and Automation,* Harbin, China, pp. 3882–3887, 5–8 August 2007.

[TIN 08] TING Y., CHEN C.-H., FENG H.-Y., *et al.*, "Glue dispenser route inspection by using computer vision and neural network", *The International Journal of Advanced Manufacturing Technology*, vol. 39, pp. 905–918, 2008.

[TOD 09] TODTONG Y., SUWANNATA N., RAKPONGSIRI P., *et al.*, "Observation of scratch on magnetic media by using thermal infrared camera", *Asia-Pacific Magnetic Recording Conference (APMRC'09)*, pp. 1–2, 2009.

[WIL 90] WILSON B.C., JACQUES S.L., "Optical reflectance and transmittance of tissues: principles and applications", *IEEE Journal of Quantum Electronics*, vol. 26, no. 12, pp. 2186–2199, 1990.

[YOS 08] YOSHIAKI U., HARAKO K., SHIMADA K., *et al.*, Defect inspection method of magnetic disk device there for and magnetic disk drive device, US Patent, 0072692 A1, 2008.

[ZHO 05] ZHONG Z.W., GEE S.H., "Analysis and reduction of ultrasonic pitting defects on hard disk surfaces", *Materials and Manufacturing Processes*, vol. 20, pp. 851–861, 2005.

[ZHU 12] ZHU S., ZHOU W., SONG Y., "Detecting oscillation amplitude and defects of hard disk rotating in high speed by laser Doppler technique", *Journal of the International Measurement Confederation*, vol. 45, pp. 74–78, 2012.

11

Inspection of Granular Microstructure of FePt Film in Heat-Assisted Magnetic Recording Media

This chapter presents an image processing method for quantitative transmission electron microscopy (TEM) analysis of recording media. Specifically, multilevel image segmentation is applied to characterize aggregated magnetic nanoparticles. This allows for the measurement of the grain size distribution. The Lennard–Jones (LJ) potential energy model is then applied to measure the dispersion of the nanoparticles. This image processing procedure allows for the rapid inspection of FePt film in industrial experimental heat-assisted magnetic recording media.

11.1. Introduction

Heat-assisted magnetic recording (HAMR) and bit-patterned media are underway for the development of next-generation technologies to meet the ever-increasing demand for higher data storage capacity. The HAMR-based

---

Chapter written by Paisarn MUNEESAWANG.

FePt media are regarded as the most promising option to extend area density beyond 1.5 Tb/in^2 [WAN 13]. An ideal HAMR thin-film recording media would consist of a layer of FePT grains which are uniformly ordered [HO 14] and uniformly distributed in sizes [PIS 13]. The existence of FePt grains obtained in the industrial experimental HAMR media is not without its defects [HO 14]. In this chapter, we report on TEM based on the quantitative study of L1$_0$-FePt media regarding the grain size distribution and dispersion.

The control of sizes and spacing of nanoparticles is necessary in the implementation of dispersed nanoparticles in devices and other developing technologies. The methods and systems that can rapidly assess dispersed nanoparticle populations are highly desirable [NON 13]. To gain an insight into the structural properties of nanoparticles and their characteristic nanoscale applications, TEM constitutes a major tool with which non-invasive studies may be conducted *in situ* at the quantum level. TEM images of nanoparticles have successfully been analyzed [COU 08]. Furthermore, image processing techniques have been implemented on images of higher magnification from atomic resolution TEM [KIM 06], scanning TEM (STEM) [ORT 09] and atomic force microscopy (AFM) [LIU 11]. The majority of the analysis method segments the images into foreground and background pixels. The most frequently reported techniques used for nanoscale applications are based on traditional image processing approaches that use boundary and edge information. Some existing methods rely on the well-known Otsu's thresholding method [HIN 11] or edge detection [WOJ 11]. Such techniques are suitable for high-contrast images but less effective in the case of agglomerated nanoparticles without clear boundaries.

The aforementioned TEM image processing methods have shown some success for the characterization of the shape and size distribution of nanoparticles. However, none of these methods discuss the characterization of dispersion nanoparticles from the resulting segmented images. Despite its importance, there is only a limited amount of literature concerning the automated dispersion analysis of nanoparticles [NAV 09, SUL 11]. We discuss this issue by proposing a two-stage approach: the first stage solves the nanoparticle segmentation and separation problems and the second stage solves the calculation of the dispersion of the nanoparticle population. The proposed procedure is tested on self-assembled FePt-based nanoparticles synthesized from different Fe compounds. Compared to traditional image segmentation approaches based on predefined thresholding [COU 08, KIM 06, ORT 09, LIU 11, HIN 11, WOJ 11, PAR 13], this work adopts an unsupervised method [DUD 11] for multilevel segmentation, allowing a more accurate analysis of foreground regions. This allows for possible successive operations to enhance the capability of segmentation in the case of agglomerated nanoparticles. In the second stage, we adopt the LJ potential energy model [BIS 09, SUL 11] to construct a dispersion index of nanoparticles at various degrees in the aggregation formula. The proposed dispersion index also offers the scale invariant feature applied to TEM images with different magnifications.

First, section 11.2 reviews the HAMR. Then, the FePt media and the synthesizing of nanoparticles are presented. In section 11.3, it presents image processing procedure which leads image segmentation and separation of aggregated nanoparticles. Section 11.4 provides experimental results and comparison to other methods. Section 11.5 presents the application of LJ potential energy model to characterize dispersion index of nanoparticles. Section 11.6 summarizes the text presented in this chapter.

11.2. Heat-assisted media recording technology

11.2.1. *HAMR*

Figure 11.1 shows the head-assisted magnetic recorder (HAMR). In this diagram, the laser needs to be integrated with the writing head. This waveguide laser source can be used to concentrate heat energy on a particular spot on the media. In addition, transducers can be used to enhance the optical field, a few nanometers away from the localized region in the media to be written. On the media side, the heat sink is the highly thermally conductive film placed below the memory film to minimize lateral heat flow.

The magnetic media is heated to an elevated temperature which is near to the Curie temperature of the material. The coercivity of the media then drops to a value less than the magnitude of the writing field. After the bit has been written, the head region is then rapidly cooled down to room temperature in the presence of the head field, provided that the head field is large as compared to the local demagnetization field, the magnetization of the media grains will remain oriented in the direction of the externally applied field.

11.2.2. *L1$_0$-ordered FePt as HAMR media candidate*

The L1$_0$-ordered FePt phase is considered to be the most promising candidate for HAMR media [VAR 14]. The structure of the FePt nanoparticle usually occurs in two forms: face-centered cubic (FCC) and face-centered tetragonal (FCT), as shown in Figures 11.2(a) and (b), respectively. Due to the alternate stacking of Fe and Pt atoms along the [001] axis, the cubic symmetry changes to FCT as shown in Figure 11.2(b). The FCT FePt nanoparticles possess ferromagnetic properties with large anisotropy constant of ~7 × 10⁷ erg/cm³, so that they can be used in magnetic recording media with sizes as small as 3 nm [WEL 00].

In order to implement FCT FePt thin films in hard disk drives (HDDs) for reaching area densities >1 Tb/in², many technical challenges need to be discussed. One of them is to reduce the annealing temperature for phase transformation of the films. Usually, as-synthesized FePt nanoparticles are in the FCC phase and high-temperature annealing must be used to transform the superparamagnetic particles to ferromagnetic ones. Unfortunately, the particles usually agglomerate into larger sizes leading to a wider size distribution. Morphology of the nanoparticles affects the magnetic properties. In this chapter, the magnetic properties of the as-synthesized nanoparticles before and after annealing are examined in section 11.2.3. The size and dispersion are measured using TEM image processing in section 11.3.

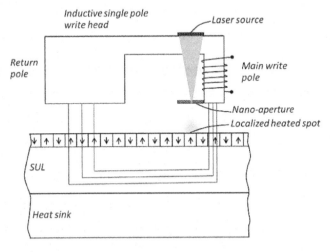

Figure 11.1. *Diagram of the heat-assisted magnetic recording*

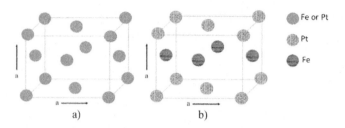

Figure 11.2. *Schematic illustration of the unit cell of a) chemically disordered face-centered cubic and b) chemically ordered face-centered tetragonal FePt*

11.2.3. *Magnetic nanoparticle*

This section presents the process for conducting the materials used for experimental media [CHO 13]. Magnetic nanoparticles were synthesized from 1.0 mmol Fe(acac)₃ and 0.5 mmol Pt(acac)₂ by a modified polyol process using the standard Schlenk line technique in an N_2 atmosphere. Dispersed in hexane, surfaces of these nanoparticles were modified by oleic acid and oleylamine of varying amounts: 1.5, 2.5, 3.5 and 4.5 mmol for samples, respectively, designated as B, D, A and C. Table 11.1 provides details of the synthesis [CHO 13].

Sample	Reagents (mmol)			
	Fe(acac)₃	*Pt(acac)₂*	*Oleic acid*	*Oleylamine*
B	1.0	0.5	1.5	1.5
D	1.0	0.5	2.5	2.5
A	1.0	0.5	3.5	3.5
C	1.0	0.5	4.5	4.5

Table 11.1. *Reagents and heat conditions in the experiments*

Images of nanoparticles were taken by TEM (FEI model Tecnai G2 20) operating at an accelerating voltage of 200 kV. The magnetic colloids were dropped on carbon-coated copper grids and hexane was provided to evaporate at room temperature overnight before the imaging. In Figure 11.3,

TEM images of nanoparticles obtained by varying surfactants concentration show different particle distributions and agglomerations. Such variation provides different scenarios to test our image processing procedure. In sample (A), nanoparticles of comparable size and spacing are uniformly dispersed over the entire image of Figure 11.3(a). In other images, orderly arrangements are not obtained and nanoparticles in Figures 11.3(c) and (d) are agglomerated by particle interaction. Clearly, this overlap did not occur by chance and the colloids were diluted enough to leave empty space in these images. In sample (D), nanoparticles densely packed in the bottom right corner are difficult to distinguish with the unaided eye. Samples may then be classified into four classes: non-overlapping sample (A), small overlapping sample (B), medium overlapping sample (C) and large overlapping sample (D).

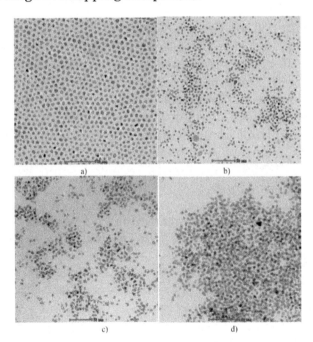

Figure 11.3. *Original input 8-bit TIFF images with 544 × 543 pixel resolution: a) sample A, b) sample B, c) sample C and d) sample D*

11.3. Inspection procedure

Image processing procedure first applies an unsupervised clustering method to segment nanoparticles. Then, the aggregated nanoparticles are separated. This procedure is explained as follows.

11.3.1. *Image segmentation*

The unsupervised clustering algorithm, the K-means [DUD 11, HAY 04], is adopted for TEM image analysis. Let χ be the set of pixels obtained from the input image. For a preselected number of cluster K, the algorithm subdivides N pixels, $\chi = \{x_1, x_2, \cdots, x_N\}$, into K disjoint clusters, according to Euclidian distance. Specifically, $\chi = \{\chi_1 \cup \chi_2 \cdots \cup \chi_K\}$, where χ_k is the membership of the kth cluster.

For initialization, let the K centroids, μ_k for $k = 1, \cdots, K$, be assigned by the random selection of pixel samples in χ. In the first step, an input pixel x_t is selected and assigned to the k^*th *winning* cluster according to minimum distance criteria. This will result in a change to the membership of the winning cluster, χ_{k^*}. In the consequent step, the centroid of the winning cluster μ_{k^*} is updated by taking the mean value of samples in χ_{k^*} (including x_t). The two-step iterative procedure is repeated again with a new input pixel.

ALGORITHM 11.1.– The K-means iterative learning algorithm is summarized as follows: Let the K cluster be, respectively, labeled by $C = \{C_1, C_2, \cdots, C_K\}$.

1) *Winner identification.* For every input pixel x_t, its distance to each of the centroid μ_k for $k = 1, \cdots, K$ is

computed. The winning cluster is determined according to a minimum distance:

$$k^* = \text{argmin}_{j=1,\ldots,K} \|x_t - \mu_j\| \qquad [11.1]$$

Then, in the updated membership, $x_t \in C_{k^*}$.

2) *Centroid update*. The centroid of all clusters will be updated as follows:

$$\mu_k^{new} = \frac{1}{N_k} \sum_{x_t \in C_k} x_t \qquad [11.2]$$

where N_k denotes the total number of vectors in C_k.

This procedure progressively improves the clustering accuracy as the total cost function monotonically decreases in every iteration. The *K*-means guarantee a monotonic convergence to an (local) optimum and must terminate at some point.

Figure 11.4 shows the result after the application of *K*-means to sample B. It can be observed that all image pixels are quantized into *K* levels. The quantized image can be segmented into foreground and background. In addition, these levels can also be used for guiding the separation of overlapping particles which is described in the next section.

11.3.2. *Separation of overlapping particles*

In order to separate overlapping particles, we labeled the foreground region as *base image* and applied the popular watershed transform [LIN 05, CHE 09] to the particles within the *base image*. However, the direct application of watershed transform usually results in oversegmentation. To overcome this problem, we formed a *top image* from the quantized pixels within the foreground regions, by using the output of the *K*-means. The *top image* was defined such that it contained pixels whose gray values were darker than the pixels around the border of the foreground region. Figure 11.4 shows the extraction of *top* and *base images* from the output of *K*-means and then the application of watershed transform in two channels. The representation of the *top image* contains small regions with emphasis on the overlapping particles and the center of the individual particles. These regions are considered the depth area, according to the principle of the watered transform. Thus, as shown by the first channel in Figure 11.4, the application of distance transform followed by watershed transform to the *top image* can avoid oversegmentation. The region representing the center of the particle may not be separated since the distances from the region center to each point of the region's boundary are quite similar. In comparison, the regions representing the overlapping particles have asymmetrical shapes, and thus the distances from their center to the boundary have a high standard deviation. Thus, the output of the distance transformation will guide the watershed transform to separate these regions, as shown by the regions around the center of the top image in Figure 11.4.

In comparison, as shown by the result from the second channel, the watershed transform of the *base image* results in oversegmentation. At the final stage, the outputs of the two segmentation channels are combined, in such a way that the segmented regions from the *base image* are merged if their boundaries pass through the same region of the *top image*. This region merging technique assumes that the regions of the *top image* are showing the area around the center of the particles and not the boundaries. The union operator combines the oversegmented regions of the *base image* to produce a more meaningful region as shown in Figure 11.4. In the experiment, we have observed that the performance of the multilevel segmentation was depending on the value K. We found that $K \geq 10$ was suitable for our experimental image data. In addition, the top image was suitably obtained by two to three levels of quantized grayscales at the dark side.

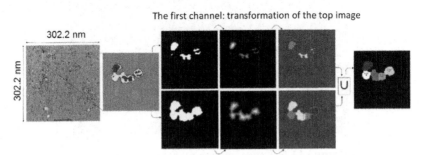

Figure 11.4. *Separation of overlapping nanoparticles by using the two-channel watershed transform*

11.4. Measurement of the size distribution

The multilevel segmentation method was applied to the TEM images of samples A–D, as shown in Figure 11.3. Here, some of the nanoparticles are overlapping. Figures 11.5–11.8 show the results of using the image processing method on 544 × 543 pixel images of samples A–D. For sample A, the number of detected nanoparticles is 868. The average diameter and area are 4.70 nm and 17.78 nm², respectively. In sample B, with some touching particles included, 1,066 nanoparticles are counted in the original image in Figure 11.6. The high standard deviation of diameters and area in sample C and sample D signal the presence of particle agglomeration.

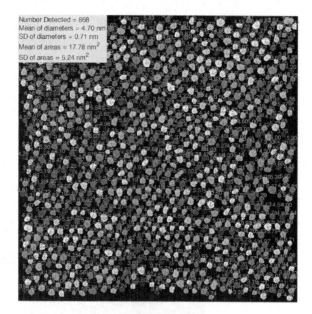

Figure 11.5. *Image processing results for sample A*

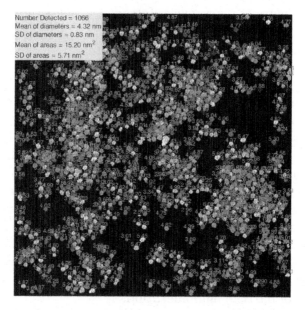

Figure 11.6. *Result of image segmentation for sample B*

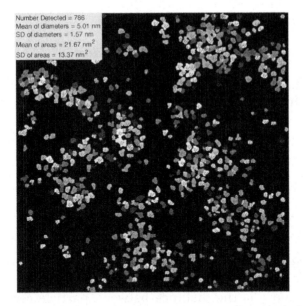

Number Detected = 786
Mean of diameters = 5.01 nm
SD of diameters = 1.57 nm
Mean of areas = 21.67 nm^2
SD of areas = 13.37 nm^2

Figure 11.7. *Result of image segmentation for sample C*

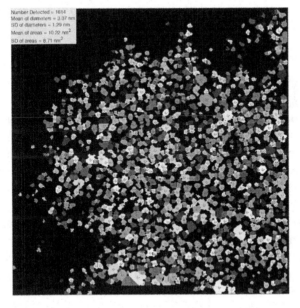

Number Detected = 1614
Mean of diameters = 3.37 nm
SD of diameters = 1.29 nm
Mean of areas = 10.22 nm^2
SD of areas = 8.71 nm^2

Figure 11.8. *Result of image segmentation for sample D*

11.5. Measurement of dispersion

11.5.1. Lennard–Jones potential index

Arranging magnetic nanoparticles in a close-packed array affects the magnetic behavior of the nanoparticles. This is due to interparticle interaction forces that can be theoretically explained [BIS 09]. A single magnetic sphere of radius a and constant magnetization, $\mathbf{M}$, generates a magnetic field as:

$$\mathbf{H} = \frac{3(\mathbf{m}\cdot\hat{\mathbf{r}})\hat{\mathbf{r}}-\mathbf{m}}{4\pi\mu_0 r^3} \qquad [11.3]$$

where $\mathbf{m} = \mu_0 V\mathbf{M}$ denotes the magnetic moment, $\hat{\mathbf{r}} = \mathbf{r}/r$ denotes a unit vector parallel to $\mathbf{r}$, μ_o is the permeability of vacuum and r is the distance between particle centers. The magnetic energy of such a dipolar particle due to a neighboring dipole is given by $U_m = -\mathbf{m} \cdot \mathbf{H}$. If two particles with moments, $\mathbf{m}_1$ and $\mathbf{m}_2$, are separated by a distance r, the dipole–dipole energy is then given by:

$$U_{dd} = \frac{\mathbf{m}_1\cdot\mathbf{m}_2-3(\mathbf{m}_1\cdot\hat{\mathbf{r}})(\mathbf{m}_2\cdot\hat{\mathbf{r}})}{4\pi\mu_0 r^3} \qquad [11.4]$$

The maximum magnetic energy is obtained when the two particles are in contact (i.e. $r = 2a$). This maximum energy characterizes the magnitude of the dipole–dipole interaction. Furthermore, this interaction is relatively long-range, decaying as r^{-3}.

Based on equation [11.4], the dipole–dipole energy is dependent on r, which is the separation of the centers of the two particles. This parameter also characterizes the dispersion or the van der Waals interaction between two particles, which is usually represented by an LJ potential [HEN 97]:

$$V_{LJ}(r) = \frac{C_{12}}{r^{12}} - \frac{C_6}{r^6} \qquad [11.5]$$

where C_{12} and C_6 are the parameters that depend on the properties of the two particles. The dispersion interaction between two large spheres of radii a and b is calculated by integrating the above interaction over the volume of the two spheres.

In this work, the LJ potential [BIS 09, SUL 11] is adopted for the calculation of interparticle potential of the spheres. This is given by:

$$V_{LJ}(r) = 4\epsilon_o \left[\frac{\sigma^{12}}{r^{12}} - \frac{\sigma^6}{r^6} \right] \qquad [11.6]$$

where σ and ϵ_o are the constantly representing physical properties of the particles. ϵ_o is the depth of the well of the potential energy function, which is a measurement of how strong two particles attract one another. σ is the finite distance at which interparticle potential is zero.

Figure 11.9 shows the calculation of the van der Waals force of four particles and the plot of LJ potential using equation [11.6], in the case of $\epsilon_o, \sigma = 1$. The particles are drawn according to their van der Waals radii such that they would just be contacting each other at the minimum energy separation. Particles try to minimize their potential energy and the contacts sitting at the bottom of the potential curve, which is at $r = 2^{1/6}\sigma$. When the particle is at the left of the minimum, the particles repel; otherwise, they attract one another. The LJ potential combines a short-range repulsive force, represented by the $1/r^{12}$ term, with a long-range attractive force, the $1/r^6$ term. The attraction force arises from the van der Waals dispersion force due to fluctuating dipoles, whereas the repulsive exchange interaction is due to the overlapping of particles. In practice, when $r = 2\sigma$, the $V_{LJ} \approx 0$, whereas when $r \to \infty$, the V_{LJ} diverges to infinity. Thus, the potential can be modified as:

$$V_{LJ}(r) = \begin{cases} V_0, & (r < R^*) \\ V_{LJ}(r), & R^* \leq r \leq 2\sigma \\ 0, & r > 2\sigma \end{cases} \qquad [11.7]$$

where $V_0 = V_{LJ}(r = \sigma)$ is a threshold.

For larger components comprising many particles, we may derive an analogous interparticle potential by summing the LJ interaction across all particle–particle pairs within the two particles [BIS 09]. Let $\mathbf{r}_i$ be the vector describing the location of the ith particle in the 2D plane. The summation of the LJ potential can be written as:

$$V_{LJ}(\mathbf{r}_1, \dots, \mathbf{r}_N) = 4\epsilon_0 \sum_i \sum_{j>i} \left[\frac{\sigma^{12}}{r^{12}} - \frac{\sigma^6}{r^6} \right] \qquad [11.8]$$

where $r = \|\mathbf{r}_i - \mathbf{r}_j\|$ for $i,j = 1, \dots, N$, and N is the number of the particles in the investigation. This is the total potential energy, which can be normalized by the number of particles:

$$\bar{V}_{LJ} = \frac{1}{N} \times V_{LJ}(\mathbf{r}_1, \dots, \mathbf{r}_N) \qquad [11.9]$$

In the experiment, the normalized version of the total LJ potential, calculated by equation [11.9], is used as the dispersion index. This provides the scale invariant feature for the measurement of the dispersion of nanoparticles in the input images taken at various scales. In addition, we let $\epsilon_0 = 1$, and obtain $\sigma = R^*/2^{\frac{1}{6}}$ for the simulation. Here, R^* is the average diameter of the particles measured from the input image.

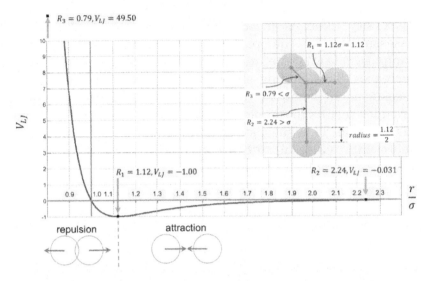

Figure 11.9. *An example of the calculation of van der Waals force of four particles and the plot of LJ potential as a function of r/σ*

11.5.2. *Experimental result*

Figure 11.10 shows samples A1–D1 used in this experiment. The segmented images obtained by multilevel segmentation method are shown in Figure 11.11. From the segmented images, the dispersion index of the nanoparticles assembly in each sample can be obtained. In order to determine the interaction among the particles, neighbors of each particle were first identified. The centers of particles were considered as data points or the center of Voronoi cell. Two particles were said to be neighbors if they shared a common edge in a Voronoi diagram. The neighbor pairs were graphically demonstrated by Delaunay triangulation, which is a dual form of the Voronoi diagram. Figure 11.12 illustrates the neighbor pairs of segmented nanoparticles. The total potential energy was calculated by equation [11.8] and then normalized by the number of particles to obtain the dispersion index $\overline{V}_{LJ}$, which was $-0.2237, -0.2807, -0.4177$ and -0.6061 for images A1, B1, C1 and D1, respectively. The dispersity index is in a good agreement with the visual assessment. As the particles get closer (ranking from samples A1–D1) the absolute value of dispersion index increases. This finding shows that the proposed dispersion measurement method based on the particle potential provides results to complement the visual inspection and size distribution. This suggests that this index value can act as a representative value to characterize the dispersion state of the self-assembled nanoparticles.

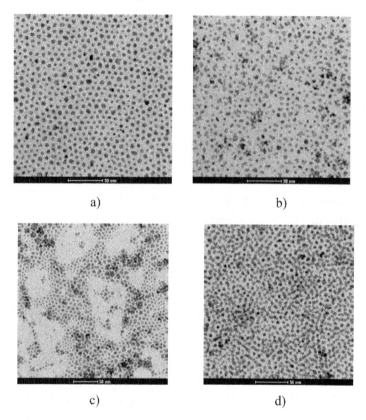

a)   b)

c)   d)

Figure 11.10. *Original input images: a) image A1, b) image B1, c) image C1 and d) image D1 with 512 × 533 pixel resolution*

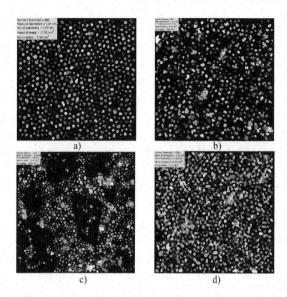

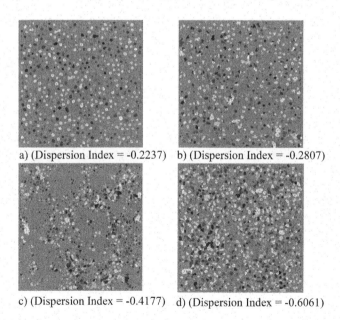

Figure 11.11. *Multilevel segmentation result and nanoparticles separation: a) image A1, b) image B1, c) image C1 and d) image D1*

a) (Dispersion Index = -0.2237)   b) (Dispersion Index = -0.2807)

c) (Dispersion Index = -0.4177)   d) (Dispersion Index = -0.6061)

Figure 11.12. *Dispersion measurement results: a) image A1, b) image B1, c) image C1 and d) image D1*

The scale invariant feature of the measurement method was also studied by applying the method to images of sample A taken at higher magnification and at different spatial locations. Figure 11.13 shows two highly magnified images of sample A, referred to as A2 and A3. Figures 11.14 and 11.15, respectively, show the results after applying the multilevel segmentation and dispersion measurement. Evidently, the proposed method offers high-accuracy measurement of particle dimensions and dispersion. The results obtained from images A1–A3 are consistent. Regardless of resolution, the dispersion index values are similar up to the first decimal, with only slight differences at the second decimal. This result shows that the proposed method for dispersion measurement of nanoparticles is highly desirable, since, in practice, the array of nanoparticles in material research is usually examined at different spatial locations and resolutions. The combination of dispersion measurement using LJ potential and multilevel segmentation offers a fast and accurate assessment of self-assembled nanoparticles.

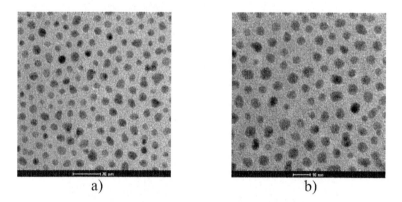

a)　　　　　　　　　　　　b)

Figure 11.13. *Original highly magnified image of sample A: a) image A2 and b) image A3*

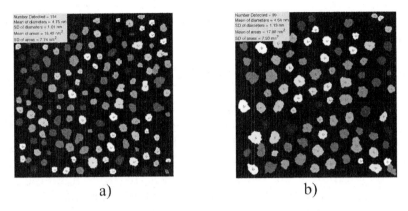

Figure: 11.14. *Multilevel segmentation result and nanoparticles separation of sample A: a) image A2 and b) image A3*

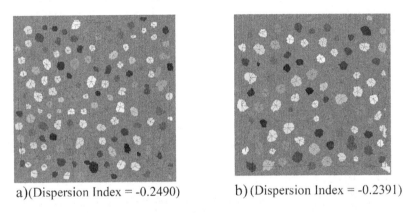

a)(Dispersion Index = -0.2490)   b)(Dispersion Index = -0.2391)

Figure 11.15. *Dispersion measurement result of sample A: a) image A2 and b) image A3*

11.6. Conclusion

This chapter presents image processing methods for segmentation of magnetic nanoparticles. The method applies unsupervised clustering algorithm to the TEM image and separate aggregated nanoparticles. LJ potential was demonstrated as a tool for characterizing the self-assembly of magnetic nanoparticles.

The original TEM images of particles synthesized by using four different Fe sources required separations of the particles from the substrate background. This was accomplished by multilevel segmentation incorporating watershed transforms, and with this method, average particle size can be determined. The dispersion index was then computed at various degrees in the aggregation formula. Based on the highest dispersion index and smallest distribution in size, Fe(acac)₃ emerged as a strong candidate in the synthesis of FePt nanoparticles. Furthermore, implementation of the method on images of different magnifications emphasized the reliability of the proposed method, yielding comparable average size and dispersion index.

11.7. Bibliography

[BIS 09] BISHOP K.J., WILMER C.E., SOH S., *et al.*, "Nanoscale forces and their uses in self-assembly", *Small*, vol. 5, no. 14, pp. 1600–1630, 2009.

[BOY 11] BOYD R.D., CUENAT A., "New analysis procedure for fast and reliable size measurement of nanoparticles from atomic force microscopy images", *Journal of Nanoparticle Research*, vol. 13, pp. 105–113, 2011.

[BUR 03] BURGEI W., PECHAN M.J., JAEGER H., "A simple vibrating sample magnetometer for use in a materials physics course", *American Journal of Physics*, vol. 71, no. 8, pp. 825–828, 2003.

[CHE 09] CHENG J., RAJAPAKSE J.C., "Segmentation of clustered nuclei with shape markers and marking function", *IEEE Transactions on Bio-Medical Engineering*, vol. 56, pp. 741–748, 2009.

[CHO 13] CHOKPRASOMBAT K., SIRISATHITKUL C., HARDING P., et al., "Monodisperse magnetic nanoparticles: effects of surfactants on the reaction between iron acetylacetonate and platinum acetylacetonate", *Revistamexicana de física*, vol. 59, no. 3, pp. 224–228, 2013.

[COU 08] COUDRAY N., DIETERLEN A., VIDAL L., et al., "Image processing nanoparticle size measurement for determination of density values to correct the ELPI measures", *Precision Engineering-Journal of the International Societies for Precision Engineering and Nanotechnology*, vol. 32, no. 2, pp. 88–99, 2008.

[DUD 11] DUDA R.O., HART P.E., STORK D.G., *Pattern Classification*, 2nd ed., Wiley, New York, 2011.

[FIS 00] FISKER R., CARSTENSEN J.M., HANSEN M.F., et al., "Estimation of nanoparticle size distributions by image analysis", *Journal of Nanoparticle Research*, vol. 2, pp. 267–277, 2000.

[GRZ 10] GRZELCZAK M., VERMANT J., FURST E.M., et al., "Directed self-assembly of nanoparticles", *ACS Nano*, vol. 4, no. 7, pp. 3591–3605, 2010.

[HAY 04] HAYKIN S., *Neural Networks: A Comprehensive Foundation*, 2nd ed., Prentice Hall, NJ, 2004.

[HEN 97] HENDERSON D., DUH D.M., CHU X., et al., "An expression for the dispersion force between colloidal particles", *Journal of Colloid and Interface Science*, vol. 185, no. 1, pp. 265–268, 1997.

[HIN 11] HINDSON J.C., SAGHI Z., HERNANDEZ-GARRIDO J.C., et al., "Morphological study of nanoparticle–polymer solar cells using high-angle annular dark-field electron tomography", *Nano Letters*, vol. 11, pp. 904–909, 2011.

[HO 14] HO H., ZHU J., KULOVITS A., et al., "Quantitative transmission electron microscopy analysis of multi-variant grains in present L10-FePt based heat assisted magnetic recording media", *Journal of Applied Physics*, vol. 116, no. 19, pp. 193510(1–8), 2014.

[KIM 06] KIM Y.M., JEONG J.M., KIM J.G., et al., "Image processing of atomic resolution transmission electron microscope images", *Journal of the Korean Physical Society*, vol. 48, no. 2, pp. 250–255, 2006.

[LIN 05] LIN G., CHAWLA M.K., OLSON K., et al., "Hierarchical, model-based merging of multiple fragments for improved three-dimensional segmentation of nuclei", *Cytometry Part A*, vol. 63, pp. 20–33, 2005.

[LIU 11] LIU Q., WANG H., LIU J., et al., "AFM image processing for estimating the number and volume of nanoparticles on a rough surface", *Surface and Interface Analysis*, vol. 43, no. 10, pp. 1354–1359, 2011.

[MON 12] MONDINI S., FERRETTI A.M., PUGLISI A., et al., "Pebbles and Pebble Juggler: software for accurate, unbiased, and fast measurement and analysis of nanoparticle morphology from transmission electron microscopy (TEM) micrographs", *Nanoscale*, vol. 4, pp. 5356–5372, 2012.

[NAV 09] NAVARCHIAN A.H., MAJDZADEH-ARDAKANI K., "Processing of transmission electron microscope images for quantification of the layer dispersion degree in polymer-clay nanocomposites", *Journal of Applied Polymer Science*, vol. 114, no. 1, pp. 531–542, 2009.

[NON 13] NONTAPOT K., RASTOGI V., FAGAN J.A., et al., "Size and density measurement of core–shell Si nanoparticles by analytical ultracentrifugation", *Nanotechnology*, vol. 24, no. 15, p. 155701, 2013.

[ORT 09] ORTALAN V., HERRERA M., MORGAN D.G., et al., "Application of image processing to STEM tomography of low-contrast materials", *Ultramicroscopy*, vol. 110, no. 1, pp. 67–81, 2009.

[PAR 13] PARK C., HUANG J.Z., JI J.X., et al., "Segmentation, inference, and classification of partially overlapping nanoparticles", *IEEE Transactions on Pattern Analysis*, vol. 35, pp. 669–681, 2013.

[PIS 13] PISANA S., MOSENDZ O., PARKER G.J., *et al.*, "Effects of grain microstructure on magnetic properties in FePtAg-C media for heat assisted magnetic recording", *Journal of Applied Physics*, vol. 113, no. 4, pp. 043910(1–6), 2013.

[SUL 11] SUL I.H., YOUN J.R., SONG Y.S., "Quantitative dispersion evaluation of carbon nanotubes using a new analysis protocol", *Carbon*, vol. 49, no. 4, pp. 1473–1478, 2011.

[VAR 14] VARAPRASAD B.C.S., TAKAHASHI Y.K., WANG J., *et al.*, "Mechanism of coercivity enhancement by Ag addition in FePt-C granular films for heat assisted magnetic recording media", *Applied Physics Letters*, vol. 104, no. 22, pp. 222403-1–222403-4, 2014.

[WAN 13] WANG X., GAO K., ZHOU H., *et al.*, "HAMR recording limitations and extendibility", *IEEE Transactions on Magnetics*, vol. 49, no. 2, pp. 686–692, 2013.

[WEL 00] WELLER D., MOSER A., FOLKS L., *et al.*, "High Ku materials approach to 100 Gbits/in2", *IEEE Transactions on Magnetics*, vol. 36, no. 1, pp. 10–15, 2000.

[WOJ 11] WOJCIK T.R., KRAPF D., "Solid-state nanopore recognition and measurement using Shannon entropy", *IEEE Photonics Journal*, vol. 3, pp. 337–343, 2011.

List of Authors

Sansanee AUEPHANWIRIYAKUL
Computer Engineering Department
Faculty of Engineering
Chiang Mai University
Thailand

Thanapoom FUANGPIAN
Department of Electrical and Computer Technology
Faculty of Technology
Uttaradit Rajabhat University
Thailand

Jirarat IEAMSAARD
Department of Electrical and Computer Engineering
Faculty of Engineering
Naresuan University
Phisanulok
Thailand

Nattha JINDAPETCH
Department of Electrical Engineering
Faculty of Engineering
Prince of Songkla University
Hat Yai
Songkhla
Thailand

Anan KRUESUBTHAWORN
Faculty of Applied Science and Engineering
Khon Kaen University
Nong Khai Campus
Thailand

Pichate KUNAKORNVONG
Data Storage Technology
College of Data Storage Innovation
King Mongut's Institute of Technology Ladkrabang
Bangkok
Thailand

Wimalin LAOSIRITAWORN
Department of Industrial Engineering
Faculty of Engineering
Chiang Mai University
Thailand

Paisarn MUNEESAWANG
Department of Electrical and Computer Engineering
Faculty of Engineering
Naresuan University
Phisanulok
Thailand

Patison PALEE
College of Arts
Media and Technology
Chiang Mai University
Thailand

Sayan PLONG-NGOOLUAM
Western Digital (Thailand) Co. Ltd.
Bang Pa-in Industrial Estate
Ayutthaya
Thailand

Pornchai RAKPONGSIRI
Western Digital (Thailand) Co. Ltd.
Bang Pa-in Industrial Estate
Ayutthaya
Thailand

Somporn RUANGSINCHAIWANICH
Department of Electrical and Computer Engineering
Faculty of Engineering
Naresuan University
Phisanulok
Thailand

Pitikhate SOORAKSA
Computer Engineering
Faculty of Engineering
King Mongkut's Institute of Technology Ladkrabang
Bangkok
Thailand

Orathai SUTTIJAK
Department of New Media
Faculty of Informatics
Mahasarakham University
Thailand

Nipon THEERA-UMPON
Electrical Engineering Department
Faculty of Engineering
Chiang Mai University
Thailand

Kittikhun THONGPULL
Department of Electrical Engineering
Faculty of Engineering
Prince of Songkla University
Hat Yai
Songkhla
Thailand

Suchart YAMMEN
Department of Electrical and Computer Engineering
Faculty of Engineering
Naresuan University
Phisanulok
Thailand

Index

Other titles from

in

Computer Engineering

2015

ROCHANGE Christine, UHRIG Sascha, SAINRAT Pascal
Time-Predictable Architectures

WAHBI Mohamed
Algorithms and Ordering Heuristics for Distributed Constraint Satisfaction Problems

ZELM Martin *et al.*
Enterprise Interoperability

2012

ARBOLEDA Hugo, ROYER Jean-Claude
Model-Driven and Software Product Line Engineering

BLANCHET Gérard, DUPOUY Bertrand
Computer Architecture

BOULANGER Jean-Louis
Industrial Use of Formal Methods: Formal Verification

BOULANGER Jean-Louis
Formal Method: Industrial Use from Model to the Code

CALVARY Gaëlle, DELOT Thierry, SEDES Florence, TIGLI Jean-Yves
Computer Science and Ambient Intelligence

MAHOUT Vincent
Assembly Language Programming: ARM Cortex-M3 2.0: Organization, Innovation and Territory

MARLET Renaud
Program Specialization

SOTO Maria, SEVAUX Marc, ROSSI André, LAURENT Johann
Memory Allocation Problems in Embedded Systems: Optimization Methods

2011

BICHOT Charles-Edmond, SIARRY Patrick
Graph Partitioning

BOULANGER Jean-Louis
Static Analysis of Software: The Abstract Interpretation

CAFERRA Ricardo
Logic for Computer Science and Artificial Intelligence

HOMES Bernard
Fundamentals of Software Testing

KORDON Fabrice, HADDAD Serge, PAUTET Laurent, PETRUCCI Laure
Distributed Systems: Design and Algorithms

KORDON Fabrice, HADDAD Serge, PAUTET Laurent, PETRUCCI Laure
Models and Analysis in Distributed Systems

LORCA Xavier
Tree-based Graph Partitioning Constraint

TRUCHET Charlotte, ASSAYAG Gerard
Constraint Programming in Music

VICAT-BLANC PRIMET Pascale *et al.*
Computing Networks: From Cluster to Cloud Computing

2010

AUDIBERT Pierre
Mathematics for Informatics and Computer Science

BABAU Jean-Philippe *et al.*
Model Driven Engineering for Distributed Real-Time Embedded Systems 2009

BOULANGER Jean-Louis
Safety of Computer Architectures

MONMARCHE Nicolas *et al.*
Artificial Ants

PANETTO Hervé, BOUDJLIDA Nacer
Interoperability for Enterprise Software and Applications 2010

WALDNER Jean-Baptiste
Nanocomputers and Swarm Intelligence

2007

BENHAMOU Frédéric, JUSSIEN Narendra, O'SULLIVAN Barry
Trends in Constraint Programming

JUSSIEN Narendra
A to Z of Sudoku

2006

BABAU Jean-Philippe *et al.*
From MDD Concepts to Experiments and Illustrations – DRES 2006

HABRIAS Henri, FRAPPIER Marc
Software Specification Methods

MURAT Cecile, PASCHOS Vangelis Th
Probabilistic Combinatorial Optimization on Graphs

PANETTO Hervé, BOUDJLIDA Nacer
Interoperability for Enterprise Software and Applications 2006 / IFAC-IFIP I-ESA'2006

2005

GÉRARD Sébastien *et al.*
Model Driven Engineering for Distributed Real Time Embedded Systems

PANETTO Hervé
Interoperability of Enterprise Software and Applications 2005